Lawrence City Hall cupula

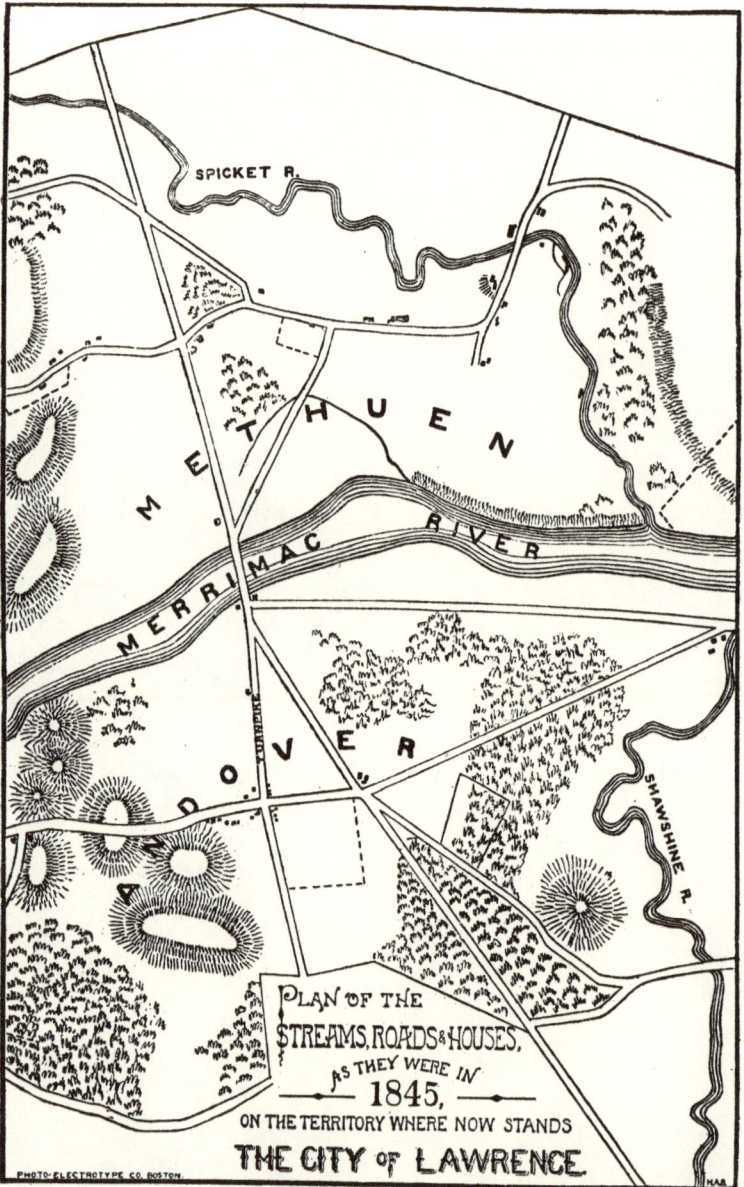

SPICKET R.

METHUEN

MERRIMAC RIVER

ANDOVER

SHAWSHINE R.

PLAN OF THE
STREAMS, ROADS & HOUSES,
AS THEY WERE IN
— 1845, —
ON THE TERRITORY WHERE NOW STANDS
THE CITY OF LAWRENCE.

PHOTO-ELECTROTYPE CO. BOSTON.

The dots seen on the above map represent the houses which were located within the territory now included in the city, when the Essex Company began operations. It will be noted that the nearest approach to a settlement was at the "cross-roads" on the Andover side of the river, where the old Lowell road (Andover street) crossed the Turnpike (South Broadway).

LAWRENCE, MASSACHUSETTS (1845 - 1918)

A CONCISE HISTORY OF LAWRENCE MASSACHUSETTS -
HER INDUSTRIES AND INSTITUTIONS; MUNICIPAL
STATISTICS AND A VARIETY OF INFORMATION
CONCERNING THE CITY

by

Maurice B. Dorgan

preface by
Louise Sandberg,

Special Collections, Lawrence Public Library
author of **Lawrence in the Gilded Age**

SICPRESS 2012
METHUEN, MA

Originally published in 1918 as "*Lawrence yesterday and today: (1845-1918) a concise history of Lawrence Massachusetts - her industries and institutions; municipal statistics and a variety of information concerning the city*" by Maurice B. Dorgan, Lawrence: Press of Dick & Trumpold.

EDITOR'S NOTE: Chapters from the earlier edition have been rearranged for clarity and readablity. New illustrations provided by the Special Collections at the Lawrence Public Library, Lawrence Mass.

editor J. Godsey
for copies sales@SicPress.com
Methuen, MA 2012

TABLE OF CONTENTS

List of Illustrations 7

Preface to the 2012 Edition 9

Preface to the 1918 Edition 11

Early Local History 13

Inventing a City 25

Early History of Lawrence 33

Industrial Growth 45

Lawrence Calamities 57

Industrial Upheaval of 1912 69

Municipal Government and Departments 79

Lawrence Schools 101

Church History 111

Social and Fraternal Organizations 119

Responses to Country's Calls 121

Public Buildings and Institutions 129

Public Transportation 143

Street Railways 143

Lawrence's Industries 149

Journalism In Lawrence 179

Old Landmarks and Designations 183

Historical Remnants 187

Who's Who in Public Life 199

General Statistics 228

Index 261

ABBOTT LAWRENCE

LIST OF ILLUSTRATIONS

Map of Lawrence, Massachusetts, 1845 .... frontis.

Abbott Lawrence, ... p. 6

Panorama of Lawrence Mills............................... p. 8

North Lawrence under construction .... p 12

Great Falls Dam, Lawrence, Mass. p.28

Charles S. Storrow p.23

Mills along the Merrimack River.. p 44

Engraving of Pemberton Mill Disaster .... p 56

John H. Tarbox School.. p.101

Grace Episcopal Church p.116

Soldiers and Sailors Monument... p.127

Lawrence Common p.128

Pacific Mills Cotton Department p.151

Pacific Mills Worsted Department..................................... p.153

Arlington Mills p.154

Everett Mills p.157

Monomac Spinning Company p.159

North Canal Boarding Houses p.177

Merrimack River p.178

Daniel Saunders, Sr. .... p. 182

Den Rock Park .... p. 186

Hon. John. J. Hurley, Mayor .... p. 199

PANORMA OF LAWRENCE MILLS

PREFACE TO THE 2012 EDITION

When Maurice B. Dorgan published his work *Lawrence yesterday and today (1845-1918)* in 1918 he prefaced the work as an historical reference book and that in large matter is what it is. There are no historical insights or conclusions to detract from a wealth of pragmatic information. There is fact after fact and simple chapters on simple subjects. For those of us who rely on facts to help answer innumerable questions about every conceivable topic related to the history of Lawrence, Massachusetts, Dorgan's two books (*Lawrence Yesterday and Today* and *The History of Lawrence*) are invaluable. They are used constantly by me and a string of researchers over the years. He usually has his facts right and we love him for it. From the history of the eagle atop City Hall to Industrial Upheaval of 1912 Dorgan has given facts and occasionally his own view of those facts.

He was writing his first book at a time of great promise: Lawrence population was at its largest, the city's industry was following the boom of the war years, City institutions worked well and second generation Lawrencians were buying houses, educating their children, becoming citizens, and supporting churches and fraternal organizations. There was much to be proud of: a state of the art water and sewer system, a successful school department, newly paved streets, electric lights, electric railway and intercity train service, the beginning of a playground program, the New England Baseball League, many beautiful churches, a bustling down town, two public libraries, and many factories looming over the city employing thousands of individuals. Everything was looking up. The country was beginning a decade of unparalleled growth for the United States and industry appeared to be the way of future growth. *Lawrence Yesterday and Today* was a mix of civic pride and Lawrence boosterism.

Dorgan did not consider himself an historian. He was largely a compiler of material taken from many sources. The two earlier city histories, Hayes and Wadsworth's volumes, were used. He also used material collected by Robert H. Tewksbury, including a manuscript owned by the widow that has tantalizingly gone missing. As a publicity tool it was remarkably successful. There are many copies of the original work still out in the community, many of them used into tatters. This new volume with an index and a number of new images will be of great value to the local community.

JULY 30, 2012

LOUISE SANDBERG,
LAWRENCE PUBLIC LIBRARY

PREFACE TO THE 1918 EDITION

In the preparation of this work, I have endeavored to produce a historical reference book, giving a compact story of the founding of Lawrence and its development up to the present day. The table of contents has been laid out in a manner that should make it easy for the reader or student of local history to find information relative to any particular phase or period of the life of the community. I have been painstaking in my search for facts, and I am confident that what is printed will prove reliable.

Much has been written about the early history of the city. The story of its conception and early development has been graphically told by able writers. But, little has been written, in a permanent form, about the activities of the last quarter of a century, during which the most marked progress has been made. In covering this great constructive period, attention has been given to all the important happenings. To many of the present residents the story is familiar; to the more recent comers it should prove instructive, as I hope, (it will be to future generations. To those outside our gates, who read, it may be convincing of the city's enterprise and progress, and its advantages.

In the research pertaining to the early history of Lawrence, valuable assistance was obtained by reference to Hayes' and Wadsworth's histories, and also to the historical sketches by the late Hon. Robert H. Tewksbury. I am deeply indebted to Mrs. R. H. Tewksbury for her cooperation in permitting recourse to Mr. Tewksbury's last manuscript on Lawrence. Thereby, I have been enabled to clear up a number of inconsistencies that have appeared, besides securing some interesting facts in regard to the early days, which have not hitherto been printed.

I wish to express my thanks to Charles H. Littlefield, William T. Kimball, and Arthur D. Marble, all of whom are well versed in the early history of the city, and who gave valuable counsel; to Charles F. Hill who was associated with me in the beginning of the research; to William A. Walsh, the public librarian, for many courtesies extended; also, to the industrial, banking and mercantile enterprises, and public-spirited men whose cooperation made it possible to produce the work.

JUNE 20, 1918.   M. B. D.

North Lawrence under construction

EARLY LOCAL HISTORY

INDIAN HISTORY AND TRADITIONS

One looking down from the encompassing hills upon the hive of industry, that is Lawrence today, can hardly imagine that a few generations past, the Red men roamed the territory within the city limits, now so densely populated by whites. Yet, it was not so very long ago that Indians camped on both sides of the river.

Reliable history of man in this vicinity begins with the Indians. The Merrimack River (Menomack by the Indians, from Mena, an island, and awke, a place, because of the number of beautiful islands in the river) furnished a locality attractive to the Indians who were great admirers of the beauties of nature. Along its banks was a favorable resort for their mode of life. There was plenty of fish in the river and numerous streams running into it; the light land near the water was suitable for cultivation of corn and beans, and the forests afforded abundant game.

At the time of the first settlements upon the Merrimack River the most powerful and important tribe along its banks was the Pennacooks. Their headquarters were on the river near where Concord, N. H., is now built. Their great chief was Passaconnaway.

He had conquered and subdued all tribes on the river, and all in some manner paid tribute to him. The Agawams inhabited the river east below tidewater, having their homes from the Merrimack to the Cape. The Pentuckets owned and occupied the Merrimack from "Little River" in Haverhill to Pawtucket Falls at Lowell; then came the Wamesits, Nashua, Souhegan, Namoskeag, Winnipesaukee, and several other tribes.

There is no evidence showing that any particular tribe had a home in Methuen, or what is now North Lawrence, but it is certain that Bodwell's Falls (then situated a short distance above the present Lawrence dam), and the shores of the Spicket River were favorite resorts, especially in the fishing season. On the Andover side, a company of Pentuckets had a settlement near Cochichewick Brook. Some writers have located the ancient seat of the Agawams at Bodwell's Falls, and to this place came to reside the daughter of Passaconnaway, who was wedded to Winnepucket,

13

a sachem of Saugus and who has been characterized by one writer as the "dog of the marshes". It turned out to be an unhappy union and war might have resulted, had not the "pale faces" appeared upon the stage at this time and diverted attention from tribal troubles.

Passaconnaway proved a friend of the first white settlers and desired peace. The residents along the river were never disturbed by Indian depredations during his life. He resigned his power as Grand Sachem of the tribes in 1660 to Wonolancet, about 20 years after the first white settlements upon the river. After Passaconnaway's death, a war sprang up between the Indians and the whites which was waged at intervals till the year 1696. During these years, the settlers of Andover had much trouble with the Indians.

It was on the extreme southern border of Lawrence that a band of northern warriors were discovered when about to fall upon and destroy Andover settlements. As late as 1722, seventy-eight years after the settlement of Andover, we find the town voting money to repair block-houses protecting "Shawsheen Fields" (South Lawrence). The severest Indian raids upon Andover settlers were nearly 50 years after settlement.

Local writers of early history have told us of an Indian village on Pine Island, and within very recent years, their places of sepulcher on the Shattuck farm in West Andover have been desecrated in the hunt for skeletons as well as stone implements, which the Indians were accustomed to bury with their dead. They had a factory for arrow points among the sand dunes where the Wood mills now stand, and quantities of their chips, the waste product of their manufacture, could be picked up there before the great mills covered the grounds.

That the Indians undoubtedly found this locality favorable, not only for fish and game, but for the tilling of the sandy fields for their supply of corn is evident. Speaking of this phase of Indian activity, Arthur D. Marble, the present city engineer, says that when he made the survey of Den Rock Cemetery in 1876 he was accompanied by two members of the Peters family in whose possession the land had been since white men first settled here. Back of the rock on a gentle slope to the southeast, towards the little brook, which runs through the valley, he was shown an old Indian corn field. The little hills were as pronounced and unmistakable as though it was but a year or so ago that the Indian squaw, with her crude stone hoe, piled up the earth around the tender blades.

On the south bank of the river were the Indian burial grounds, one at the western limit of the city near Laurel grove, already mentioned, and another for their chieftains just east of Cold spring, through which South Union street now runs. To this crude sepulcher of savages, wandering

14

Indians have made pilgrimages, within the memory of man now living. The burial ground on Shattuck's farm, just below the old steamer landing at Laurel grove, was extensive. Whether a battlefield, a burial site in the days of pestilence (when ninety percent, of the savages died and Merrimack valley became a vast charnel house), or a usual place of burial, is not known.

There is a tradition that Tower Hill was an important outlook or signal station in Indian warfare; that from the summit smoke of fire signaled wandering bands.

Of the Indian village, referred to, on Pine Island, four miles above Lawrence, Nancy Parker was apparently the last remnant. She was remembered by the very old settlers as a tall, wild looking, but harmless and industrious Indian woman, making her rounds among the farmers of the region,— "little dreaming that spinners would crowd to the valley by the hundreds, and that the noisy river-rapids would be harnessed to the wheels at which they toiled. From Nancy Parker's spinning wheel to the monster mill wheel is a long step."

In 1676, a party of savages crossed the river at Bodwell's Ferry (about a mile above the dam), chased the people of Andover, killed a young man named Abbott, and took his brother captive.

There is a tradition that old Bodwell, standing on the spot now occupied by Davis' foundry, with a long English musket, shot an Indian spy skulking through the tall grass on the opposite side of the river. He not only probably saved the Andover settlements from harm, but secured a fine wolf-skin robe, which he found on the dead savage.

There is another tradition that a thieving Indian, seeking to enter one of the old dwellings on the plain, was shot through the chinks of the timber wall, and buried beneath a great tree, standing near City hall; also that an early settler, seeing a movement in the grass near the site of the South canal, discovered a creeping savage working his way towards a pioneer's cabin. He shot the wily Indian, when three others broke from cover and made good their retreat. A story is told of a young pioneer who, returning from a courting visit to the fair daughter of an up-river settler, had his dream of bliss suddenly disturbed by the whizzing of a tomahawk past his head. Finding two Indians in chase, he saved himself by his knowledge of by-paths.

There are other traditions that relate the perils of the hardy pioneers in this section, all of which are interesting but too numerous to mention.

It is difficult to determine who were the first white settlers in the territory, which comprises Lawrence today, but it is said that lands along the riverbank were occupied by whites as early as 1655, and pioneers named Messer, Frye, and Cross appear to have been the first comers in this section. An interesting tradition is handed down, which relates how, for a roll of cloth a pioneer purchased of the Indians their rights in all the lands he could surround in a day's travel through the forest. Commencing on the river, with his savage companions, he took a course northwestward over highlands about Spicket Falls, thence southward along the slopes of Tower Hill to the Merrimack, and by the north bank to the point of starting; thus compassing a favorite hunting ground, and including the site of a future city. Indian sachems received, in 1642, for their rights in Haverhill lands, including the site of the town of Methuen, three pounds and ten shillings. For six pounds, and a coat, the Andover territory was secured. As Lawrence is but a speck in those great townships, the little over seven square miles comprising it, according to the valuation placed on it by the Indian owners, would not have exceeded five shillings. It is not probable that many whites had permanent residence within Lawrence limits prior to the year 1700, though Shawsheen Fields (South Lawrence) were cultivated by residents of Andover Village, protected by block houses, and Methuen Intervales (North Lawrence) were mown by commoners, from the direction of Haverhill, for years before that date.

Probably the first permanent habitation was a rude dwelling occupied by one Bodwell, and located on the Merrimack River bank near the mouth of the Spicket. This old dwelling was removed to a location where East Haverhill street now crosses Elm street. Here it still stands, enlarged and remodeled, almost the only relic deeply marked by time in the central wards of the city. It has a history, which goes back into dim obscurity. The pioneer who occupied the original house controlled a large area of land, and he may have been the hardy settler referred to in the chapter on Indian traditions, who slew a savage on the riverbank.

An ancient house, known as the Swan house, stood on the line of the common, just east of Trinity church. The stones of the cellar underlie the much-traveled Haverhill street. Tradition locates a rude log fort, or refuge for settlers, in Jackson Terrace; by some, it is said to have stood nearer the mouth of the Spicket River. There was also, it is said, a timber fort or stockade on the slope of Tower Hill, overlooking this valley.

The pioneers were mainly from the agricultural districts of England, and upon locating here most of them continued to follow the industrial pursuit to which they were accustomed, while others got their living as raftsmen or fishermen on the river. When Methuen was set oft' from Haverhill in 1725 probably not over fifty persons resided within the site of Lawrence. It was an isolated spot before the bridging of the Merrimack. World's End Pond was a sort of inland boundary of civilization, beyond which pioneers ventured with fear. The Andover tract was known as the "Moose Country" or the Plain of Sodom, and the chief innkeeper at the cross roads was familiarly called Lot. The Methuen district was in retaliation referred to as Gomorrah by dwellers on the opposite bank. The phrase, "out of the world into Methuen," was commonly used.

Nearly 100 years had rolled on after the incorporation of Methuen, bringing little change to the isolated farmers. The future site of the city had been converted into peaceful farms. Dams had been built upon the Spicket River, and small paper mills and the Stevens shop for the manufacture of pianoforte cases had been erected, but the Merrimack flowed in its natural channel, undisturbed by the arts of man. At this time, dwelling houses were not numerous, and, as in other farming towns, were somewhat remote from one another. The number of buildings in the now thickly populated portion of Lawrence could have been counted upon the fingers of the hand.

No church spires pointed to heaven; three small schoolhouses offered their primitive accommodations. There was no hum of machinery except the simple movements of the small paper and gristmills on the lower Spicket and activity of Stevens' box-shop further upstream. In this sleepy hollow was born the wonderful industrial city of today, and the change that came in 1845 was so rapid, radical and entire, that it completely overshadowed the leaven of original population, till only here and there we find a descendent of a pioneer family, and but few landmarks of the early days.

The site of Lawrence in the olden time was not the place of sand heaps and swamps, such as some writers have represented it to be. The great central farm of Hon. Daniel Appleton White and his ancestry included at one time 300 acres, divided into tillage, pasturage, and woodland. These lands are now covered by large mills and the most compactly settled districts of Wards Two, Three and Four. The farms of Daniel Merrill and Phineas M. Gage, that lay along the lines of Jackson, Newbury and Union streets, between the Merrimack and Spicket rivers, had thriving orchards and many fertile acres. The great Trull farm on Tower Hill was a fertile tract, a portion in forest. The poor farm lands of the Town of Methuen along the west side of the turnpike (Broadway) were rich in pasturage. Joshua Thwing's lands, including all the central common and the compactly settled portions of Ward Two, were fertile, as were the farms, north of the Spicket River, owned by Herrick, Huse, Stevens, Graves, and Tarbox. The cornfields, rye fields, and orchards of the Poor, Richardson, Stevens, Saunders, and Shattuck families in South Lawrence gave evidence of a good soil and of careful, old-time husbandry.

Among the very early pioneers of South Lawrence were the Barnards, Stevenses and Poors; later came the Parkers and other families. The first named family traces back the title to lands nearly 250 years. To North Lawrence came, as early pioneer settlers, who remained, the Bodwells, Swans, Sargents, Barkers, Poors and Marstons; possibly others, whose descendents do not remain. Notable among the sturdy yeomen, native residents, who had homesteads on the plain before the forming of the town, were Capt. Nathan Shattuck and Joseph Shattuck, Daniel Saunders, Ebenezer Poor, Phineas M. Gage, Benjamin Richardson, Asa Towne, Nehemiah Herrick, John Tarbox, Michael Parker, Thomas Poor, Caleb Richardson, Nathan Wells, Abiel Stevens, James and Edwin Sargent, Adolphus Durant, Samuel Ames, Fairfield White, Stephen Huse, John Graves, James Stevens and Henry Cutler. Abiel Stevens and Adolphus Durant were men of marked character, being the first manufacturers in this section.

The few dwellings of the pioneers dotting the plain on the northside were mostly upon the road leading from Lowell to Haverhill, now straightened, graded and known as Haverhill and East Haverhill streets, and upon the Londonderry Turnpike (now Broadway). Opposite the ancient dwelling on East Haverhill street, already mentioned, was the more modern house of Adolphus Durant, built about 1830. The farmhouse and buildings of Phineas M. Gage stood in the fields on the spot now known as Jackson Terrace; the farm orchard was in the section of the city now crossed by Orchard street, his garden extending along the line of Garden street. Thus, the names of two city streets are naturally accounted for. One old house was removed to make room for the original High school building opposite the Haverhill street mall of the common. The ancient homestead of Capt. White stood near the corner of Haverhill and Lawrence streets. His son, Judge Daniel Appleton White who gave the citizens of Lawrence the White Fund, by which has been established an instructive course of lectures besides material aid for the maintenance of the Public Library, was born beneath its sloping roof. The farmhouse of Fairfield White was located at the corner of Amesbury and Haverhill streets. Another farmhouse at the corner of Franklin and Haverhill streets was known at one time as the Sargent house. It was torn down about the time the city was incorporated.

The original farmhouse of the Methuen poor farm, formerly owned by Nathaniel Sargent, stood near the corner of Bradford street and Broadway, then the corner of Haverhill road and the old turnpike. The town farmlands lay along either side of the turnpike from Andover Bridge northward, with a great pasture on the easterly slope of Tower Hill, the lands of Alpheus Bodwell being in the Ward Five lowlands. West of the railway near the corner of Haverhill and May streets was the dwelling of Capt. John Smith. The Bodwell farm buildings stood on the hill, just westward of the ferry road. The old farmhouse has been supplanted by a modern brick structure. On the farm of Levi Emery (now cut up into house-lots) was the old farmhouse of one Ordway, a Bunker Hill patriot.

A rickety dwelling, known as the Rogers house, stood at the upper guard locks, and was demolished and replaced at the founding of the city. The Samuel Ames farm was also located in Ward Five, and below, on the riverbank near the ferry, were two ancient houses, once much resorted to in the days of ferries and fords.

On the lower Spicket was the Foster house, just below East Haverhill Street Bridge, and the paper mill of A. Durant, long since supplanted and removed. The little old school house at the corner of East Haverhill and Prospect streets was replaced by the present school building; the one on Tower Hill was years ago removed, and the one in South Lawrence was made into a dwelling.

Where are now the Arlington Mills, stood the piano case factory of Abiel Stevens, afterwards turned into a hat factory, and in the immediate neighborhood were the residence of father and son, the Susan Huse place, and the square house in which resided Nathan Wells.

In South Lawrence, the crossroad settlement, where Andover street crosses Broadway, was the nearest approach to a village within the present city limits. Here were located the Essex Tavern (later converted into a dwelling), the Shawsheen Tavern (later the Revere House which was torn down several years ago), the old pioneer county store, and the brick building occupied by Daniel Saunders, founder of the city. The Shawsheen House was built by one John Poor with bricks made at Den Rock in a brickyard run by the Peters family in the olden days. On the Lowell road westward from this corner were the farmhouse of Theodore Poor, the Caleb Richardson estate, and the old dwellings erected by the pioneers Barnard and Stevens. On the corner of Andover and Parker, streets stood the dwelling of Capt. Michael Parker. Parker street perpetuates his name.

The present City Farm is a part of the old farm of Col. Thomas Poor who saw service, with a company of 50 young men from North Andover, at Lexington and Concord, and took part in several other important engagements during the Revolutionary War.

Among the most noticeable of recent landmarks were the Tarbox dwelling at the foot of Clover Hill (one time known as Graves Hill), where the late Hon. John K. Tarbox was born, and the old dwellings of the Sargents and Swans, to the eastward of Prospect Hill. Some still remember the remnants of the rude fish wharves along the line of the Merrimack. In the old days these were busy localities in the fishing season; there were five of them between the dam and the Essex County Training School, simple structures of rough stone and logs, each creating an eddy where the fish gathered in immense numbers. They disappeared before the onrush of progress, started with the building of the dam.

Topography of Lawrence

The topography of the territory hereabouts has undergone most remarkable changes, according to geologists and early historians. Far back in the dim past, we are told, the region comprising Lawrence and the surrounding towns constituted a vast lake, and that by some upheaval in nature the surface of the earth was changed, leaving a few ponds as slight remnants of that inland sea. Cochichewick, Mystic, Haggett's and World's End (Stillwater) Ponds are said to be puddles remaining after subsidence of waters let loose from their beds by an unusual convulsion of nature.

We are also told that during the glacial period the Merrimack flowed in a closed tunnel under the ice and emptied its waters into Boston harbor. The glaciers gradually melted away and slowly retreated northward. At Lowell was left a pile of drift, which formed a dam so strong that the river was turned to its present course, in a northeasterly direction, through Lawrence, Haverhill and Amesbury, thus finding its ocean outlet at Newburyport.

Therefore, to this phenomenon we are apparently indebted primarily for the creation of Deer Jump, Peters' and Bodwell's falls, which furnished the unlimited waterpower that made Lawrence possible.

However, let us get down to a less remote period and briefly consider the appearance of this locality just prior to the construction of the dam : There was a deep depression east of Union street, and the very bottom of that part of the North canal rests on made land. The eastern part of the site of the common was an alder swamp drained by a brook running through Jackson street and emptying into the Merrimack. There was another low basin between Amesbury, Haverhill and Franklin streets, which found its drainage outlet southward through Lawrence street. This basin, long since filled and drained, has become the heart of population in Wards Three and Four. There was a fourth depression near the

North depot filled with muddy water, from which hornpouts were sometimes taken. The lowlands beyond the depot and those extending along West street in Ward Five are still remembered. There were sand hills in several places and a bluestone ridge extending south of, and parallel with Essex street, between Lawrence and Newbury streets. South of the river was a rolling, sandy plain, parts of which were covered by thick growths of trees.

The topography of Lawrence has seen changes beyond what is shown by the foregoing. It is almost impossible to believe the Spicket River ever ran in the very crooked channel the old maps show. Yet it was even more crooked than these small scale maps can show. Several small ponds in various sections have disappeared with the improvement of the land.

Today the position and appearance of Lawrence is well described as follows: The city lies in latitude 42 deg., 42 min., 13 sec, and in longitude 71 deg., 10 min., 13 sec. west from Greenwich; has a little over seven square miles (4,577 acres) area, of which 2,216 acres are in the northern district, taken from the town of Methuen; 2,097 acres, south of the Merrimack River, were taken from the town of Andover. The estimated water area is 264 acres. Excluding water surface, railway rights of way, public and church lands exempted, 3,102 acres remain as taxable estates.

The city proper lies in a broad and open plain. The central and populous wards are upon the rolling swell of land on the north bank of the Merrimack River, where that stream curves about the great mills. The southern district, less thickly populated, is a wide plain extending westward from Shawsheen River, somewhat rolling and broken near the western limits. The highlands west of the city, known as Tower Hill, and the rolling ridge, Prospect Hill, eastward, are sites of picturesque residences, having an elevation of 80 to 150 feet above the dam. These heights command wide views, their southern slopes rising abruptly from the bank of the Merrimack. The valley enclosed by these ridges is nearly two miles broad, extending northerly and southerly to higher lands beyond city limits.

The towns of Methuen, Andover and North Andover encircle the city. They are rich in tradition, their early history including the history of the region where now is Lawrence.

EARLY ROADS AND FERRIES

In the early days there were few roads in this locality, and traveling had not near the pleasure that accompanies it in these days of comfortable conveyances and smooth, well-packed roadways. The old ferry roads had much travel before the building of Andover Bridge; they compassed the valley, now the site of the city.

The westerly road approached from the north, reaching the Merrimack at Bodwell's ferry, near the pumping station, by the way of what is now Reservoir, Ames and Doyle streets. The easterly road ran as it now runs, over and a little to the eastward of Prospect Hill, by the way of what is now Ferry street, reaching the Merrimack at Marston's ferry, near the Lawrence poor farm, where was also, in the olden time, a ford.

These were the principal crossings on the river. The latter, Marston's, was established, primarily, to enable settlers to pursue northern Indian bands, who often appeared on the north bank, doing much mischief and escaping unpunished. Both ferries were discontinued when Andover Bridge was built in 1793.

After the building of Andover Bridge, a rough roadway ran from the bridge, northeasterly, across the lowlands to a point just west of the First Baptist church, corner of Haverhill and Amesbury streets, where it joined the Haverhill road.

Haverhill and East Haverhill streets follow substantially old county roads, changed somewhat in grade and direction; Broadway is a section of the old turnpike laid out in 1806, from Concord, N. H., to Medford, Mass. Portions of Cross, Arlington. Berkeley and Marston streets in North Lawrence, and of Lowell road, Salem turnpike (Winthrop Avenue) and Merrimack street in South Lawrence, with the ferry and back roads in the outlying wards, also follow substantially old thoroughfares.

ANDOVER BRIDGE

Andover Bridge, the first bridge to span the Merrimack River at Lawrence, was built by a corporation known as the "Proprietors of Andover Bridge." This was the oldest corporation within Lawrence limits. In March, 1793, in the closing year of the first administration of President George Washington, an act was passed by the General Court of Massachusetts incorporating Samuel Abbott and John White, esquires, with Joseph Stevens, merchant, and Ebenezer Poor, yeoman, and associates, as the "Proprietors of Andover Bridge", for the purpose of erecting a bridge over the Merrimack River from Andover to Methuen, at Bodwell's Falls, close to where the Broadway bridge now stands. The charter provided that the bridge should be built within three years, should not be less than 28 feet wide, should have a centre span of no feet reach, over the main channel, to insure easy passage for great timber rafts. Tolls were fixed by the act for foot passengers and every kind of carriage from a chariot to a wheelbarrow.

The first structure stood on huge wooden piers, and cost about $12,000. The opening of the bridge, November 19, 1793, was a great local event. A company of infantry and a company of cavalry did escort duty at the celebration which was attended by many notable people from miles about a boy named Stevens, while attempting to pass a guard stationed to keep the bridge clear for invited dignitaries, was fatally bayoneted by a soldier. Otherwise, the occasion was of a joyful nature.

The corporation had a hard time of it. Adversity perched on its shoulders at the start, and frequently bore heavily on its patience and resources. Bridge building experience was limited then and the new structure had an ailing existence for eight or nine years. On August 28, 1801, a part of the bridge fell in ruins while a drove of cattle was passing over it. Some of the herd, 59 sheep, 6 cows and a saddle horse, perished in the waters of the river, and were paid for by the "proprietors." In the winter of 1802-03, the superstructure was re-built, but shortly afterward, the great centre span collapsed. It was promptly repaired. Yet, four years thereafter, February 15, 1807, a great freshet and run of ice swept away the larger part of the bridge.

The structure had stood on the site of the present railroad bridge, but prior to the next rebuilding it was moved upstream to the present location, and permanent stone piers were substituted for wood. These piers at times were terribly damaged by ice and logs. They were demolished, with the exception of one, when the present iron structure was erected in 1881. The remaining pier still stands in the bed of the river under the Falls Bridge, but it does not sustain the structure.

In 1837, the old bridge was built, upon which many of the first comers to the new city rode over. It was a primitive affair without sidewalks. The entire width of 20 feet was reduced by huge strengthening timbers within the high board railing, leaving but 17 feet of passageway crowded with travelers flocking in and teams loaded with material for the dam, canal, new buildings and mill foundations from the ledges of South Lawrence and elsewhere.

In 1846, the bridge was absorbed by the Essex Company, and in the spring of 1848, the structure was raised nearly ten feet to the level of the railway line. This new structure was of a frame truss type. In the freshet of 1852, the tollhouse, south abutment and fish way all went down in the rush of waters. In 1858, the bridge was thoroughly reconstructed by the late Morris Knowles.

The bridge remained a toll bridge until 1868 when it became free, as a public highway, the city paying the larger part of the value and assuming the care of the bridge under the county commissioners' award. At the same time, Lawrence Bridge at Union street was made free in a like manner. The latter had been built in 1854–55 for the purpose of accommodating North Andover and Lawrence, and avoiding the railroad crossing, at grade, near the Andover Bridge. Both bridges were destroyed by fire, Andover Bridge in 1881 and Lawrence Bridge in 1887, and were replaced by the present iron structures.

Andover Bridge, for over half a century, prior to the building of the dam, was the centre of activity in this locality and at the time of the influx to the "new city," it was the busiest place in the valley. But a short distance from the south end were the taverns at Shawsheen corner (corner Andover street and South Broadway), the scene of many joyous as well as bibulous gatherings. The half mile from the bridge to this corner was the racetrack in the old times. On muster and training days, the old militia marched over the swaying arches, here and there in the ranks revolutionary patriots.

About 1814, some 15 British officers, prisoners, were quartered at Shawsheen corner to keep them away from the shipping of the ports. They proved quite an attraction, especially to the women of Shawsheen Fields, who found them to be excellent dancers.

On June 20, 1825, General Lafayette passed over Andover Bridge in his triumphal journey from Boston to Concord, N. H. In was on this bridge that Daniel Saunders and his associates stood in March 1845, when they conceived the idea of harnessing the waters of the Merrimack River for the use of industry, and of laying the foundation of the city.

Inventing a City

The Essex Company

The history of the Essex Company is practically the story of the founding and early development of Lawrence. This corporation conceived the idea upon which the city is built, the harnessing of the waters of the Merrimack River and turning their power to the promotion of manufacturing industry. With the construction of the great dam was laid the corner stone of Lawrence, one of the foremost textile manufacturing cities in the world.

From the very beginning, the Essex Company was closely identified with the growth of the community. Not only did it make possible, through the wonderful waterpower it established, the foundation of the city's great industries, but it was a tremendous factor in inaugurating many of the public improvements and utilities, the benefits of which the present generation is enjoying.

The Merrimack Water Power Association, formed in 1843, with Samuel Lawrence as president and treasurer, and Daniel Saunders as agent, with associates, mainly from Lowell, was the forerunner of this more powerful-chartered company. The pioneer association secured lands and made surveys that greatly simplified and facilitated later operations. It had been demonstrated that, at and about Bodwell's Falls by the historic Andover Bridge, there lay a tract of land resting upon foundations of imperishable blue stone and so shaped and environed by nature as to be a rare site for a permanent dam and a connected system of canals, and for the building of a manufacturing city. Industries having been established at Lowell and elsewhere in New England, from 1825 to 1845, enterprising operators were already convinced that great opportunities for the employment of capital and labor lay in the establishment of textile industries by waterfalls on Merrimack River.

It, therefore, came to pass that the Essex Company was incorporated March 20, 1845, on that very day the active promoters visited the site of Lawrence and perfected general plans for future operations. In less than one month from the granting of the charter, the company was duly organized and the capital of one million dollars had been subscribed without the issue of circular or prospectus. The directors were Abbott Lawrence, Nathan Appleton, Patrick T. Jackson, John A. Lowell, Ignatius Sargent, William Sturgis and Charles S. Storrow, all manufacturers or financiers of high character.

The work of this company at Lawrence in early years was primarily important, it controlled and forced the situation. Aside from operations at Lowell there were really few models for guidance, and founders were required to design and also to execute plans. Fortunately, at the outset, Charles S. Storrow, the pioneer railroad superintendent and engineer, who for several years had successfully managed the first passenger railway in New England —the line from Boston to Lowell— became the resident manager of the company's affairs, and, with a corps of assistants, immediately commenced locating and constructing the dam and canals and laying out the new town in accordance with a definite and well considered plan.

Abbott Lawrence was president of the company during all the early years. These two men, both enthusiastic and forceful in the execution of plans, pushed forward the work of development and of town building with a rapidity that won the admiration of those who watched every step of progress. Daniel Saunders was upon the spot, a shrewd adviser and a judicious purchaser of needed lands.

It has been said that Lawrence was, at the beginning, purely a business enterprise, but it is also conceded that the needs of a future community were clearly foreseen by the promoters and that steps were wisely taken to provide for coming population in advance of the then prevailing conception of public needs. Seldom do promoters encounter at the start more difficulties than did the founders of Lawrence. Textile manufacturing, in monster mills, was then an experiment in America. The works designed were upon a large scale, requiring heavy outlay and years of working and waiting for conclusive results. When operations were fairly begun adverse legislation and financial depression came to hinder and disturb, but the directors and managers of this company were men of courage, integrity and loyalty. Their fortunes and their reputations were staked upon the success of an enterprise that would affect the lives of thousands of men and women in this and in other lands, and provide new opportunities for breadwinners. Failure would result in loss to the stockholders and would also prove a public calamity and a blow at industrial development in America. The leaders, doubtless, had an eye for ultimate profits, but there was also a philanthropic spirit manifest in their action.

The public at this day probably does not fully realize the extent of the activities of the Essex Company, prior to the incorporation of the city.

Besides building the dam, canals, the first streets and drainage system, and fitting lands for habitation, the company built, equipped and for years operated the great machine shop, with foundry and forge shops, all of stone, (afterward controlled by a company organized as the "Lawrence Machine Shop", and now included in the Everett Mills group); also built fifty brick dwellings and a large boarding house, and made expensive improvements in deepening and straightening the Spicket River from the Machine shop raceway to its mouth.

As a protection against fire, at the joint cost of the company and the Bay State Mills, the Prospect Hill reservoir was built and connected with a system of water mains. Andover Bridge was purchased and repaired by it; a fine brick hotel (in later years enlarged and now the present Franklin House) was erected; gas works were needed, and this company, joining with the Bay State Mills, built the first works; the lumber dock, on Water street, was excavated, and lumber manufactured and sold in immense quantities during the busy early construction period.

In the loft of the machine shop, a full set of worsted machinery was set up and operated experimentally, the first attempt to develop that since important and growing industry of the city. Flumes, raceways, wheel pits and protecting walls were built, at great cost, at the central mill site. The company also engineered and built for owners, and, in some cases, built and sold to the original owners, the first Atlantic Cotton Mills, the Upper Pacific Mills, the Pemberton, Duck and Machine Shop buildings.

The central and beautiful Common, Storrow Park, Bodwell Park, Union Park and Stockton Park, besides a large tract of land on the west bank of the Shawsheen River, from Market to Andover streets, were reserved by the company and conveyed by deed of gift to the inhabitants of Lawrence to be forever used as public grounds. Besides, for recreation, it gave freely of lands for religious and educational purposes. In fact, there was hardly an activity working toward the development and advancement of the "new city," in which this corporation was not concerned. It was only after the progress of Lawrence was well under way and new enterprises took up the task of further development that the Essex Company turned its entire attention to the care of its own works, and the business of the company is now practically confined to the rental of its mill powers and the improvement of its remaining lands.

It may be truthfully said that few incorporated companies have been operated continuously, for more than 70 years, along definite lines so little changed. In the whole history of the company there have been but two treasurers in general management, Charles S. Storrow and Howard Stockton. The engineers in charge have been Capt. Charles H. Bigelow,

27

Great Falls Dam, Lawrence, Mass.

Benjamin Coolidge and Hiram F. Mills, although of late years Richard A. Hale, assistant engineer of the company, has practically filled the position of engineer. George D. Cabot, Capt. John R. Rollins, Henry H. Hall, Robert H. Tewksbury and Roland A. Prescott have in turn served as accountant and cashier. George Sanborn was connected with the company for 52 years, from 1845-1898, the most of the time as superintendent of outside construction. At his death, in 1898, he was succeeded by his son, George A. Sanborn, who still holds the position.

A large percentage of titles to real estate in Lawrence originated with the Essex Company and its records of deeds and surveys, open or public inspection, greatly simplify the work of examiners in perfecting titles.

BUILDING OF THE DAM

The construction of "The Great Stone Dam", perhaps the greatest contributing factor in developing Lawrence as one of the leading manufacturing cities of the country, was begun in the summer of 1845 and completed three years later. At the time of building, it was the most massive structure of the kind in the country and it remains, after more than three score and ten years, as permanent and complete as when first imbedded upon the solid rock foundation.

Within a few months of the organization of the Essex Company, July 5, 1845, the contract for the construction work was let to Gilmore & Carpenter. Excavations commenced August 1, 1845. The first stone was laid in the foundation line of headers at a point near the centre of the river by John A. Carpenter of the firm of contractors on September 19, 1845, and three years afterward, September 19, 1848, on the same day of the month and hour of the day, the last stone of the completed structure was laid at a point above the first bed stone, under the direction of the same contractor. The engineer in charge of the construction was Charles H. Bigelow, a captain of engineers in the United States Army. Under his supervision, the north canal was also constructed.

The dam is constructed of huge granite blocks, laid in hydraulic cement firmly embedded and bolted upon the river rock bed. The thickness at the base is 35 feet, narrowed gradually to about 13 feet below the crest stone. The greatest height of masonry is 32 feet and the average plunge of water 25 to 26 feet without flashboards. The masonry, including wings extending inland, is 1,629 feet in length. The overflow of water is 900 feet wide from wing to wing, the crest line curving slightly upstream. A solid filling of earth, backing the masonry and sloping back, one foot in six, protects the structure. The south wing wall is 324 feet long and the north wing 405 feet. The original cost of the structure, at the time of building when prices of labor and material ruled low, was about $250,000.

It is conceded to this day that the dam and guard locks were an advance upon engineering methods at the time. No rebuilding or special repair has been needed as no weakness or defect has been apparent since its completion. It stood the test of the flood of 1852, the most destructive on record for the Merrimack River, when the old tollhouse, part of the Falls Bridge and the fishway went into the swirl of water, ice, logs and debris.

THE NORTH CANAL

The building of the North Canal went on simultaneously with the construction of the dam. Water was let into the upper portion of this canal, to test the banks, on November 29, 1847. The guard locks were finished the same month. The entire canal was not filled until a year later, however. The North, or principal canal, is 5,330 feet in length and 100 feet wide at the beginning, narrowing to 60 feet at the outlet and is 12 feet in depth, the bottom being graded to a fall of one foot in 10,000 or six inches in its course. About 12,500 horsepower or 140 mill powers for ordinary working hours in the driest season was developed.

The banks of the canal are, to a large extent, artificial, necessitating a vast amount of thorough construction. The stream follows the line of the river, and the intervening space, measuring about 400 feet, is now the site of a continuous line of some of the city's most important industrial plants.

The South Canal, built by stages in more recent years, now measures three-quarters of a mile in length, is 60 feet wide and 10 feet deep.

The magnitude of this great waterpower development is conceivable in the fact that the great pond or reservoir formed by the building of the dam has an area of about one square mile. This large storage area, and the system of natural reservoirs, the lakes and ponds upon the Merrimack and its tributaries, covering more than 100 miles, fed from about 4,600 square miles of drainage area, prevent fluctuation and scarcity in dry seasons.

FIRST COMERS TO THE "NEW CITY"

The influx of population, following the beginning of the construction of the dam, brought a great number of people from various walks of life to the "new city" Business and professional men, and mechanics and laborers of all kinds began to settle here, coming from the country for miles about.

Among the first comers was Amos D. Pillsbury of Georgetown, who came to procure a shop for the manufacture and repair of boots, but, finding no available place, he purchased a gondola at Newburyport, 32 by 12 feet, on which he built a "stateroom", put in a stock of boots, shoes, leather, tools, cooking utensils and provisions, arrived at the "new city" just before the first land sale, anchored in the river below the bridge, threw out his plank and commenced business. Here he continued until cold weather, when he removed to Essex street into one of the new stores. He built in 1847 a building near the lower end of Common street, which he called the Montezuma House, one of the first hotels here. It was built without plan or system; the usual order of procedure was reversed by commencing at the top and leaving off at the cellar, it being raised and the roof covered before the cellar was dug. After a slight application of Spanish paint and the painting of the word Montezuma in large letters where no one would expect to see it, the building was completed. The walls of the house were covered with religious mottoes, and the guests were regaled with a constant flow of Scriptural quotations from the proprietor in place of the intoxicating beverages that were to be found at the other hotels. Both the Montezuma and its proprietor were noted for their peculiarities. About this time, Horace Greeley visited the town and stopped at the Montezuma, having been directed there upon inquiring for a hotel where liquor was not dispensed. Being of the same mind as regards the use of intoxicants, the famous journalist probably found his host interesting.

Another early trader was John C. Dow who for several years conducted a book and stationery store. John Colby opened a similar establishment about the same time, October 15, 1846. The first dry goods dealer was Artemus W. Stearns who opened a store on Amesbury street in 1846. Mr. Stearns erected the building on Essex street in 1854, which is now a part of the block occupied by the A. B. Sutherland Company. The first clothing dealer was William R. Spalding who came here in 1846. Hezekiah Plummer the first lumber dealer, erected a steam mill in South Lawrence for supplying lumber for the growing wants of the new town. Joseph Couch was the first trial justice. The first druggist was Nathaniel Wilson who came June 24, 1846. The first baker was Jeremiah S. Field who commenced running a cart Monday, January 25, 1847. The first mechanic locating in Lawrence was Henry Goodell who came here in the employ of the Essex Company, May 15, 1845. The first attorney was Henry Flanders who settled here March 10, 1846. Dr. Moses L. Atkinson, the first physician in Lawrence, opened an office on Turnpike street (Broadway) on January 1, 1846.

On February 6, 1849, the Lawrence Brass Band was organized. This early musical organization still exists. The first private school was opened on March 1, 1847, in the Essex Company's building on Turnpike street, which was later removed to the "plains." The first grammar school was established in 1848 on the site of the Unitarian church on Jackson street. The following year the High school was opened.

The pioneer Shawsheen House, the Oak Street House, the Montezuma and the United States Hotel were among the first hostelries, the last mentioned being destroyed by fire on August 12, 1859. Another was the Coburn House, opened in November 1847, by the Essex Company, now greatly enlarged and called the Franklin House. The Merrimack House was built about the same time at the corner of Broadway and Tremont street. This was burned in 1849, and not rebuilt. The Franklin is the only one of the early hotels to remain. The first boarding house was opened by Timothy Osgood at 2 Turnpike street on December 4, 1845. This was the first dwelling house raised here after the starting of operations on the dam.

The first brick store buildings on the south side were erected by J. N. Gage, near the bridge, in 1846; the first on the north side by Albert and Joseph Smith and Daniel Floyd on Common street below Newbury street. Ground was broken for the first block of brick stores on Essex street, afterwards known as Merchants Row, about the first of January 1847.

The first fraternal organization here, a lodge of Odd Fellows, was organized May 10, 1847. Ground was broken for the first mill, the Bay State, June 9, 1846. The first post office was opened September 7, 1846, and named Merrimack. The first house of worship was erected by Grace Episcopal Church in 1846. The first printing ever executed here was a handbill issued September 26, 1846, announcing that *the Merrimack Courier* would be issued October 9. The first brick for a brick block was laid August 12, 1846. It was the block at the corner of Methuen and Hampshire streets, being No. 1 of the Atlantic Mills boarding houses.

The first grocery store was opened in 1845 on the south side of the river by Josiah Crosby. This store with stock was afterward bought by Joseph Shattuck, who, with his brother Charles, conducted the business in the brick block, built by them on Essex street, until 1887, when they retired and were succeeded by Henry A. Buell & Co. This block is now occupied by the Lawrence Gas Company, and the Buell concern is doing business at the corner of Common and Newbury streets.

EARLY HISTORY OF LAWRENCE

The history of the territory, now comprised within the limits of the city, as Lawrence literally begins with the incorporation of the town, though the foundation from which the town sprung, and upon which the city grew, was started on August 1, 1845, with the excavating for the great stone dam of the Essex Company. When the Town of Lawrence was incorporated, April 17, 1847. The gigantic scheme of establishing a textile centre about Bodwell's Falls was well under way. In 1846, the construction of several of the mills was commenced, as was also the erection of an immense machine shop and foundry.

At the time the Essex Company began operations here the population was probably not over 200, but population rapidly followed enterprise. A boarding house was erected on the Turnpike. The frame was raised on September 12, 1845, and on December 4, following the finished house was occupied by Timothy Osgood who not infrequently lodged all the way from 100 to 200 beneath his roof. The rush was so great that no one thought of complaining of the lack of proper accommodations, if he were fortunate enough to gain admission inside a dwelling. For two years, the rush for houses continued almost unabated. Some of the laborers in the employ of the Essex Company walked nearly three miles every morning and night for months, so lacking were housing accommodations.

The news of the "new city" building attracted a great influx of mechanics and laborers into the whirlpool of activity, a term which probably best describes the scene during the construction period. There were no idle men, no idle teams. Every one was employed. Masons, carpenters, stonecutters, laborers were all doing their utmost. Laborers earned at that time 84 cents to $1.00 per day; mechanics, $1.50 to $2.00 per day.

In all the region in which the city now stands, there was no spot where one could escape the din and dust of bustling industry. Beginning at the gneiss ledge, situated nearly two miles south, the stone from which composes the river wall and mill foundations, —or at North Andover, three miles east, then the depository of bricks and lumber by railway, —or at Pelham, some eight miles west, from whence came the granite for the dam, there was an almost endless string of slow plodding teams, loaded to the utmost, all centering from the dam to the Spicket River to deposit their

33

loads, but here were not the only signs of activity. All over the place, buildings were rising with most astonishing celerity. For 12 hours a day the heavy teams, here removing hills, there filling valleys, or loaded with building materials, plodded through the suffocating dust of dry weather, or the almost bottomless mud of the rainy season. For months together the railway company delivered from 100,000 to 200,000 bricks per day at North Andover, all destined for the "new city."

The year 1846 saw the greatest number of big enterprises started, and this year and 1847 and 1848 might be regarded as a group of years forming the construction period, when nothing was manufactured for market and little productive machinery was operated. Sums, then considered vast, were expended in perfecting the huge plants designed to use the waterpower developed by the dam. The financial resources of the Essex Company were taxed to the utmost, and the confidence of its stockholders was severely tested at this time. The plan was of such magnitude that it required years for completion, and there could be no hope for an immediate return on the money invested.

Gaze, in imagination, upon the scene in the autumn of 1847, when the town was still in the first year of its infancy, and the following features will appear prominent. The heavy work on the dam was well in progress, the grading and walls of the canal taking shape along the north bank of the river; the Atlantic Mills were going up where they (what is left of them) now stand, the Bay State Mills were rising into view at the present site of the Washington Mills, and, below, upon the Spicket bank, the stone building of the great Machine Shop and Foundry, now the property of the Everett Mills, was coming into view. Boarding houses were in the process of construction for expected operatives; large saw mills, with a lumber dock and yard, were in operation at "Essex Yard", so-called; four projected railway lines were rapidly approaching the new town; groups of dwellings were scattered here and there upon the wide area, and, before electric lighting, gas, or kerosene even, the darkness, on starless nights, was profound; there was not a paved street, permanent sidewalk or public sewer. To the southwest of the dam, and above the north end of same, were the shanty villages, built upon leased land by Irish laborers who were attracted to the site by news of the "new city." These were the vanguard of a coming host, then new to the country. Many of them brought their whole wardrobe upon their backs, their entire possessions in a small bundle, but, by hard labor and thrifty ways, they attained to substantial competence. The shanty has given place to a modern dwelling, and their descendents are prominent in the professional and business life of the community.

All these enterprises, excepting the work at the Bay State Mills and upon the railroad lines, were carried along simultaneously by the Essex Company.

April 28, 1846, the first public sale of lands was made by the Essex Company. The highest price then obtained was for a lot at the corner of Jackson and Essex streets, which realized 70 cents per square foot. To-day this same lot is worth about $12.50 a square foot. Much land passed to individual ownership at that sale. The second public sale of land by the company did not occur until December 6, 1855, when 600 lots, located in almost every part of the city, were offered for sale.

On September 7, 1846, a post office was opened in a little building on the Turnpike, within a stone's throw of the site of the present post office building. The coming of this important adjunct of a busy community took many by surprise. The idea of establishing a post office here originated with George A. Waldo of Methuen, whose son, George Albert Waldo, was made the postmaster. The work of securing the necessary support of the idea at Washington was performed by Samuel J. Varney of Lowell, and at his suggestion, the office took the name of Merrimack. Prior to this, from the commencement of operations on the dam, the place was known by such names as "New City", "Essex", "Andover Bridge", etc.

In 1846 and early 1847, there was a large accession to the population. Mechanics, merchants, physicians and lawyers began to locate here, and order commenced rising out of chaos. In 1846, the first religious service was held, and by the following year, most of the leading sects were established here. In October 1846, the first newspaper was issued under the name of *The Merrimack Courier*, by J. F. C Hayes.

The name of Merrimack, given officially to the place by the establishment of the post office, was continued until the Town of Lawrence was set off from Methuen and Andover by legislative enactment in the winter of 1847, which separation, by the way, was made in face of strong opposition from both towns. The question had arisen just prior to this as to what name the proposed town should take, and, on January 13, 1847, a meeting of a considerable number of residents was held in the office of the Essex Company, with a view to an understanding. The name of Lawrence was agreed upon as a token of respect to a distinguished family of that name, two of whom, Abbott and Samuel, were among the most energetic businessmen in New England. In fact, in point of investment the family had as great an interest here as had all others combined. They had staked a fortune on the success of the project, and Abbott, as the first president of the Essex Company, and Samuel, as the head of the Bay State Corporation, were prominently identified with all the leading enterprises. Naturally, their family name was embodied in the petition to the legislature for the town charter. So when, on April 17, 1847, the charter was granted, the town became known as Lawrence, and the city has retained that name.

In accordance with the provisions of the charter, the first town meeting was held on April 26 in Merrimack Hall (on the corner of Jackson and Common streets, then the largest hall in the place), and the first town officers were elected and moneys appropriated for the various functions of the government. At this meeting, the nucleus of the present police department was formed with the appointment of 10 constables, and the community, which had lived hitherto almost without law, in territorial independence, came under proper restraints. Money was voted for the purchase of two hand engines for the fire department, just organized. Prior to that, the only apparatus for fighting fires was the "Essex," the first fire engine in use here, which had been purchased by the Essex Company and manned by its workmen. This engine was sold to the town and was soon followed by more powerful machines and hose and hook and ladder companies until, at the introduction of the steam fire engine, the department was well equipped.

At the same town meeting, money was also voted for two schoolhouses to augment the accommodations of the three little district schools that had served since and prior to the laying of the foundation of the dam. The year following, 1848, two grammar schools were opened, and in January 1849, the High school was established. This was the beginning of the fine public school system of which the people of Lawrence are so justly proud. In 1847, an important educational institution was also established in the Franklin Library, founded by private subscription, which in 1872 was donated to the city and. formed the basis of the present well equipped Public Library.

The first bank, the Bay State, afterward becoming known as the Bay State National and the only national bank in the city today, was established in 1847, as a bank of discount. In October of the same year, the first savings institution, the Essex Savings Bank, was started.

In 1847, the Bay State Mills, the Atlantic Mills and the Essex Company formed into an association and erected suitable buildings for the manufacture of gas for their own use. In February, 1849, the association disbanded, and a stock company, known as the Lawrence Gas Company, took over the works and began lighting the streets and running its pipes into private residences.

At the time of the first town meeting, the people were comparatively strangers to one another, and it was somewhat difficult to select for office, according to the usual rule, by party lines. Therefore, the best possible

36

selection for town officers was made irrespective of party. Not so, the following year, when party lines were sharply drawn and the election of town officers was one of the most animated ever held in this vicinity. Ballot after ballot, without affecting a choice of officers, consumed the day and the business, which was to be acted upon, was not half finished when night compelled an adjournment. The sites for the Town hall and Oliver schoolhouse were among the questions laid over. These articles in the warrant came up at an adjourned meeting. No one seemed inclined to interfere with the arrangement in regard to the schoolhouse, but when the question of the location of the hall came in order to be acted upon, there was a noisy opposition to every proposition for location, with no definite aim at reconciliation. The matter was finally determined, however, and the present building erected.

The year 1848 was one of the most progressive years in the early history of Lawrence. In that year the group of industrial enterprises in construction was practically completed and some cloth manufactured, though it was not until 1849 that the production of goods for market commenced at the several mills, and machinery was turned out at the great machine shop. In later years, the building of other mills followed, and new enterprise, taking up this phase of the work of the Essex Company, encouraged the growth of the city's industries. The dam was completed in September of 1848, and the water was turned into the North canal.

It was during 1848 that streets and parks were laid out and suitable drainage provided. One might think to look over the valley stretching between Prospect and Tower Hills that the civil engineers of the Essex Company, when they began operations here, had a snap in laying out streets and lots. But the present land surface offers little suggestion of what the original was.

Deep gullies cut up the valley, through which little watercourses ran to the river. One of them was so long and important that the company built a costly stone culvert through it. Vast amounts of filling were necessary, for while an Indian trail could run down a steep path into a gully and up again on the other side, the great drays which were destined to team the product of the busy multitude that would throng the valley, would need to travel in lines of far less resistance. Then too, there would come the problem of drainage, with the need of continuous and fairly uniform gradients.

The big stone culvert, which the Essex Company built, served Lawrence for a main sewer for many years. The course of the culvert was quite a circuitous one, and it played a very important part in the early plans of the city sanitation. For years, it received all the house drainage and street wash between Jackson street and Broadway, and north as far as Haverhill street.

An attempt was made to establish a water supply by conveying water from Haggett's Pond, Andover, but it developed that the scheme was impracticable. Subsequently the Bay State Mills and the Essex Company built a reservoir on Prospect Hill, particularly for fire protection for the mills, and kept it filled by pumping from the canal. A few houses were piped with the water and it was used to some extent for domestic purposes. Most of the inhabitants, however, clung to the wells, the original source of supply, until the establishment of the city water works.

About this time, June 8, 1848, the first police court was held in a building on the northerly side of Common street near Broadway; in the rear was the lock-up. Judge William Stevens of North Andover was the presiding justice. After the Town Hall was built, police court for a time was held in what is now the council chamber, the judge's office being in the little coatroom at the westerly end, now occupied by the assistant city auditor. The cells for the prisoners were in the basement. Before the Civil war, disturbances becoming lively on the "plains," the city for a time maintained a lock-up on Elm street near Lawrence street. These were the police court facilities until the building was erected which occupied the site of the present station at the corner of Common and Lawrence streets. The first Superior court was located in the auditorium of the Town Hall, railings and fixtures being removed on town meeting days.

Early in 1848, the importance of securing and laying out a place for the repose of the dead began to receive serious attention. The original lot designated for this purpose embraced but about three acres. Subsequently this sacred enclosure was enlarged and it became known as Bellevue Cemetery. The Catholics early consecrated the ground on the summit of Currant Hill. Later Father O'Donnell secured the tract for the second cemetery on the west of the old ferry road, and his successors obtained a still larger tract extending from the northern line of the second to the southern line of the first Catholic burying-ground.

Direct railway communication was opened with Boston, Lowell and Salem, and Lawrence became an important railroad centre. The Boston & Maine railway, having changed its location from Andover to North Andover, constructed between April, 1845, and March, 1848, the five miles of road between those places by way of this city, together with bridges across the river and canal, and on February 28, 1848, ran their passenger cars across the bridge for the first time to the station on the north side of the river. On July 2, 1848, the Lowell railway was completed between

Lawrence and Lowell. The Essex railway, from Lawrence to Salem, was opened on September 4, 1848. The Manchester and Lawrence railway was opened for travel in October 1849. railroad facilities followed the growth of the city, and constant improvements were made in the service. Eventually the need of a Horse Railroad was apparent, and in 1867, the first track was laid from the Woolen mill in Methuen to the Everett mills at the foot of Essex street.

In June 1848, the first important step was taken in the movement for the navigation of the Merrimack above tidewater. On the 6th of that month, the steamer "Lawrence" came up from Newburyport with a delegation from that place and adjoining towns, landing her passengers about opposite the foot of Hampshire street. Since then sundry attempts have been made to navigate the river, but with little success.

In 1848, the town had a population of nearly 6,000. Of that number, 3,750 were of native birth; 2,139 were natives of Ireland; there were one German, one Italian, three Frenchmen, two Welshmen, nine natives of Scotland, 28 people of English birth and 16 negroes. Not so, cosmopolitan as today, but it was largely representative of the dominating races at present.

It was in 1848 that the town rejected the offer of the Common as a gift, but at a subsequent meeting wisely accepted. The Essex Company had stipulated that the town must fence the tract, and spend $300 a year for 20 years to beautify it. It seems as though in that day, too, the cry of "influence of corporations" was effective. At any rate, it nearly caused the loss of this boon to the community. On October 7, 1868, the Common became the property of the city, without restriction.

Town meetings continued turbulent until the town became a city, and adjourned meetings were frequent. During the summer of 1849, a sort of mania for town meetings pervaded the people. Generally speaking, the Whigs were in the ascendancy, although now and then a Democratic selectman or other town officer was chosen. No public meeting ever assembled in this city equaled the last meeting of the electors of the town. During the melee, General Oliver lost his coattail.

The city charter was passed by the legislature, March 21, 1853, and was accepted by the people on the 29th of the same month. The first election under the charter was held on the 18th of April following, and the city government was duly organized on the 18th of May, the same year (for personnel of city or town governments see General Statistics). At the first city election, there were about 1,000 names on the voting list, and from the vote cast it is apparent that nearly every one took an active interest in the proceedings.

There was not a rod of paved street in the city in 1853 and not forty rods of brick or of any permanent sidewalk. Concrete had not been used for walks at that time. The few walks that had been laid were of gravel and planks or boards. The entire south side of Essex street and a considerable portion of the north side was open, undeveloped land. The City Hall stood in an open field, abutted by buildings only on a portion of the Essex street side. The City Hall, the Jail and the Oliver schoolhouse (the last mentioned much smaller than the building recently razed to make room for the Central Grammar School) were the only public buildings constructed of permanent materials. The Jail or House of Correction was built that year.

*Charles S. Storrow, the first mayor, was elected by the Whig party. He was succeeded in 1854 by Enoch Bartlett, a candidate of the Democratic party and a young lawyer of considerable promise. It was during his administration that the "Know-Nothing" uprising commenced. That was a trying experience for Mayor Bartlett. Not long after his election, he had suffered a loss of health, and the worry and excitement attendant upon the popular demonstrations, at times threatening the peace of the community, taxed his waning energy. Shortly after the end of his official term, he went home to New Hampshire, his native state, to die.

In 1855, the "Know-Nothings" swept the city, electing Albert Warren as mayor. Their cry was "Nothing but native Americans in public office." The Whig and Democratic parties had dwindled down to a very few on either side, who had little fear of the Pope of Rome making America his immediate headquarters. The sweep in Lawrence, however, was no more general than throughout the state. In 1856, the election was a repetition of the year before, Warren being reelected. The Democratic party made no nomination, and John R. Rollins received the support of all voters not affiliated with the "Know-Nothings."

In 1857, party lines were not so strictly defined. The "Know-Nothing" party had just expired. John R. Rollins was elected mayor over Thomas Wright. Both Rollins and Wright were Whigs. The city at the time was strongly anti-Democratic. Rollins was re-elected in 1858, over N. G. White, also a Whig, the Democrats throwing their support to Rollins' opponent as in the preceding year.

The Republican party supplanted the Whig party in 1859, and Henry K. Oliver, the Republican mayoralty nominee, was elected, though Daniel Saunders, Jr., the Democratic candidate, had the support of some of the most active Republicans. On the other hand, General Oliver was sup-

* Hon. Charles S. Storrow died April 30, 1904, aged 95 years.

ported by influential Catholic Democrats and their followers. Feeling ran high, but the Irish vote being finally secured for the general, he was elected by a decided majority. The following year the political pot was turned over, and Daniel Saunders, Jr., was elected. It was during the first month of his administration that occurred the terrible disaster, the fall of the Pemberton Mill.

Party politics in municipal affairs continued to attract a keen interest in succeeding years, until party lines were wiped out at the adoption of the new city charter in 1912. For a number of years prior to then the Democrats were the dominating party. and are still, locally, in state and national elections.

In patriotism, Lawrence has never been lacking, and in 1861, she gave one of the first martyrs of the Rebellion, when Sumner H. Needham fell in Baltimore on the memorable 19th of April. Lawrence furnished 2,497 men for the war, 224 over and above all demands. Ninety-two were commissioned officers. The whole amount of money appropriated and expended by the city on account of the war, exclusive of State aid, was $115,630.10. The total amount of State aid paid to families of volunteers, and which was afterward repaid by the Commonwealth, was $192,233.05. The nation has never looked in vain to Lawrence in her need.

Lawrence has passed through numerous crises, and in the early years of the city, the blows have been most severe. The tariff enacted soon after the first manufacturing here nearly paralyzed the industries just then started. The great and memorable panic of 1857-58 gave the city a setback from which it slowly recovered. The Pemberton disaster came upon its heels, and the boom times of the war were followed by the rapid and demoralizing shrinkage in values in 1872-74. Nothing in the way of a serious calamity occurred from then up to within the past 27 years, except the cyclone in South Lawrence in 1890, which resulted in the loss of eight lives and great damage to property.

During her early history, Lawrence suffered from both flood and fire. In 1852, the town was thrown into almost a panic by the great freshet of that year, when the highest pitch of the water was ten feet above the crest of the dam. This freshet washed out the abutment of the bridge and the tollhouse on the south side of the river, and, at intervals, the water reached the woodwork on the railroad bridge.

There was dread of an overflow of the wing walls of the dam, and, to protect the town, a train of cars and a large number of teams were run night and day in conveying earth for an embankment. The lowlands on the riverbank were flooded, and on a number of occasions since during heavy spring freshets, these sections have been overflowed, though in recent years there has been little damage in this respect. The nearest approach to the freshet of 1852 was that of 1896, when the water reached nine feet nine inches, or within three inches of the great flood.

Destructive fires have been numerous, especially in the early years. One of the most disastrous fires that occurred in the city broke out on August 12, 1859. in what was known as the "United States Hotel," which was located on Essex street, midway between Appleton and Jackson streets. That structure soon went down, killing in its fall two young men. From this the fire spread east, destroying one or two stores, and west to Appleton street, wiping out what was then known as the "Church Block", embracing the Second Congregational church, with stores under same, and thence traversing north, carried down the courthouse. The Unitarian church, some distance removed, was ignited by the sparks and cinders, and badly damaged.

Another conflagration, which should be given special mention, was that started by the burning of the steam mill of Wilson & Allyn on May 2, 1860. The mill, formerly the meetinghouse which stood, in the pioneer days, on the hill near the farmhouse of Fairfield White, was a two-story building, and filled, from base to attic, with combustible materials. A brisk wind carried the burning embers high in the air and scattered them upon the roofs of buildings as far as Tower Hill. By the aid of ladders and water buckets many buildings in the path of the flying coals were saved, and every structure west of the railway escaped destruction. Several wooden workshops between the mill and the railway went down, and the large carriage manufactory of General Gale was saved with much difficulty.

Although there have been fires with greater amount of damage than the aforesaid conflagrations, none have occurred that covered so large an area. It has been frequently predicted that Lawrence will yet experience a terrible conflagration in one of its congested tenement districts, but it is to be hoped that the prospect will continue as a prediction only. An efficient, well-equipped fire department, with a favorable combination of circumstances, has kept the number of destructive fires in recent years comparatively small.

Beyond a slow, steady growth of the city, there were few extraordinary public improvements during the 25 years that followed the Civil War. A notable improvement was the straightening of the Spicket River and the building of the main sewer through that section during the years 1883 to 1886. It might also be mentioned that street letter boxes were introduced here November 15, 1867; that the first fire alarm telegraph system was

CHARLES S. STORROW

completed July 25, 1869, and that the legislative act to provide for a water supply was accepted May 7, 1872. In November of the following year, ground was broken for the reservoir on Tower Hill.

It is worthy of mention, in closing this chapter, that during the hard times of 1857, an invention of incalculable importance to the world was brought out successfully in this city by two of the employees of the Lawrence Machine Shop. We refer to the steam fire engine. The inventors were Thomas Scott and N. S. Bean. Although there were other engines built elsewhere at the same time, it remained for Lawrence to produce the most practical. This city was awarded the palm at a test of machines at Boston. The first engine built here was called the Lawrence and was purchased by the City of Boston. The invention was bought by the Amoskeag Company of Manchester, N. H., where the engines were manufactured for many years. These machines completely revolutionized fire departments, and Lawrence was not slow to adopt them.

Mills along the Merrimack River

Industrial Growth

No history of Lawrence would be complete without a chapter devoted to the industrial growth of the city. Over half of the city's valuation comes from the 40 or more industrial concerns, and most of it represents property of the textile manufactories, their plants alone covering a land area estimated to be about 283 acres.

The development of the great mills has been the most remarkable feature of Lawrence's history. They are the backbone of the community, the city's greatest asset. Their army of operatives would make a good-sized city in itself. They give directly employment to about one-third of the population and, as the channels of trade are filled largely by the earnings of the textile workers, they are the lifeblood of the remaining two-thirds. Their presence has attracted other manufacturers in a great diversity of lines, and they have been a means of stimulating general enterprise. They have not only gained a worldwide recognition for themselves, but they have put Lawrence on the map as one of the greatest industrial centers.

The story of the small beginnings of these hives of industry, their prodigious growth, their present mammoth proportions and gigantic operations outrivals even the tale of the "magic growth" of western cities.

Prior to the building of the dam, the only industries here were the little Durant paper mill on the south bank of the Spicket, east of Newbury street, the Stevens' box shop on the site of the Arlington Mills, engaged in the manufacture of cases for the Chickering pianos, and the old Graves soap factory at the foot of Clover Hill; and in the whole area within the city's limits were less than 200 souls. Through out all this territory were a few scattered farmhouses, the nearest approach to a settlement being the "Four Corners," or cross-roads, where Andover street now crosses South Broadway. Through this small habitation flowed the Merrimack River with its latent power.

Briefly, that was the industrial prospect when Daniel Saunders and his associates conceived the idea of turning the tremendous water power of the Merrimack at Bodwell's Falls to the use of manufacturing industry. That they built well is evidenced by the great textile centre which today occupies the site of their operations.

During the three years required for building the dam, the foundation of the present industrial growth was laid. On April 11, 1846, the Bay State Mills (now the Washington Mills plant of the American Woolen Company) were laid out and put in operation in 1847. Construction work commenced on the Atlantic Cotton Mills on June 9, and on the Essex Company's machine shop and foundry (now the property of the Everett Mills) on June 10, 1846.

The Pacific Mills and the Pemberton were incorporated in 1853; the Lawrence Duck Company in 1853; the Everett in 1860; the Lawrence Woolen Company (now Kunhardt's) in 1864, and the Arlington in 1865.

For the first quarter century, after the starting of the pioneer mills at Lawrence, manufacturing in America was a matter largely of experiment. Machinery and methods of operation had not been perfected; the prejudice against homemade fabrics had not been overcome by actual and extensive tests. It 'would take a volume of goodly proportion to fully narrate the experiments, the trials, the partial failures and the eventual successes of local enterprises, and a larger volume in which to pay due tribute to the patient labor and hard study of scores of men who within the walls of our mills have by investigation and by trial brought processes of textile manufacture to such a state of perfection that it is now mostly a contest between rivals as to which shall be entitled to preference and public favor when all have attained to model methods and have discovered and applied processes differing only in degree.

Many things, all-important in modern life, had their beginning here. The worsted industry was made practical and leading in the mills of Lawrence. The use of wood pulp and Manila grass in paper manufacture was demonstrated to be practical at the orginal Russell Paper Mills. Machinery for the sewing of leather and other devices in the perfection of shoe machinery were first attempted and brought to some degree of perfection in the old Lawrence Machine Shop, a concern that, while it failed as a corporation, left much that was valuable to its successors elsewhere. There is nothing the value of which it is so hard to estimate as the value of a practical and useful invention in processes of manufacture, for millions eventually share in the benefits secured. In every branch of textile and paper manufacture, important inventions and improvements have been made by Lawrence mechanics and manufacturers.

Our industrial plants are constantly reaching out for improvements and, notwithstanding the impression among some people abroad, who are not familiar with the requirements of the work, a vast amount of skill and ingenuity are necessary for the successful operation of the big, textile mills. As the head of one of the large plants of the city has very aptly put it, "the factory of today calls upon almost every department of human knowledge for its development and maintenance. It demands the services of the civil, mechanical, hydraulic and steam engineer, the carpenter and the builder of brick and stone, wood and iron, the foundry and the machine shop, the inventor, the mechanic, the skilled artisan, the engraver, printer and dyer. It also needs the chemist, the electrician and the man of scientific research."

It was with the operative population of Lawrence, that the Pacific set up the first combing machines used in the country; the Washington made the first all-wool dress goods, the famous Bay State shawls and blue flannel coatings being originated by these mills; the Arlington was the first to successfully manufacture, in the United States, black alpacas, mohairs and brilliantines, in which class of goods England formerly had monopoly. With the Lawrence operatives originated Paul's self-acting mules, the Pearl spindle for cotton spinning, the Wade bobbin holder which revolutionized the process of spooling, the high speed steam engine, and the successful steam fire engine, to mention but a few of the notable inventions originated and developed here.

The financial crisis of 1857 struck a severe blow to Lawrence's industries, and the growth of the city during its first decade was very much retarded. Nearly all the mills suspended for a short time; then occurred the failure of the Bay State Mills and their reorganization. The terrible Pemberton Mill calamity of 1860 was an added blow. But, owing to a big demand for the products of the local mills during the war of the Rebellion, Lawrence took a new start. The boom times during and after the war, however, were followed by the rapid and demoralizing shrinkage in values in 1872-74. Other depressions have occurred, coming about once in every 10 years, though not as serious as those experienced in the early years. But the Lawrence industries have weathered the gales in a manner that indicated a sound stability.

The most marked development in the industrial growth came in 1905 when William M. Wood of the American Woolen Co. conceived the plan of procuring yarn for the various mills of the concern without being dependent upon other manufacturers. Thus, it was that the mammoth plant which bears his name came into being. The building of the Wood Mills started a decade of mill construction in Lawrence such as has probably never been witnessed in any other textile centre. Within a few years most of the leading plants made big additions. The erection of the Ayer Mills (named for the late Frederick Ayer, a manufacturer of note) followed and the Arlington Mills were greatly enlarged, several new buildings being constructed by this corporation at a cost estimated to be nearly a million dollars. Large additions were made to the Pacific, Washington,

Everett, Kunhardt and Duck. The big, new print works of the Pacific, besides the large coating mill of the Champion-International Paper Company (into which concern were merged the Russell paper mills), were built during this construction period; also the Uswoco Mill of the United States Worsted Company, the Katama Mill and the worsted and merino yarn mill of the Monomac Spinning Company. Many of the minor industrial plants have also increased their facilities for production. Besides, new industries have come to the city, the most notable of the recent arrivals being the Walton Shoe Company, which has occupied the old Stanley machine shop building on Haverhill street, and the Diamond Match Company, opposite the Wood Mills, the scouring liquor waste of which it uses in the manufacture of its product.

The Everett, Kunhardt and Lawrence Duck are listed among the big textile mills, but the American Woolen, Pacific and Arlington stand out as the mammoth plants of the city, their immense proportions and their great volume of production amazing all tourists. These three, in their groups, have single buildings that dwarf the average factory structure. In the case of the American Woolen Company, this is especially true. In fact, in size, there is no other to compare with the Wood Mills. Some idea of the size of this immense plant may be gained by recalling that the main building is a quarter of a mile long, 123 feet wide and six stories high; that there are 29 acres of floor space under one roof, and that from three-quarters of a million to a million pounds of wool are consumed each week by the plant when it is running to its full capacity. The Washington and Ayer, the other big plants of the American Woolen Company in Lawrence, are huge in size, though not nearly as large as the Wood.

Not only is the plant of the Wood Worsted Mills the largest single mill plant in the world, but it has the distinction of having been erected in a shorter time than any other manufacturing establishment of magnitude. Conceived one day, it was, as it were, in operation the next. Cloth was being manufactured in April 1906, where a long line of willow trees and birches were swaying in the breezes of the previous August.

Had the prediction been made in the summer of 1905 that machinery would be humming in a mammoth mill eight months later where, at the time of the prediction, there existed only a rough, half-wooded field along a winding river bank, it would have been regarded as preposterous. Yet 900 men accomplished this seeming impossibility. There was no magic to it. It was not an Arabian Nights dream. It was a twentieth century wonder, made possible by foresight, industry, energy, persistence and skill.

It remained for a man who had risen from the bottom to the top of the, mill ladder to startle the industrial world with this example of what dash, pluck and push can do when backed by brains. The Wood Mills stand today a monument to the enterprise of William M. Wood.

The growth of the Arlington Mills has also been most remarkable. From the small wooden structure that was wholly consumed by fire in 1866 to the great system of mills that reach out beyond the city limits into the adjacent town of Methuen is a long step in factory development. The top mill of this group is one of the largest mill buildings in the country. This concern is famed for its most extensive variety and its quality of yarns, besides its specialties in plain and fancy fabrics. Notable improvements in the process of the manufacture of dress goods originated at the Arlington. The record of the corporation for regular payment of dividends for 40 years has been interrupted only by the omission of a dividend on Jan. 1, 1914, and this lapse was made up on July 2nd of 191 7, when a special dividend of $2 a share was paid in addition to the regular quarterly dividend of $1.50 per share. Joseph Nickerson, Albert W. Nickerson, William Whitman and Franklin W. Hobbs, the present head, have been the controlling minds in the building up of this great institution.

The Pacific Mills, also, have had a marvelous growth. Their buildings cover an immense area. The main mill is one of the most prominent structures in the city; it is 806 feet long by 72 feet wide, and seven stories in height. To go through the various rooms of this building would necessitate the walk of more than a mile. The new print works, located on a seventeen-acre lot, have absorbed the Hamilton works of Lowell, besides the works of the Cocheco Mills of the corporation at Dover, N. H. They are reputed to be the largest plant of their kind in the world. The Pacific stand pre-eminent among the mills of their class in America. Their products are world-famous. Locally the plant is regarded as the most steadily operated in the city. In March 31, 1913, this corporation bought at auction the Atlantic Cotton Mills, thus securing a valuable site for a new mill and much desired room for further expansion later when the pioneer Atlantic is torn down. The guiding heads of the great concern are Robert F. Herrick, president, and Edwin Farnham Greene, treasurer.

Remarkable improvements have been made in the mills, tending to the physical and mental comforts of the workers. Not only have the hours of labor been greatly reduced, but the sanitary arrangements have been much improved. At the very beginning of manufacturing here, operatives began work at 5:30 o'clock in the morning; there was a half hour for breakfast and a half hour for dinner; the day's work closed at 7 o'clock in the evening and was a day of 13 hours. Later the noon respite was increased and the breakfast recess discontinued while the working day has been reduced to 11 and then to 10 hours, and now the 54-hour law sets the length of time at 54 hours a week. Instead of starting work at 5:30 a. m., the operatives in the mills now begin at 6:45 a. m. In the early days, lighting and ventilation were poor. Besides, there was little chance for rest or recreation, while the wages were very small as compared to what are paid today, and the method of paying not so convenient as the weekly system in use now.

During the earlier years of Lawrence, the principal industries were the large cotton and woolen mills, located mostly upon the North canal and dependent upon the dam in the river for their power. But after the Civil war, many industries of wide range of character were drawn to Lawrence. A second canal was constructed on the south side of the river, and as the calls for more mill sites were made, this canal was extended in length. Steam power is also used in many factories and shops, and, within a few years, electrical power has been introduced, the Pacific Mills having in operation a large electric powerhouse a short distance from the plant. Paper mills, machine shops, iron and brass foundries, woodworking establishments, shoe factories, and many others have been added to the industries of the city. A notable feature of the expansion of the larger plants is the gradual disappearing of the old corporation boarding houses.

The diversified nature of the textile industries of Lawrence has done much to keep it on the level keel of prosperity when other manufacturing cities staggered under the depression in their one line of production. When the cotton goods market is poor the worsted goods market is apt to be all right, and, as Lawrence manufactures both lines extensively, the city is not so seriously affected when one market falls off. This city does a tremendous business in worsteds, being according to the United States Bureau of Statistics, the second largest producer of fine worsteds in the country, Philadelphia alone leading it.

The relationship between capital and labor, between the employer and the employed, is always an important factor in any manufacturing community. Lawrence, with a few exceptions, has been free from strikes and labor troubles. The only controversy that could be considered as very serious was the big strike of 1912, which was attended with violence and, through the misrepresentations of unscrupulous or ignorant writers, brought the city into ill repute. As a rule, the corporations and employers have been liberal and fair in their management of affairs and the laboring classes have been reasonable and patient in their demands, each preferring peaceable arbitration to compulsory measures for the settlement of their difficulties.

The many small property owners in Lawrence bear testimony to the thrift and industry of its wage earners. The city is noted for the large percentage of working people who own their homes.

TWENTY-SEVEN YEARS OF PROGRESS

From 1890 to 1917, Lawrence had its greatest development. These years are remarkable for the great number of public improvements made, and the extraordinary expansion of the city's industries and subsequent influx of population and growth of property valuation.

The year 1891 saw the passing of the horse car and the applying of electric power on the street railway, whose lines soon began reaching out through all parts of the city and to surrounding cities and towns. The removal of Gale's hill and the filling in of the low lands of Ward Five were started, and steps were taken toward the establishment of a filtration system in connection with the city's water supply that year. The following year the construction of the filter beds was begun. In 1896, the high service system was added to the water works. In the meantime, there was a radical departure in schoolhouse construction with the building of the Rollins school, which was soon followed by the erection of the Tarbox school in 1895 along the same modern lines. The State armory was completed, as was the Public Library building during this construction period. Great improvements were made in the sewerage system, the Water street sewer, draining the lowlands of ward five, being built in 1893, the construction of the Shanty Pond sewer, draining the section of South Lawrence west of South Broadway, being started in 1895.

In 1896, Engine 7's house and Engine 6's house were completed. The following year the Weatherbee school was built. In 1898, land was purchased and plans selected for the new; High school on Lawrence street, and on June 17 of the following year the corner stone of the building was laid. The same year land was secured for the erection of the Bruce school. In 1900, Engine 8's house was built. The construction of the present courthouse was started and the new General hospital building dedicated in 1902. The following year the United States government purchased land for the post-office building in Depot Square. In 1904 the erection of the Bay State block, Lawrence's tallest building, was begun, and work started on the post office and Hood school buildings. In 1905, two attempts were made to secure an auxiliary water supply from driven wells, but all borings failed. About the same time an agitation started for the covered filter, located north of the original filter bed. In 1906, the high-pressure water service for fire protection was installed in the business district.

The year 1905 saw the beginning of the greatest period of building construction since the founding of the city. In the three years that followed, it has been estimated, there was $10,000,000 expended in building operations. The magnificent Wood mills were erected in this period, also the Ayer mills and great additions to several of the other industrial plants. The enormous increase in manufacturing facilities attracted thousands of people to the city, and in providing accommodations for them hundreds of dwellings were erected, besides a number of business blocks. Public improvements kept pace. In 1907 the erection of the large Central fire station was started, and was completed the following year, when Engine 9's house was also built.

In 1908, began the movement for permanent street pavement, with the paving of Common street. The following year Essex street was repaved, and it is today one of the finest roadways in New England. In 1912 paving operations were taken up on a still larger scale and in the next five years over a half million dollars was spent by the city for street paving. All of the main thoroughfares have been paved with granite blocks, besides many other streets. In 1909, the Tuberculosis hospital was built, and in 1910, Engine 4's house.

In the fall of 1911, the question of a new city charter was taken up by the voters, with the result that the old original charter was abolished and the commission form of government adopted. The same year the Breen school was built.

The year 1912 goes down in history as probably the most eventful since the incorporation of the city, important because of the radical change in the management of the city under a new charter, but in the main because of the big strike of mill operatives, that through the misrepresentations of itinerant agitators and unscrupulous writers attracted international notice, and cost the city, county, state and corporations hundreds of thousands of dollars, besides reflecting discredit upon the community.

The strike and subsequent happenings did not give the people much time to look into the workings of the new charter, but it has since proven its worth, though there are some features of it which might be improved upon. A notable event of 1912 was the establishment of the supervised playground system, which has met with remarkable success. A deep interest in the city playgrounds followed with the result that the park system has been extended and big improvements have been made on all the grounds.

In 1913, definite steps were taken toward the construction of a Central bridge over the Merrimack River. About the same time, a survey of the Merrimack River was made for a proposed deep waterway. A regrettable event of this year was the disaster which occurred on June 30, when 11 boys were drowned in the Merrimack River as the result of the collapse of a gangplank at one of the bathhouses. The use of these houses was discontinued in consequence, and it is expected that they will be replaced in the near future by a suitable municipal swimming pool.

A notable improvement in 1914 was a revision of the building ordinances, the city council adopting a building code prepared by the planning board. That year work was started on the construction of a new police station. In the year 1915 was experienced a business depression, when the city government was confronted with a difficult problem in providing work for the unemployed. The construction of the Ward One sewer was started, and the building of the new central Oliver grammar school was also begun, on June 2, that year.

The years 1916 and 1917 were the busiest and most prosperous years in the city's history. The great demand for textile products, caused by the European war, kept every mill running to its full capacity, and labor was in great demand. Municipal and general business interests shared in the beneficial results. The value of mill stocks reached such a point that the most unprecedented increases in corporation tax revenue were secured by the city. Big voluntary raises in pay were given the mill operatives. Outside the extra-ordinary activity of the industries, the notable events of these years were two calls to arms by the national government. In June 1916, the local militia units were called to the Mexican border, when trouble threatened with Mexico. In April 1917, a more serious summons came when war was declared against Germany.

Lawrence Today

AREA : 4,577 acres, about equally divided by the Merrimack River; 2,216 acres in North Lawrence; 2,097. South Lawrence; 264; Merrimack River.

SITUATED : Within easy reach of seaboard. Twenty-six miles from Boston, on lines of Boston & Maine Railroad, with 150 passenger trains daily, also centre of street railway system, carrying 9,000,000 passengers yearly. Excellent waterpower. Merrimack River which flows through city turns more spindles than any other stream on earth.

POPULATION : Over 100,000, including 47 nationalities. Three suburban towns adjoining depend almost entirely upon city's industries and mercantile enterprises. Combined population of Lawrence and contiguous towns, over 130,000.

INDUSTRIES : New England's greatest textile centre. Largest woolen textile manufacturing centre in the United States (aside from Philadelphia carpets). Third city in Massachusetts in value of general products, Boston and Worcester only exceeding it. Has largest print works and worsted mills in the world. Mills cover nearly 300 acres. Over 30,000 employed in the textile plants alone. Annual payroll of over $32,000,000; annual production of over $150,000,000; invested capital of over $127,000,000. Wide diversification of industries, manufactures including: Worsteds, woolens, cotton cloth, print goods, paper, paper mill machinery, shoes, shoe machinery, braids, rugs, carriages, wheels, bobbins, fibre board, boilers, chemicals, soap, loom. harnesses, mill supplies, besides various products of foundries, machine and woodworking shops, granite works, etc.

PUBLIC HEALTH : According to mortuary statistics for July 1917, Lawrence leads the cities of the country in health conditions, notwithstanding the mixed nature of population. City has excellent water supply system. First successful municipal filtration plant installed here. Reservoir, pumping station and 103.5 miles of water mains. 90 miles of sewers. 17 parks and playsteads, comprising 164.67 acres. General, municipal and tuberculosis hospitals. Medical inspection and dental clinics in connection with schools. Sanitary arrangements in the factories of the very best. Strict enforcement of health regulations.

PUBLIC SAFETY : Well equipped police and fire departments. Police station, district court and nine engine houses. High-pressure water service in fire hazard district. State armory and three units of state militia. Well-lighted thoroughfares. 108 miles of streets. 70 miles of accepted streets. 18.8 miles paved with granite with cement grouted joints.

EDUCATIONAL : In educational advantages compares .favorably with any other city of its size in the country. public schools, including evening courses, elementary, grammar and high grades. Eight parochial schools. Well equipped industrial school. Two commercial schools. Public library with 70,000 volumes. Free lecture courses. 43 churches, all denominations, besides a large number of other organizations active in the interest of the moral and physical development of the community. Over 200 fraternal and charitable societies. Four enterprising daily newspapers. Live Chamber of Commerce.

GOVERNMENT : Commission form, including the initiative, referendum and recall. Concentration of responsibility and a close relationship to the electorate are prominent features of plan. Number of voters, 13,000, including 380 women who are privileged to vote for members of the school board. 19 voting precincts, included in six wards. 21,000 male polls. One of the lowest tax rates in the state, $18.80 per thousand. Assessed property valuation (1917), $84,077,651.

MERCANTILE : Centre for several surrounding towns. Shopping district lined with finely appointed, well equipped stores, several of which are metropolitan in proportions.

BANKS: One national bank, three trust companies, three savings, and three co-operative banks, besides a Morris plan bank for handling small loans. Over $30,000,000 of saving deposits in banks of Lawrence.

REMARKS : A shire town of Essex County, with courthouse and registry of deeds. Post Office of the first class. A city with a most cosmopolitan population, industrious, thrifty, law-abiding people, living in harmony. Comparatively free from labor troubles. A city of homes, remarkable for the number of workers who own their homes. A progressive city, ever ready to welcome enterprise and encourage it.

PEMBERTON MILL DISASTER

LAWRENCE CALAMITIES

DISASTER IN LAWRENCE

The first disaster or accident of unusual seriousness to occur in Lawrence was recorded on October 12, 1847. It was in connection with the building of the Merrimack River dam. Two men were killed, two seriously injured and three slightly hurt.

At the time of this accident about 300 feet of the dam on the south side and 100 feet on the north side of the river was completed, the water meanwhile running through the unfinished space of 500 feet. It became necessary during the progress of the work to shut off the water from this by a coffer dam. The timbers were all in position and supposed to be securely boarded, and workmen were engaged in putting down flashboards. Without warning that portion of the dam upon which they were engaged rose up on the surface of the water and 15 men were carried amid broken timbers by the rush of the flood upon the rocks 25 feet below.

L. A. Wright, superintendent of the wood-work, and Captain Charles H. Bigelow, the engineer in charge, were in a scow at the time, and barely escaped with their lives, the latter being badly injured.

It was intended to raise the water to a level required to supply the Bay State Mills, then nearing completion.

THE FALL OF THE PEMBERTON MILL

"No cyclone or whirlwind had swept the fain: no torrent had undermined; no lightning stroke had rent; no explosion had shattered the fair structure. Some inherent and fatal defect invited and caused collapse so complete that it came without warning and overcame every element of strength and solidity." The late Hon. R. H. Tewksbury in his history of the calamity.

We of this generation have had our trials, but they are as nothing compared to those of the early residents of Lawrence who experienced the shock of the most dire calamity that has ever befallen the city, the Fall of the Pemberton Mill. Coming in all its appalling magnitude just as the city was recovering from the stagnation following the crisis of 1857, it fell upon the community with terrible and crushing force.

To fully understand the gloom into which Lawrence was plunged, those living in the flush times of today must remember that the three years, 1857, '58 and '59, immediately preceding this calamity, had been years of financial depression. Lawrence had suffered in common with, but more than other localities.

The Bay State Mills, then the largest woolen industry in the country, had failed and ceased operations. The great stone Machine Shop building (now part of the Everett Mills) was silent and deserted. The Pacific Mills were in the experimental stage, struggling to survive; there were rumors of failure or stoppage of all work at the Atlantic Cotton Mills, and actual closing at the Pemberton Mill. Building had almost entirely ceased; the population had decreased fifteen percent and valuation had shrunk from former figures; real estate was for sale at ruinous prices. Only when the great demand for manufactured goods, growing out of the war of the Rebellion, came, with the prosperous years that followed, did the city fully recover lost ground and start upon a progressive course that has had no serious setback.

The Pemberton Mill was built in 1853 by the Essex Company for a manufacturing corporation of which John Pickering Putnam was the managing director. It was constructed in accordance with plans made by Capt. Charles H. Bigelow, the architect and engineer, and the work was superintended by him and his assistants. It was one of the lightest, most attractive, and apparently most substantial structures in the city. It had been in continuous operation, except during the financial depression of 1857-'58, and early in 1859 had been purchased by David Nevins of Methuen and George Howe of Boston, who paid $325,000 for the plant which had originally cost about $840,000.

Under their management the mill had again been put in operation and there were signs of prosperity, when on the 10th of January, 1860, shortly before 5 o'clock in the afternoon, while the machinery was in motion, without a moment's warning, the whole structure trembled, tottered and fell, burying beneath its shapeless, broken ruins the mass of humanity, teeming within its walls. There went down amid that pile of brick, mortar, timbers and broken machinery, 670 men, women and children. The tidings flew like wild fire throughout the city and immediately a sturdy corps of volunteer mechanics and workers of every occupation covered the ruins, clearing away debris and rescuing the trapped operatives.

Had no further calamity occurred the loss of life by this downfall would have been greatly lessened, but, about 10 o'clock, just as the rescuers were reaching many of the victims, there was a cry of alarm that appalled the stoutest hearts. A lantern in the hands of a workman was broken by a chance blow from a pickax, wielded by another rescuer, and the ignited fluid fell among inflammable cotton and oily waste that burst into flames, unquenchable by means at hand. Fed by saturated cotton, shattered timber and crude waste, tongues of flame darted like serpents from openings in the huge smoking ruin.

Firemen labored incessantly to reach and subdue the flames, but so completely were the layers of broken machinery covered by the bent and twisted floors that it was well nigh impossible to effectively reach the spaces where many living employees were pinned among broken fragments of machinery, shafting, and material in process of manufacture. Between these layers of flooring, there was a draught that fanned relentless flames creeping through every aperture and space and destroying all hope of escape for imprisoned sufferers.

The scene, lighted by bon-fires and the flames from the burning mass, in the smoke that hung about it, was weird, awe-inspiring and indescribable. All about the streets, from every available outlook, an excited, hushed crowd gathered from the homes of the city and from the country about, looking on filled with fear and foreboding.

There were 918 persons employed by the corporation but of these nearly one-third were at work in outbuildings or in the yard and were therefore out of danger. Of the 670 persons in the mill when it fell, 307 escaped unhurt, 88 were killed, 116 badly injured and 159 slightly injured. It seemed almost miraculous that such a large percentage of employees escaped with their lives.

The City Hall was transformed into a hospital and morgue for the wounded and dead by order of Hon. Daniel Saunders, Jr., who was mayor at the time, and the physicians of the city, as well as those of neighboring towns, volunteered their services and labored untiringly for the relief of the sufferers. The scene at the City Hall was one long to be remembered. Here the wounded were cared for during the night and the dead were carried for identification. At one time there were 54 wounded patients in the hall, and the services rendered by many women, not only there but in the homes of the sufferers, were invaluable. The heart-rending pathos witnessed in the identification of the dead can be left to the imagination.

The calamity stirred the charitable impulses and awakened the sympathy of an entire country. A relief committee was organized, of which Mayor Saunders was chairman and Hon. Charles S. Storrow was treasurer, and by every mail came such a flood of unsolicited contributions that it was soon deemed advisable by official notification to stay the generosity of the givers who were anxious to assist in alleviating the suffering caused by the disaster.

All movements for the relief of the injured, the care of and wise and just distribution of money and supplies contributed by the charitable were carried out with surprising promptitude. Scarcely had the first shock subsided when the machinery for rendering all possible relief was fully in operation. In the work of bringing order out of the chaos Hon. Daniel Saunders, Jr., the mayor, was a most competent leader. The committee of relief comprised Hon. Daniel Saunders, Jr., Charles S. Storrow, Henry K. Oliver, William C. Chapin, and John C. Hoadley. The district inspectors were Sylvester A. Furbush, J. Q. A. Batchelder, Edward P. Poor, William D. Joplin, Henry Withington, Elbridge Weston, and Daniel Saunders, Sr.; they constantly conferred with the committee, giving assistance and confining aid to deserving and proper cases.

The total amount of the contributions received was $65,834.67 and of this sum $51,834.67 was disbursed in aid of the sufferers and for funeral, medical and other expenses and the $14,000 remaining was invested for annuities in trust in the Massachusetts Hospital Life Insurance Company. The larger part of this trust fund has been expended for the relief of more cases needing continuous aid. The trustees employed Pardon Armington, afterwards mayor of the city, as clerk of this relief committee and he made accurate and complete records of the receipts, disbursements and doings of the faithful trustees.

Four days after the catastrophe Mayor Saunders issued a proclamation appointing a day for fasting and prayer and calling upon the people to abstain from labor and to hold religious services in the various churches. The propriety of the call was acknowledged by the people and never was a fast day so universally observed in the city.

A jury was summoned by Dr. William D. Lamb who was then the coroner, and after hearing the evidence of eye-witnesses and experts found that the cast iron pillars used for supporting the several floors of the building were weak on account of defective casting, and it was agreed that this was the cause of the terrible disaster.

It was the recollection of eye-witnesses that the roof of the mill first sank at the southerly end and the whole roof, freeing itself from wall supports, came crashing down upon the floor below. The great weight and force of the falling roof carried down the upper floor with all the load of machinery and nothing could withstand the descending mass from this point, through all the stories, until the solid earth was reached. Every timber acted as a lever to tilt and crush the walls. The collapse of the main

60

building was utterly complete and can be conceived of only by those who saw the ruin as it lay. The wall of the northerly end was thrown outward, a portion falling upon the ice that covered the canal. The upper floors, as they lay in ruin, overhung the lower at the north end toward the canal. Measuring from outside, the building had been 284 feet in length and 84 feet in width.

The wing building at the northerly end (60x37 feet dimension), of the same height as the main mill, five stories, did not fall with the main structure. In this wing were the counting room, cloth room and offices. There were also several low, detached buildings, as the dye house, picker house, cotton house, etc. The chimney at the south end remained standing with some crumbling walls attached. Only the main building fell.

Of the dead bodies removed from the ruins, 13 were mutilated beyond recognition, and the remains were buried in a lot in Bellevue cemetery, over which was erected a plain granite monument, with the inscription: "In memory of the unrecognized dead who were killed by the Fall of the Pemberton Mill, January 10, 1860."

The present Pemberton Mills occupy the site of the old plant. Immediately after the calamity a new company, with David Nevins, George Blackburn and Eben Sutton as controlling owners and directors, organized as "The Pemberton Company", and rebuilt the works on the old foundations, commencing operations anew in 1861. Since that time they and their successors have continuously operated the mills at a profit. At the time of the disaster Frederick E. Clarke was the paymaster and cashier for the corporation. John E. Chase was the agent.

LIST OF DEAD

The killed and fatally injured (death resulting very soon) were as follows

Adolph, William
Ahern, Ellen
Ashworth, Augusta
Bailey, Joseph
Barrett, Mry
Bannan, May Ann
Branch, Lafayette
Broder, Bridget
Brennan, Owen
Burke, Mary
Callahan, Mary

Callahan, Peter
Callahan, Hannah
Cain, William
Clarke, Catherine
Colbert, Ellen
Conner, Ellen
Conners, Catherine
Corcoran, Margaret
Coleman, Margaret
Cooney, Catherine
Cronan, Joanna
Crosby, Bridget

Crosby, Irene
Cullen, Alice
Culloten, Mary
Dearborne, John C.
Dineen, Ellen
Donnelly, Margaret
Dunn, Elizabeth
Fallon, Margaret
Flint. Lizzie D.
Foley, Margaret
Gallan, Bridget
Gilson, Lorinda
Griffin, Mary
Hamilton, Margaret
Harty, James
Harrigan, Catharine
Harold, Dora
Hannon, Catharine
Hickey, Ellen
Hickey, Catharine
Howard, Mary
Hollifield, Bernard
Hurley, Joanna
Hughes, Martin
Hughes, John
Jewett, Mary
Jordan, William
Kelly, Bridget
Kelleher, Catharine
Kimball, Elizabeth R.
Leonard, Dennis
Loughrey, Bridget
Lunney, Richard

Mahoney, Ellen
Martin, Asenath P.
McAleer, Margaret
McCann, Mary
McNabb, John
Metcalf, William
Midgeley, Richard
Molineux, Hannah
Murphy, Alice
Murphy, Mary
Nash, Orin C.
Nice, Mary
O'Brien, Michael
O'Connor, Patrick
O'Hearne, Jeremiah
Orr, Eliza
Palmer, Morris E.
Roach, Ellen
Roberts, Julia
Rolfe, Samuel J.
Ryan, Matthew C.
Ryan, Bridget
Ryan, Mary
Shea, Hannah
Smith, Maggie J.
Stevens, Celia A.
Sweeney, Catharine
Sullivan, Ann
Sullivan, Margaret
Thomas, Jane
Towne, Lizzie
Turner, Margaret

Note : Two employees, Maria Hall and Augusta L. Sampson, were crippled for life and received life annuities.

THE LAWRENCE CYCLONE

9:15 o'clock on a Saturday morning, July 26, 1890, a whirlwind swept over the whole length of the southern ward of the city, Ward Six or South Lawrence, killing eight persons, injuring 65 and causing damage to property to the amount of approximately $45,000.

The tornado swooped down from the west at a velocity of a mile a minute. The morning had been oppressively hot, and shortly before 9 o'clock a furious rain-storm set in. Just as the rain ceased falling, a black funnel-shaped cloud was seen approaching. It was high above Andover street and near West Parish road. It descended straight down on the cricket club grounds, a fenced enclosure of several acres in what is now known as Carletonville. The entire eight-foot tight board fence was leveled and, except for a short distance on the southwest corner, was thrown outward from the centre in every direction.

Farther on the tornado struck two dwellings on Emmet street. One of these was carried easterly and nearly ruined, and the other was completely demolished. Just east of this the Essex Company's "Old Blue Ledge", an abandoned stone quarry close by the present Wetherbee school, deflected the tornado upward over a thickly populated region in the vicinity of Durham and Newton streets and the houses escaped with the loss of shingles and a chimney here and there, but little damage being done until Broadway was reached. A portion of the roof of St. Patrick's church, at the corner of Broadway and Salem street, was raised from the walls, and the Cutler house nearby was destroyed. The superstructure of the Boston & Maine railroad bridge on Salem street was bent and twisted. Michael Higgins, a switchman of the railroad, was killed here, and little Helen Cutler was blown from the bridge and also killed.

From this point, the progress for some 100 rods or more was across open ground to Springfield street where the most damage was done to buildings and where the greatest loss of life occurred. Houses were piled in the middle of the street, and large blocks were torn and twisted. Thence the gale swept through South Union Park, uprooting and leveling great trees. Then it struck Portland street where much damage was done. It spent itself at the entrance of the Shawsheen into the Merrimack River.

LIST OF DEAD

Elizabeth O'Connell, 32 years
Annie Collins, 6 years
Michael Higgins, 21 years

Elizabeth Collins, 25 years
Mary Lyons, 34 years
Hannah Beatty, 8 years
Mary Ann O'Connell, 11 years
Helen H. Cutler, 10 years

The storm had barely passed before the mayor, Dr. John W. Crawford, was upon the scene of destruction surrounded by other members of the city government. The fire department at once began a careful patrol, and continued it until after all danger of fire bursting from the ruins had disappeared. The chief of police and the heads of the street, health, and public property departments were also promptly on hand with a large force of men and teams. Their efforts with those of the firemen, seconded by hundreds of ready volunteer workers, soon extricated the dead, and wounded from the wreck. The wounded were quickly conveyed to the General hospital and the Orphan Asylum, where they were received by skillful and tender hands and efficiently cared for.

Within an hour after the storm the mayor and aldermen had constituted themselves a relief committee and had opened the Packard schoolhouse as a refuge for the homeless. Here many persons were lodged on Saturday and a few succeeding nights, and here also they were supplied with meals until their homes could be re-established.

Early in the evening a military guard, consisting of Battery C, Field Artillery, under command of Captain L. N. Duchesney, and Company F, Ninth Infantry, under Captain Joseph H. Joubert, was thrown around the wrecked district.

On the following day, Sunday, it was estimated that 50,000 strangers visited the city for the purpose of seeing the ruins. So effective were the measures for keeping order that no arrests were necessary.

On Saturday evening in response to a suggestion of Mayor Crawford, the Board of Trade held a meeting, at which its president, Franklin Butler, its treasurer, H. L. Sherman, Hon. Charles A. DeCourcy and Rev. Clark Carter, the city missionary, were added to the general committee for the purpose of receiving funds and disbursing relief. The committee included the following: Hon. John W. Crawford, chairman; Fred A. Libbey, Charles T. Main, George B. Elliott, Arthur A. Bailey, Otis Freeman, Jr., and Lewis P. Collins, aldermen; Franklin Butler, Henry L. Sherman and Hon. Charles A. DeCourcy, from the Board of Trade, Rev. Clark Carter, city missionary, and William T. Kimball, city clerk, who was also secretary of the committee. J. R. Sherman served as the fund treasurer.

Throughout Sunday and Monday the work of clearing the wreck was pushed rapidly forward under the direction of John Battershill, superintendent of public property, and William S. Marsh, superintendent of streets.

Monday evening a mass meeting was held at city hall, which was cheered by messages of sympathy and offers of aid from other cities, and at which a large sum of money was subscribed by the citizens. A committee, comprising Rev. Clark Carter, Rev. Michael T. McManus, pastor of St. Patrick's church, and Michael F. Collins, was appointed to attend to the immediate needs of the wounded, homeless and destitute. A committee was also selected to estimate the losses on buildings and to grant aid in repairing and rebuilding. Of this committee the Hon. James R. Simpson was chairman, ably supported by John K. Norwood, William R. Pedrick, A. A. Currier and John F. Hogan.

The total amount of the contributions to the relief fund was $37,560.65. The smallest amount given by any Lawrence party was ten cents and the largest $500. Lawrence donated $27,249.35; Boston $6,853.00; Lowell $2,090.30; Haverhill $1,059.00; Salem $218; Manchester, N. H., $66.00 and Worcester $25.00.

The amount of money drawn by the building committee to pay awards was $29,879.23. The estimated damage was $37,000, and the actual damage aggregated $42,000, which includes all money paid out to replace damage done by the cyclone.

Tornado of 1910

In the evening of August 4, 1910, Lawrence was again visited by a tornado, which, although not as terrible as the disaster of 1890, was very destructive. Passing through the heart of the city, the storm left a trail of destruction. Trees were uprooted, buildings unroofed, the lives of many were endangered and one young man was seriously injured. Charles A. Mahoney was struck by a falling branch of a tree and knocked from a wagon while driving along the lower end of Oak street. Although it was the next day before he regained consciousness, he eventually recovered. Probably the greatest havoc was wrought in the Common. Many of the paths were blocked by a tangled mass of uprooted and torn trees. The huge flag pole that stood opposite where the beautiful Shattuck staff is now located, was snapped off at the base like a pipe-stem.

THE VICTIMS

Secundo Allegbro, 10 years
Roland Jones, 9 years
William Bolster, 10 years
Joseph McCann, 15 years
Joseph Belanger, 8 years
Flower Pinta, 11 years
John Cote, 8 years
William Thornton, 10 years
*Ronaldo Gaudette, 10 years
Michael Woitena, 14 years
Joseph Hennessey, 15 years

* Gaudette was visiting with parents at the residence of his grandfather, Alfred Parent, and was to have returned to his home in Fitchburg on the day following the accident.

Not since the cyclone in 1890 did Lawrence experience such a calamity as the so-called bathhouse tragedy. This disaster occurred on June 30, 1913, when a runway leading from the northerly bank of the Merrimack River, a short distance above the dam, to one of the municipal bathhouses, collapsed and 11 boys, ranging in age from eight to 15 years, were drowned. Scores of others were saved through the heroic work of volunteer rescuers.

The bathhouses were to have been opened that day, and boys from all parts of the city were attracted there, to escape the sun's hot rays, in the cooling waters of the Merrimack. It was nearly 2 o'clock, the hour the doors were to open, and the youngsters crowded on the board walk which extended out over the water to the entrance of No. 1 bathhouse, restlessly awaiting the arrival of William Blythe, the attendant, who was to admit them for the first swim of the season.

Without warning the runway collapsed. A panic ensued, and immediately the water was a mass of struggling boys. Their wild cries for help, mingled with those of their companions who were out of danger, attracted a few men who were in the vicinity of the scene.

Indeed, the one bright spot in the whole sad affair w-as the heroic way in which men and boys alike went to the work of rescue and resuscitation. Many a boy who figured in that terrible happening owes his life to some police officer, doctor, or civilian who assisted either in his rescue or in the application of first-aid principles after his removal from the water. But for such commendable work the loss of life might have been at least three times what it was.

The heroism of young Joseph McCann, a 15-year-old crippled lad, who numbered among the victims, perhaps outshone that of all others, for he gave his life that somebody else's son might live. Young McCann was on the river bank when he saw his companions suddenly thrown into peril. Without hesitation he jumped into the river. Although a cripple, he was a good swimmer, and he struck out bravely toward the mass of struggling boys. But, as soon as he reached them, he was desperately grasped by several of the terrified lads, and drawn down to a watery grave.

Many other valiant acts were performed which space will not permit recounting. One young man, Henry Hinchcliffe, then 16 years of age, has since been awarded the Carnegie medal for bravery, and afforded a college education by the Carnegie Hero Fund. He was one of the first to the rescue, and under great difficulties succeeded in bringing a number of the drowning boys to safety. Lyman Parker and Charles Patterson were at the Lawrence Canoe Club on the opposite shore when they heard the outcries. They crossed the river in a power boat. Both dived for bodies, and, assisted by John Keefe, recovered a number that were afterwards resuscitated. Sgt. Timothy J. O'Brien of the Police department directed the first aid work.

The scene upon the river bank until darkness set in made even strong men weep. It was a pitiable sight, as parents, brothers and sisters wrung their hands in agony and called for their little ones. A pathetic fact also was that two hours after the accident happened, when it was taken for granted that there were no more bodies in the water, some doubt was expressed that all had been recovered. This was given weight when a woman in the crowd that surged the river bank declared that her son was missing. The search was resumed, and half an hour later the appalling force of the calamity was brought home to the saddened crowd, when seven other lifeless forms were brought to the surface.

An expert diver was employed, and the search was continued until late into the night, and resumed early the next day, but all the missing had been recovered. Shortly after the catastrophe the city government abolished the bathhouses. The relatives of each of the 11 victims were compensated in the sum of $100 to defray the funeral expenses. Afterwards some families sought to recover damages from the municipality, but the Supreme Court decided that under the laws of the commonwealth they could not prosecute a claim for injury or loss of life sustained at a place of public recreation from which no revenue was derived. City Solicitor

Daniel J. Murphy defended the City of Lawrence against the several suits in which the addendum was $90,000.

Judge Jeremiah J. Mahoney of the District court held an inquest into the fatalities. In his finding he declared that the accident was due to the insufficiency of the fence or railing which crumpled away under the great and unusual weight thrown against or upon it when the runway settled, and that the settling of the runway was due to the fact that only one ledger board supported it instead of two. He expressed the belief that had the runway been supported by two ledger boards the accident would not have occurred.

MASSACHUSETTS MILITIAMEN SURROUND STRIKERS

INDUSTRIAL UPHEAVAL OF 1912

The year 1912 goes down into history as an eventful one in the annals of Lawrence, for it had hardly made its advent when there began the great textile strike which was not alone a history-making and history-marking event in Lawrence, but an occurrence in which interest was centered throughout the entire United States if not beyond the confines of this country.

The strike lasted just nine weeks. It actually began on Friday, January 12, 1912, and was formally declared off on Thursday, March 14, of that year, although most of the strikers did not resume work until the following Monday.

It affected directly 27,000 operatives in the Lawrence mills. Its cost has been figured at approximately $3,000,000, including the loss of wages to the workers, the loss of business to the mills, the extra expense of policing the city and the harm to the general business of the community.

The direct result was an increase in wages ranging upward from five to twenty-five per cent, a modification of the so-called "premium system," and a twenty-five per cent increase in pay for overtime work. Its effect was even broader in scope. Besides the 27,000 operatives in the Lawrence mills, practically all textile workers in New England were given an increase in wages as a result. Conservative figures place the number thus benefiting at 125,000. By the ordinary ratio, accepted in figuring vital statistics, this means that more than 500,000 people had their standard of living raised thereby.

In the way of explanation it might be said that the modification of the "premium system" meant that workers producing more than the required amount of work were allowed a premium or extra compensation every two weeks instead of every four, as was the case prior to the strike. The workers claimed that bad luck with their work during the third or fourth week of the four-week period often nullified the extra work of the first two weeks. The bonus system was in vogue only in the American Woolen Company's and Kunhardt Mills, though in the Kunhardt plant it was based on weekly earnings.

The strike was conducted by an organization known as the Industrial Workers of the World by methods never before seen in a textile strike in this country and which came in for bitter criticism. The regular police force was not sufficient to handle the mobs. Assistance was rendered by the Metropolitan Park police department and enough special officers were sworn in to increase the force from 84 to 200. The aid of the State militia was invoked, and in all 56 military companies saw service in Lawrence during the progress of the strike. The maximum number on duty at one time was 25 companies, averaging about 55 per company.

The enforcement of the 54-hour law, with its attendant loss of two hours' pay per week, was attributed as the cause of the whole trouble. The measure prohibited women and children from working in the mills more than 54 hours a week. But as the work of the women and children feeds the work done by the men the new law meant a reduction of two hours in the week's working schedule and, while the wages per hour were not changed, the amount of compensation received by the workers under the 54-hour law was less than under the 56-hour law.

The workers demanded that they receive the same wages regardless of the change in the schedule of hours and when the first pay day arrived following the date that the 54-hour law went into effect they resented the reduction, as they saw fit to regard it, and the trouble started. This was on January 11. Five hundred weavers and spinners in the Everett, Arlington and Duck Mills were the first to quit their work.

The forerunner of this great industrial conflict was a strike of 50 weavers at the Duck Mill on January 2, owing to a controversy over the new 54-hour law. On Wednesday, January 10, at a mass meeting of Italian mill workers in Ford's Hall, it was voted to go on strike the following Friday. There was, however, the small strike on Thursday, January 11, forecasting the greater movement the next day when the storm broke which plunged Lawrence into turmoil of strife, such as had never before been witnessed in its history.

Friday morning, January 12, snow began falling at 7.30 and through the whirling whiteness ran the constantly growing crowd of strikers. It started from the Washington Mills with 500 and by ten a.m. had 12,000 people out of the mills and the riot call sounding for the police. The mob marched over Union street and entered the Wood Worsted Mills. Weapons were brandished, belts were thrown off, obstacles were hurled into the machinery and workers were actually driven from the mills. Next the army of strikers went to the Ayer Mills to get the workers out. Here occurred the first clash with the police, who were under command of Assistant City

Marshal Samuel C. Logan. Marching across the Duck Bridge the mob attacked the Duck and Kunhardt Mills, breaking many windows.

The Industrial Workers of the World had a small organization of perhaps 300 in Lawrence, although little or nothing had ever been heard of it until the strike. Immediately its local leaders sent for Joseph Ettor, an Italian organizer of that body, and he arrived from New York Saturday morning, addressing a mass meeting in City Hall. He remained as chairman of the strike committee, which was organized on the following Monday, and the real leader of the strike until his arrest on January 30, on the charge of being accessory to the murder of Anna LoPezzi, an Italian woman, who was shot on January 29.

By Saturday night 15,000 of the mill workers of Lawrence were out. On Sunday, January 14, Ettor and the strike committee had a conference with Mayor Michael A. Scanlon and the members of the Board of Aldermen, when the strikers were advised to observe law and order and not invoke trouble or continue the destruction of property. Fearing a further demonstration upon the part of the strikers on the following Monday morning, however, every police officer was ordered to report for duty early and the three local militia organizations, Battery C of the Field Artillery, Company F of the Ninth Infantry and Company L of the Eighth Infantry, were ordered to report at the Amesbury Street Armory.

The next morning, Monday, January 15, there was a clash between the troops and the strikers and there was general disorder. Thirty-five arrests were made. A strikers' parade started in the vicinity of Union street and proceeded along Canal street to the Washington Mills. Here the mill gate was stormed and a number succeeded in getting into the mill where they were arrested. Then the mob moved up street along the canal to the Pacific Mills where they were received with hose streams. After they had been repulsed a crowd armed themselves with sticks from a freight car standing on the north side of the canal and smashed many windows in the Atlantic Mills. Shots were fired from the mob at the mill watchmen, and one rioter was bayoneted, though not fatally, by a member of Company F in an attempt to rush the Atlantic mill gates.

This marked the entrance of the militia into the situation which had got beyond control of the civil authorities. Governor Foss ordered militia companies from other cities in the state to Lawrence, and from that day till several weeks later, when the need of the military was no longer apparent, the iron grip of the soldiery was felt. Cordons of militia were thrown about the mills, and sharpshooters were located in the factory towers as a precaution against prowlers who might get by the line of soldiers. Later a portion of the militia did police duty in the foreign quarters and business section of the city. Col. E. Leroy Sweetser was ordered to take command of the troops in Lawrence. Police from numerous other cities and towns were also brought in to reinforce the local police.

The City Council members endeavored to bring about a conference between the strikers and the mill men but without success, and all efforts of the State Board of Arbitration to settle the strike were futile.

On Wednesday, January 17, there was another clash between the strikers and the militia, when the former tried to go into the mill district from which they had been ordered to keep out. In fact, hardly a day passed without a mix-up between the strikers and the police or militia. The troubles between the two sides grew constantly.

On January 20, the discovery of dynamite in three buildings on the "plains" gave rise to rumors of a plot to blow up the mills. It later developed, however, that the explosive was "planted." An attempt was made to prove that the "plant" was the result of a conspiracy to discredit the strikers, but a trial in the courts failed to show that the mill operators were connected with it.

On the morning of January 29, at the mill-opening time, before daylight, hundreds of windows were smashed in the trolley cars bringing the people to work. This took place on Essex street, east of Jackson street, and on Broadway. Many were driven from the cars and forced back to their homes by threats of the strikers. The police were unable to cope with the situation. That same night a big crowd assembled in the vicinity of Garden, Union and Haverhill streets and attempted to parade through Union street. The police interfered and numerous shots were exchanged. Anna LoPezzi, an Italian woman, who was in the vicinity, was shot and instantly killed. During the mêlée Police Officer Oscar Benoit was seriously, though not fatally, stabbed in the back.

Ettor and Arturo Giovannitti, another Italian leader in the I. W. W. movement, were arrested on the following night, charged with being accessories to the alleged murder of the LoPezzi woman. It was claimed by the authorities that they had incited the crowd by alleged incendiary speeches and were responsible for the rioting. They were indicted by the Essex County grand jury but after a lengthy trial, which aroused interest even outside the country, they were acquitted. William O. Haywood, who was accused, but acquitted, of being implicated in the murder of Governor Steunenberg of Idaho in February, 1906, when the latter was killed by a bomb during the big miners' strike at that time, Carlo Tresca and Elizabeth Gurley-Flynn, who afterwards were arrested in connection with strike rioting in Paterson, N. J., were also identified as leaders in the Lawrence strike. Haywood took charge following Ettor's arrest.

An outstanding feature of the presence of the soldiers in the city, which reflected a great deal of credit upon Colonel Sweetser, his officers and men, was that, notwithstanding the ugly demeanor of the strikers and the fact that many of them were armed, only one life was sacrificed in the clashes between the soldiers and the strikers.

On Tuesday morning, January 30, John Remi, aged 18 years, was fatally bayoneted on White street when about 200 strikers, mostly Syrians, attempted to hold a parade. Company H of Salem was stationed there and one of the soldiers ran his bayonet through Remi's lung in a charge on the mob which had defied the militia.

In the midst of all the excitement of the strike, on the night of February 2, the city was plunged into a frenzy of fear by the discovery of one of the most sensational murders in police annals. Four persons were found dead in a tenement on Valley street, with innumerable knife wounds in their bodies. The murderer was never apprehended, although the crime was committed when the city was practically under martial law. It is believed that the motive was robbery, Shaef Maroon, 26, one of the victims, having drawn $485 from the Essex Savings Bank a few days before. The theory is that he was lured to the death house and slain, the murderer disposing of the other three victims to remove all witnesses of the crime. Besides Maroon, Joseph Savaria, 23, his wife, Mary, 18, and Evelyn Denis, born Tanguay, were killed by the mysterious assassin. Fortunately, there was no connection between the murder and the strike, and the terror of its revelation in the public mind was soon allayed. In a few days the murder was overshadowed by the deeper interest in the strike.

Further complications arose when the strikers attempted to send some of their children away to other cities to be cared for, which move the authorities believed to be for the purpose of exploitation. Special trains were engaged and the incident was attended with quite a demonstration on the part of the strikers. Capt. John J. Sullivan, who had relieved City Marshal James T. O'Sullivan as head of the police department, interrupted the procedure when on Saturday, February 24; he sent a number of officers to the North Station and caused 15 children with their parents to be taken to the police station. This interruption put a stop to the sending away of children, but it also resulted in Congress ordering Attorney General Wickersham to make an investigation. The entire affair was aired in Washington where Alderman Cornelius F. Lynch, who was director of the Department of Public Safety, including the police department, and Captain Sullivan, were called to explain the situation. Besides this investigation, there were at different times during the strike inquiries into the phases of the controversy by the Federal Bureau of Labor, a committee of the State Legislature and the attorney-general of the State.

The last serious clash between the strikers and the authorities occurred on February 26. Before sunrise that morning there was a sharp encounter at the lower end of Common street between the police and men supposed to be strikers. There were 25 to 30 shots exchanged. One man, an Italian, was wounded in the shoulder.

During the strike relief funds were received from all over the country, approximately $65,000. More than 2,500 persons were cared for daily. A well-organized relief station was maintained by the American Federation of Labor, where food, clothing and fuel were distributed to the needy.

Funds to the amount of $45,000 were received by the I. W. W. Shortly before the close of the strike, leaders of that organization were accused of mismanagement and misuse of these funds. Legal proceedings were instituted to obtain information as to the manner in which the funds were handled. The investigation dragged along with many delays, but finally the Supreme Court found that certain funds were improperly used and the defendants were ordered to make a proper accounting of the same.

FACTS OF THE STRIKE IN A NUTSHELL

Began January 12, 1912.

Lasted 63 days.

Twenty-seven thousand operatives involved.

Cause Reduction in pay with enforcement of new 54-hour law.

Two regiments of infantry, two troops of cavalry, besides Metropolitan Park police, assisted augmented Lawrence police force in preserving order.

Anna LoPezzi and John Remi slain in clashes between strikers and police and strikers and militia.

Joseph J. Ettor and Arturo Giovannitti, strike leaders, arrested on charge of being accessories before the fact to the slaying of Anna LoPezzi. After Jury trial both acquitted.

Parties of children sent to New York, Philadelphia and Barre, Vt., for care until the close of strike. One group stopped by police and several arrests made.

Investigation by Congressional Committee, the United States Attorney General, the Federal Bureau of Labor, a committee of the State Legislature and the Attorney General of the State.

Cost to mills, estimated at nearly $1,000,000;.

Estimated loss of wages to employees, $1,350,000

Estimated cost of maintaining regular and special police by the city, $75,000.

Estimated cost to State in maintaining militia, $200,000.

Relief funds sent in from all over the country, approximately $65,000.

More than 2,1oo persons cared for daily during period of strike.

Forty-five thousand dollars collected by I. W. W. Leaders of that organization accused of mismanagement and misuse of funds.

Estimated number of arrests, 500, of whom about one-half paid fines ranging from $1 to $100.

Strike ended March 54, 1912.

Concessions of mills, 5 to 25 per cent increases in wages.

Wage advance spread over New England. A general increase of 5 to 7 per cent.

Estimated cost to 5,500 textile manufacturers, $5,000,000 a year.

AFTERMATH OF THE STRIKE

During the big textile strike of 1912 Lawrence was infested by a stream of free-lance investigators, sociological cranks and so-called "sob" writers, the last mentioned doing the city much harm by the way of misrepresentation in distorted newspaper and magazine articles, which continued long after the controversy between the mill operatives and the manufacturers had been adjusted.

To offset this calumny and restore Lawrence's good reputation, a citizen's organization was formed in the fall of 1912 and a campaign of publicity was started to set the city right in the eyes of the nation. The climax of this movement of rehabilitation came in the great patriotic demonstration on October 12 of that year. The motto was "For God and Country," and it was a direct rebuke of the I. W. W.'s sacrilegious slogan, "No God; No Master."

Although March 14 saw the formal close of the strike, it was really several months later before conditions became normal. The leaders of the I. W. W., apparently not content with the concessions from the mills, managed to keep the foreign element in a fitful frame of mind and now and then there were disagreements and walkouts, although nothing very serious occurred until September 27

On that day a second general strike took place when about 11,000 either walked out of the mills in sympathy with Joseph J. Ettor and Arturo Giovannitti, or were compelled to quit work through fear or the enforced closing of departments. It was claimed at I. W. W. headquarters that this move was without the sanction of the organization, although after it had occurred it was approved. At a mass meeting of the sympathizers it was voted to hold what was termed "a protest strike" of twenty four hours' duration on the following Monday, as a demonstration in protest of the imprisonment of Ettor and Giovannitti whose trial as alleged accessories to the murder of Anna LoPezzi was scheduled to begin on that morning. Rioting marked this demonstration and operatives were assaulted by strikers on the way to the mills.

On the day preceding, however, Sunday, September 29, a parade was held in direct violation of the permit issued by the police authorities, and the demonstration developed the most disgraceful scenes ever witnessed in Lawrence. Red flags and sacrilegious banners were carried through the city's streets and the Stars and Stripes was trampled on. At the head of the procession rode Carlo Tresca, an I. W. W. leader, and behind him was flaunted a large banner, bearing the inscription, "No God; No Master." Wild scenes followed the attempt of the police to break up the parade and one pistol shot was fired on Lawrence street directly in front of the entrance to the police station. Before the demonstration was checked two police officers were severely battered.

This anarchistic outbreak was the death knell of the I. W. W. in Lawrence. Public opinion crystallized and turned with potent force on that organization. The City Council started a movement for a gigantic parade of the loyal, patriotic, law-abiding people of Lawrence, to be held on October 12, as a rebuke of the lawless demonstration of September 29, and a citizens' committee cooperated.

A protest meeting against lawlessness was held Thursday evening, October 3, in City Hall. Men and women of all classes and creeds, all imbued alike with patriotic fervor and the desire for peace and security, cheered the speakers till the hall rang. The sentiment spread through the city and the interest in the proposed flag demonstration became feverish. The city took on a gala dress, and as the day approached Lawrence was a mass of national colors.

On October 12, Flag Day, as it came to be called, Lawrence had a new breath of life and patriotism. With no flag but the Stars and Stripes to be seen anywhere along the line of march and every parader carrying the national emblem, 32,000 people from all walks of life, men, women and children, marched through the streets amidst patriotic airs from countless bands and the cheers from the thousands of spectators who lined the route of procession. The parade ended on the Common, where flag-raising exercises were held.

The men who flaunted red flags in their parade of anarchy a week or so before did a thing for Lawrence which the citizens of the city had not been able to do for months. It aroused them to a sense of their dignity. It stirred the civic pride in them and, as a result, the community was thrilled anew with patriotism, and the anarchistic spirit which had stifled it was stamped out. This was the end of the detrimental influence of the I. W. W. It was crushed so completely that it never again became manifest.

The committee on parade for the Flag Day demonstration comprised: Mayor Michael A. Scanlon, Aldermen Cornelius F. Lynch, Paul Hannagan, Robert S. Maloney and Michael S. O'Brien; Gen. W. H. Donovan (chief marshal of the parade), Charles E. Bradley, Leonard E. Bennink, Michael J. Sullivan, Capt. Louis S. Cox of Battery C, Field Artillery, Capt. Daniel C. Smith of Company L, Eighth Regiment, Capt. Martin Foley of Company F, Ninth Regiment, Major Frank L. Donovan, Major Charles F. Sargent.

The work of rehabilitation began with the organization of the Citizens' Association. Approximately 5,000 citizens enrolled themselves as members. A comprehensive campaign of publicity was launched, and the true facts about Lawrence and the strike were placed in the hands of every newspaper editor in the country. Thus Lawrence's good reputation was to a great extent restored.

The committee on publicity which had direct charge of this work comprised: A. X. Dooley, chairman; E. J. Wade, secretary; Mayor M. A. Scanlon, Rev. James T. O'Reilly, C. J. Corcoran, L. E. Bennink, A. B. Sutherland, R. H. Sugatt, F. N. Chandler, K. G. Colby, A. H. Rogers, W. S. Jewett, the last three mentioned being publishers of the city's daily newspapers.

These were the officers of the Citizens' Association: President, Charles E. Bradley; secretary, Edward J. Wade; treasurer, Cornelius J. Corcoran. Vice presidents: Michael J. Sullivan, Thorndike D. Howe, Emil C. Stiegler, Robert F. Pickels, James L. Rolley, Richard Carden, Narcisse E. Miville, Simeon Viger, John F. Hogan, William T. Kimball. Executive Committee: Frederic N. Chandler, A. X. Dooley, Alvin Hofmann, James H. Bride, Harry B. Musk, Otto Mueller, R. H. Sugatt, L. E. Bennink, James R. Menzie, Maynard W. Stevenson, John P. Kane, James Martin, Rev. James T. O'Reilly, Peter Carr, Rudolph Bernard, John Hart, William S. Jewett, Arthur O'Mahoney, Frank L. Donovan, Joseph White, Dr. J. J. Bartley, George Hey, Thomas E. Andrew, Maurice Cooper, Alexander H. Rogers, Andrew B. Sutherland, John Daley, James A. Dineen, Samuel Lemay, Joseph McCarthy, Fred F. Flynn, Michael P. Fleming, William Greenwood.

Lawrence City Hall

Municipal Government and Departments

Lawrence is under a commission form of government, so called. The general management and control of all the affairs of the city, except the public schools, is vested in a city council, consisting of a mayor and four aldermen, known as commissioners or directors. The general management and control of the public schools and property pertaining thereto is vested in a school committee of five, the mayor being a member ex-officio. All of these officers are elected at large, by the registered voters of the city, for terms of two years.

On November 7, 1911, at the State election, the present city charter was adopted, and it went into effect at ten o'clock on the morning of January 1, 1912, when the government under the old charter was abolished and the newly elected city council and school board took office. The adoption of the new charter was the result of a vigorous movement for a change in the form of government. When the question pertaining to the project was submitted to the voters by the Legislature public sentiment was strongly in favor of a reform. On the question as to whether the old charter should be repealed the vote was: yes, 6,027; no, 2,214; blanks, 840. The vote on the question as to the new form was as decisive. Two plans were presented: Plan One, which was to establish a city government of a mayor and a council of nine members; and Plan Two, which was to establish a government by commission. The latter was adopted by a vote of 6,077, as against 1,358 for Plan One, with 1,646 blanks.

The old charter had been in vogue since the incorporation of the city in 1853, and in the nearly threescore years of its existence it had been but slightly modified and amended. It had provided for what is familiarly known as a two-branch government, consisting of mayor and board of aldermen, and a common council. Subordinate officers and boards were either appointed by the mayor or elected by the city council. The board of aldermen comprised six members, one from each ward though elected at large, and the common council was composed of eighteen members, three being elected in each ward. The school committee had, besides the mayor, twelve members, two being elected in each ward.

No provision being made in the new charter for a board of fire engineers and a water board, both these boards were abolished, upon the adoption of the commission form of government, their powers and duties being put under control of the director of public safety and the director of engineering, respectively.

Under the present charter the administrative affairs of the city are divided into five departments, namely: department of finance and public affairs, department of engineering, department of public safety, department of public property and parks, and department of public charities. The department of finance and public affairs includes all the sub-departments, boards, and offices connected with it, such as the treasury, auditing, purchasing, assessing, sinking funds, tax collection, and claims, registration of voters, city clerk, and legal. The department of engineering includes the highways and other ways, street watering, sewers and drains, water and water works; bridges and engineering. The department of public safety includes the police and fire departments, lighting, wiring, weights and measures and conduits. The department of public property and parks includes municipal buildings, parks and public grounds. The department of public health and charities includes the health and poor departments, city physician and municipal hospitals.

The following are known as administrative officers: city clerk, city treasurer, collector of taxes, city auditor, purchasing agent, board of overseers of the poor, consisting of five persons, city engineer, city physician, board of health, consisting of three persons, of whom the city physician is one, city solicitor, board of park commissioners, board of sinking fund commissioners, board of assessors, board of trustees of the public library and a board of cemetery directors.

Prominent features of the present charter are the recall, initiative and referendum. These provisions are intended to bring the government and the people into closer relationship, and they provide an immediate and direct means of adjusting serious difficulties that may arise in the administration of government affairs. Provision is also made for publicity in all municipal matters, and there are restrictions tending to prevent hasty action on matters involving the expenditure of large sums of money. An outstanding feature is the concentration of responsibility.

Party or political designations or marks are abolished, and elective officers are chosen solely on the ground of personal qualification or fitness. When the new charter was adopted provision was made whereby the city council designated by majority vote the head of each department, except in the case of the mayor who acts as director of the department of finance and public affairs. In 1914 the charter was amended to provide that the office of each director be designated on the ballot at the time of his election by the voters of the city.

The powers of the city council are broad. The mayor has no veto, and no measure which the city council makes or passes is presented to him for, or requires his approval to become effective. The council determines the policy to be pursued and the work to be undertaken in each department, but each member has the full power to carry out the policy or have the work performed in his department, as directed by the city council. The council has full supervision of the erection, alteration and repair of all public buildings, including school buildings.

The public library of the city is under the management and control of a board of trustees, consisting of the mayor, three trustees of the White Fund (these four being members ex officio), and five citizens elected by the city council.

The annual budget is made up by the mayor, after he has received estimates, from the department heads, of the appropriations required, and it is adopted by a majority vote of the city council. A four-fifths vote is necessary to change any item in the budget as submitted by the mayor, and then only to reduce the amount.

THE CITY HALL: ITS HISTORY AND TRADITIONS

The City Hall stands substantially as it stood in 1850, a building of bold and impressive outlines, architecturally a triumph of its day. This public hall has probably served more varied uses than any other building in New England. On its stage platform have appeared many of the world's famous lecturers, orators, authors, actors, musicians and politicians. The county courts were held in this hall prior to the time of building the court house. Many of the first local churches worshiped there before becoming established in their own edifices. It was a drill room for departing volunteers and in it, wrapped in the American flag, lay the remains of Needham, the first martyr of the Rebellion. There was a week, many years ago, When the hall, on Monday night was used for a brilliant ball; on Tuesday evening, for religious revival services; on Wednesday night, for a political caucus; on Thursday, for a Sabbath school convention; on Friday, for a dog show; on Saturday, for a Fenian mass meeting, and on Sunday, for regular worship by an unhoused church, and that week was not altogether exceptional. It was a morgue at the time of the Pemberton disaster, a house of mourning when Presidents Taylor, Lincoln and Garfield died and memorial services were held, and the funerals of a number of prominent soldiers and citizens have been held from it.

Prior to the building of the Town or City Hall, town meetings were held in Merrimack hall during the year 1847, but at the March meeting in

81

1848 the townsmen gathered in the Free Will Baptist meeting house, a one-story wooden structure, standing on the north-easterly corner of White and Haverhill streets. In the warrant presented at that meeting was an article which read: "To see if the town will choose a committee to obtain a plan of a Town House, and to appoint an agent to superintend the building of the same."

On April 17 following, it was voted that a Town House be erected for the use of the town, "to include a town hall and such offices as may be judged necessary for the present and future needs of the town government". Discussions immediately started as to its location, and several sites were proposed. Finally, it was decided to erect the building in its present location, on Common street between Appleton and Pemberton streets.

The lot at the time of its purchase from the Essex Company had a frontage of 150 feet on Common street, but in 1855, eleven feet and six inches were taken for the laying out of Pemberton street, in which year also the iron steps that formed the original approach to the westerly entrance to the hall were constructed. The town paid $8,000 or fifty cents a foot for the land.

The contract for the construction of the building was let August 25, 1848, to Eli Cook, William I. Stetson and Alexander Mair of Boston, the plan of construction being prepared by Melvin & Young of Boston, classed with noted architects of the time in this section. The contract price was $27,568, and out of this amount were reserved $1,000 for a clock and bell, $700 for heating and $100 for ventilating apparatus.

The building is 120 feet 8 inches long, and 68 feet 8 inches wide, exclusive of the granite base which projects three inches all around the brickwork, with a tower 23 by 24 feet in size on the front side. The contract price, besides the above amounts mentioned as reserved for special purposes, included the cellar masonry, the ashlar or granite base, the brickwork of the walls, all woodwork, slating and painting, also a sidewalk of brick with hammered granite edgestones, and a fence along the Common street side, "equal in cost and quality to that in front of the house of Capt. Bigelow". This house stood at the corner of Lawrence and Haverhill streets, and was removed to make room for the Pacific mansion now standing there. Charles Bean was chosen by the selectmen to superintend the construction. No building of its kind was ever more economically erected.

The Town House was accepted by the architect and building committee from the contractors and it was delivered to the selectmen on December 5, 1849. On the following day the town clerk, E. W. Morse, moved into the office prepared for him and became the first occupant of the building. It was dedicated with appropriate ceremonies on the evening of December 10, 1849.

At the close of the financial year, March 1, 1850. the value of the building and land was reported to be $37,292 and the furniture $2,166, which included the furniture for the Court of Common Pleas (now called the Superior Court) that sat for a while in the large audience hall on the second floor, and also that for the Police Court which occupied the present City Council chamber. According to the town report for the year ending in March, 1851, however, the value of the property should be stated as $41,119, there being an account of additional claims paid, which had possibly been disputed.

The two brick safes between the city clerk's and the mayor's offices were the only ones built when the building was constructed. The brick safe in the treasurer's office was not constructed until 1855, that under the city engineer's office in 1874, and the one in the auditor's office in the fall of 1901. To heat the building, upon its completion, there were furnaces and at least one stove, and other furnaces and stoves were added in after years. There was a stove in the city clerk's office, to supplement the furnace heat, as late as 1875, when the steam apparatus was put in.

A prominent decorative feature of the City Hall is the large eagle on the tower. The eagle, with the ball and pedestal on which it stands, was designed and carved by John M. Smith, a member of the Board of Selectmen in 1848, who had charge of the woodwork construction at the Essex Company machine shop. It cost $500. Perched, as the bird is, about 156 feet above the ground, one does not realize that it is nine feet and six inches from the tip of the bill to the tip of the tail, with other dimensions in proportion, and that the ball on which it stands is three feet in diameter. The eagle is in a position of preparing to spread its wings to fly, and in a description printed at the time it was regarded as a fit emblem for Lawrence, and the wish was expressed that the young community, so full of promise, might ever be actuated with the noble inspiration "to spread and bear learning, virtue and wisdom to all parts of the world".

The building is acknowledged to have no superior in construction in Lawrence, and it is admired by critics of good work even today. There are no better plain brick walls in the world than the walls of this old structure. Though age has toned its colors and mellowed somewhat its outlines, and far more costly and elaborate structures have since become common, the historic building still retains its charm.

The face brickwork was laid plumb bond, that is, all the joints are exactly over those of the second course below, which was the prevailing style of the best construction in those days. On the Appleton street side of the building at the corner of the alleyway in the fifth course above the granite base, is a brick bearing the names, "S. Lawrence. A. Lawrence". When the central mill of the Bay State Company, now the Washington Mills, was built, Samuel Lawrence, the treasurer of the company, having had some bricks made bearing the above inscription, had one of them built into the corner of the central doorway of the mill a little above the sill. Another was the one built into the corner of the Town House or City Hall where it still is. The S. was the initial for Samuel and the A. for Alison, his wife. The placing of the brick in the wall of the Town House was another mark of respect for the family which so greatly assisted in the founding of the community.

The two shot displayed on either side of the doorway in the tower of the City Hall came from Fort Sumpter. They were picked up there after the evacuation of the fort by the Southern forces following the surrender of Charleston, February 17, 1865. As a token of regard, they were presented to the City of Lawrence by G. V. Fox, Assistant Secretary of the Navy, and a former citizen of Lawrence and at one time agent of the Bay State Mills. These fifteen-inch shot, with many others, were found among the ruins of Sumpter, having been fired from the Federal fleet of monitors during the bombardment of the fort on April 7, 1863. No gun of a bore greater than ten inches had been used on any other vessel or by the army during the war. In the week ending December 25, 1865, the shot, each weighing 350 pounds, were placed in position on the tower of the hall. The mountings were designed by Alderman Payne, and they consist of an iron wall plate in the shape of a shield embroidered by molding in the form of a rope. On the shield is illustrated a monitor in relief, and from it projects a forearm and hand in which the shot rests. The arm is clothed with a naval sleeve, bearing the cuff of a rear admiral, ornamented in proper form with two bands of gold and a five-pointed star. The identification inscription was provided by Ericson, the inventor of the monitor.

On December 18, 1849, soon after the town took possession of the building, the Court of Common Pleas opened a term of court in the audience hall with Judge Perkins on the bench. This court continued to sit here until October 1854, when an order was adopted by the City Council providing that arrangements be made for it in Lawrence hall, which was located on the southeasterly corner of Amesbury and Common streets, known now as Music hall.

In 1850, the town sold the old lock-up which had been located in the rear of the post office near the corner of Broadway and Common street and fitted up cells for prisoners in the basement of the Town House, in the brick arches which support the safes connected with the office of the city clerk. These cells soon fell into disrepute. *The Lawrence Courier* of March 15, 1851, described them as "narrow, dark, unventilated, reeking with moisture, loathsome places, a disgrace to the town, and a dangerous piece of property", accommodations for the purpose were sought elsewhere. The police court was then located in the present City Council chamber, and the small room at the westerly end was partitioned off for the judge. In June 1854, a committee of the City Council recommended that the police court be removed to the Empire building, formerly the Empire Hotel, located on the northwesterly corner of Essex and Appleton streets. It sat in what was for many years Needham hall, the old Grand Army headquarters, which is said to have been the dining room of the hotel; and here the court remained until the original police station building was completed and opened June 24, 1867.

The original plan of arrangement of offices was as follows: "Beginning with the room in the southwesterly corner of the building and going east, the rooms on the south side of the corridor were occupied by the common council, the city clerk, the board of aldermen, the mayor, the assessors and the city treasurer in the room the latter now occupies, his present office including the one originally occupied by the assessors, the partition being removed some time in the 80's. Opposite on the north side of the corridor, beginning at the easterly end and going west, the order of offices proposed was the school committee, the city marshal, the board of fire engineers, and the police court. (We were unable to find a record of where the auditor was located at that time.)

When the police court vacated, the common council immediately took possession of that room, and the board of aldermen moved into the room the common council had. There was much rearrangement of offices at first, but as near, as can be determined the original layout was as above described. The school committee and the city marshal moved to quarters provided in other buildings later, as did the board of fire engineers and any other officials who may have had places in the hall and whose offices are not now located there. In 1874, a city engineer was appointed and given the office now occupied by that official.

Frederick H. Garfield was elected the first janitor of the Town House and of such schoolhouses, not exceeding three, as the school committee might designate. His compensation was one dollar per day, not including Sunday, but he was to exercise the same care over the Town House on Sundays as on other days. It was evidently proper for him to work on Sunday, but wrong to receive pay for it.

The clock and bell in the tower are interesting reminders of the early days. They are the only markers of time, connected with the building, that do not pass into oblivion. The clock at one time chimed the hour. For years after the fire alarm was installed the clock did not strike. In 1895, however, a sentiment for the old timepiece revived. The hammer was rearranged so that it would not interfere with the fire alarm mechanism, and on May 3, 1895, the clock again for a time struck the hour, after a silence of a quarter of a century. From this tower, along with the other bells of the city, ""the curfew tolled the knell of the parting day"; when it ceased to do so. No one remembers, but the sweet tones of the bell still call the children to school. The bell was made by H. N. Hooper & Co. of Boston, and cost $999.96. It is one of the largest in Lawrence, and before the bell on the John R. Rollins School was placed in position, it was the largest. It weighs 3446 pounds.

The free evening school, a few years after its inauguration in the winter of 1859-'60, was provided with quarters in the basement of the City Hall, where the city grocery is now located. For a number of years this room was used as a wardroom, and occasionally as a supper room for entertainments held in the audience hall.

The auditorium on the second floor, which was originally designed for the use of the public in town meetings, was at first but a large unattractive hall except for its noble proportions. There was a gallery over the entrance at the easterly end, and at the westerly end, a rostrum about 14 feet deep, as devoid of attractions as the remainder of the hall. Eagles seem to have been much in vogue in the early days and a favorite object of the carver's skill. An eagle, carved in the repair shop of the Atlantic Mills by B. D. Stevens, for some time occupied a position on the wall above the rostrum. It was purchased by the city in 1858 for $45, and $14 was expended for the bracket on which it rested. When the City Hall was remodeled in 1872, this eagle was placed on the front of the Garden street engine house where it has since remained.

The audience hall was closed for repairs on June 25, 1872, and reopened for public inspection on the following October 9th. To break up the space, add to the beauty, and increase the seating capacity, galleries were placed on three sides of the remodeled hall, which were made architecturally beautiful with pilasters and heavy cornices in the Corinthian order of architecture, and the ceiling was handsomely frescoed. The original plan for remodeling the hall did not include a stage with scenery for theatrical performances, and there were those who questioned with puritanical prejudice the right of the city to spend money for such purpose. However, good sense prevailed, and all remains as then finished, except for the dust and stains consequent upon 45 years of constant use. The original seating capacity of the hall was 900, it now accommodates 1400. The original windows were so short that their tops would be hidden behind the sloping floor of the galleries, so it became necessary to lengthen them about four feet. It required a great deal of skill to make this renovation, but the work was successfully performed by Capt. Chadbourne, one of the city's skillful masons. The windows in the second story of the tower show the original height of those all around the building. New and improved stairways leading to the hall at the Appleton street entrance were added in 1877, at the same time the porch was built, and the entire corridor was wainscotted.

With the exception of lengthening the windows in the second story, the construction of the porch with the enclosed stone steps on Appleton street, which replaced in 1877 the pyramidal stone steps similar to those now leading up to the tower entrance on the Common street side, the construction of the stone steps at the westerly or Pemberton street entrance, which in 1881 replaced the old iron steps that were built in 1855, the exterior appearance of the building is the same as when first constructed.

The hall was used as a theatre for a number of years, and some of the most prominent actors and actresses of the country have played upon its stage. It has been used for about every possible kind of gathering, social and educational, political and religious. It is impossible to mention all the important events that have taken place within its walls or the uses to which the hall has been put. It has witnessed far more scenes of joy than sorrow, and the walls have echoed time and again the festal music of the dance and song. It has been the scene of the largest social events of the city since the time the hall was opened in December 1849.

In recent years, the demand for office room has greatly outgrown the accommodations of the building, and, with the exception of practically the administrative officials, all the city departments have quarters in other buildings. In 1910, plans were drawn for remodeling the City Hall, so that all department heads might be located under one roof. It was proposed that the auditorium be abolished and that the Common street wall be carried out flush with the sidewalk. Thus would three floors be provided, besides a larger area to the floor. The scheme has been considered practical and satisfactory, but its execution has been held up for the want of money. Before a great while, however, it is expected that this extensive improvement will be made, if an entirely new building is not erected.

FILTRATION SYSTEM AND WATERWORKS

For twenty-five years, the inhabitants of Lawrence secured their water for domestic purposes largely from wells and cisterns. This was the principal source of supply until the present water works were established.

From that time till the installation of the filtration system, which was designed by Hiram F. Mills of the Essex Company, chairman of the committee on water supply and sewerage of the State Board of Health, the water from the river was used without any attempt at purification.

Prior to the building of the filter, typhoid fever made heavy inroads upon the inhabitants of Lawrence annually, but with its installation, it developed that the disease germs could be removed, and the Merrimack River water made harmless and healthful. This has been evident in the high rating of Lawrence among the cities of the country, for health conditions.

In recent years, however, the filtration facilities have been regarded as inadequate to meet the rapidly growing requirements. The tremendous growth of Lawrence and the demand made upon the filtered supply has created a situation so serious that, at this writing, a commission is engaged in studying the possibilities of a new source of supply.

While the slow sand filter now in use has demonstrated its worth in preserving the health of the community, its capacity has not kept sufficiently in excess of the demand notwithstanding the expansion of the plant. The installation of a mechanical or rapid sand filter has been proposed to tide the city over until the State Board of Health determines a permanent source of supply. A comparison of figures extending over the past twenty-eight years shows an enormous increase in the consumption of filtered water during that period. The consumption for the year 1922 was 1,656,000,000 gallons, as compared with 1,150,000,000 gallons in 1894. The average daily consumption was 4,500,000 gallons in 1922, as compared with 2,876,543 gallons in 1894.

The first steps looking toward the providing of a water system for Lawrence were taken in 1848 when, the "Lawrence Aqueduct Company" was chartered. John Tenney of Methuen, Alfred Kittredge of Haverhill, and Daniel Saunders of Lawrence, with associates, formed the corporation. Their project of bringing water from Haggett's Pond, now the source of supply for the town of Andover, was deemed impracticable. The authorized capital of the company was $50,000. The projectors based calculations upon the estimated use of eighteen gallons per day by each consumer. Experience showed that a supply three or four times that quantity must be provided to cover use, waste, and leakage.

In 1851, the Bay State Mills and the Essex Company, sharing the cost, built a reservoir of 1,000,000 gallons capacity on Prospect Hill. Water in this reservoir, raised from the canal by pumping through tested iron pipes, was kept on a level of about 152 feet above the crest of the Merrimack River Dam. The property was owned and operated by associated corporations, forming the Lawrence Reservoir Associated, each company having its own system of distributing pipes.

For twenty-four years, pipes and hydrants in corporation yards and principal business streets were supplied from this reservoir. The old common pond was also filled from this source. In 1871 and 1872 municipal water works were agitated, and in consequence of a petition signed by Henry Barton and eighteen other citizens the City Council caused an investigation of the project to be made by a special commission which recommended that the supply be taken from the Merrimack River.

An act passed by the Legislature and signed by Governor William B. Washburn on March 8, 1872, provided for the appointment of three commissioners by the City Council to execute, superintend, and direct work done by authority of the act or subsequent acts. Upon the approval of the act by the voters in May 1872, a joint special committee on water supply was appointed in the following June. An exhaustive report was submitted and on April 18, 1873, an ordinance was passed providing for the election of a board of water commissioners.

The present pumping station and reservoir were constructed in 1874-75. On October 19, 1875, water was forced up into the reservoir for the first time. In 1893, the original filter was completed. This was the first municipal filtration system for the elimination of bacteria established in the country. The water was turned on the bed in September of that year. It has an area of two and one-half acres. In 1907, the capacity of the filtration system was increased by the construction of a covered filter west of the original bed. The water area of this is three-quarters of an acre.

In 1916 work was started on the reconstruction of the east unit of the open filter. The original bed was divided into three units with separating walls in 1902. This reconstruction consisted of the laying of a concrete bottom and walls with piers which will support the roof later when it may be decided to cover this section. The work is intended to increase the capacity of the beds by excluding the iron from the ground water which found its way into the upper drains.

The reservoir has a capacity of 40,000,000 gallons, and the pumping capacity of the old Leavitt engine at the pumping station for 24 hours is 4,600,000 gallons each side, one side being operated at a time. A turbine engine, installed in 1912, with a pumping capacity of about 3,000,000 gallons in 24 hours and a Barr pump with a capacity of about 1,900,000 gallons a day are used in connection with the high service water tower on Tower Hill, which regulates the flow on the hills and in the mercantile or so-called fire hazard district. The turbine can be used on either the high or the low-pressure service.

89

The high-pressure service was put in originally to supply Tower and Prospect Hill sections. The original main was extended from the standpipe on Tower Hill down Haverhill street, and East Haverhill street to High Sstreet. In 1906, upon petition of the Merchants' Association, the Legislature authorized the City of Lawrence to borrow $50,000, outside the debt limit, for the purpose of extending the high-pressure water service for the better protection against, fire in the business section of the city. The main on Haverhill Street was tapped at Lawrence street, and also at Broadway. A pipe was laid extending from the distributing main on Haverhill Street down Lawrence Street to the south side of Essex street. From this point, a main was extended up Essex street to Broadway, Broadway to Common, Common to Union, Union to Essex, and thence up Essex to Lawrence street, completing the circuit. The whole system is laid out so that in case of accident there will be but a small unit out of service at one time.

The high service water tower was built in 1896. The enclosed steel tank is one hundred and two feet high and thirty feet in diameter. At one hundred feet, there is an eight-inch overflow pipe that conveys the overflow back into the reservoir. In case of the necessity of repairs on the enclosed standpipe, the water can be pumped directly into the mains through a Ross pressure-regulating valve. The capacity of the standpipe is 528,768 gallons.

The water tower is octagonal, with the shortest inside diameter 33 feet, 4 inches. The thickness of the masonry walls at the bottom is two feet, and just above the balcony floor 16 inches; the balcony floor, where lookout is, 107 feet above foundation; window sills, 109 feet; sills of triangular windows in roof, 138 feet; top of finial, 157 feet above base. The foundation of the tower has an elevation of 250 feet. Cost of construction: Metal standpipe, $11,161; masonry tower, $21,718.

The reservoir when full, with depth of 25 feet, has an elevation of 202 feet, and the top of the embankment, 207 feet. The logical location for the reservoir was on "Emery Hill" at the top of Lowell street, which has an elevation of 248 feet, with a plateau broad enough for this storage basin. Why it was not located there has been attributed to "politics", although it has been said that a dispute over the price of the land was the cause. At any rate, the first water commissioners chose the Bodwell land instead of the proposed Emery location.

Connected with the reservoir are 110 miles of water mains. There are over 950 hydrants. The original cost of the water works was $1,363,000. The cost today, with the several improvements, is estimated to be $2,611,551. Beginning with 1903, with few exceptions, the department has been each year self-sustaining, there having been a surplus of receipts over expenditures.

THE FIRE DEPARTMENT

The first engine house, erected in the limits of Lawrence, was a small one-story structure, with large doors but minus windows in front, at the corner of Essex and Turnpike (Broadway) streets, on the site of the Brechin block. This was constructed shortly after the beginning of operations on the dam. In it was stored the hand engine "Essex", purchased by the Essex Company and manned by its employees for nearly three years, when it was sold to the town, and the building used for other purposes. The engine was transferred to a wooden building on Morton street, which was subsequently used as a fire station and is still standing. The structure was used until recently by one of the departments of the Industrial school, it having been remodeled and enlarged. This particular engine house was replaced by what is now known as Engine 4's house at the corner of Lowell and Oxford streets.

In 1847, the town purchased two more hand engines, and two small wooden buildings were built for their storage. One of these was erected on Newbury street, but it was afterward removed to Garden street. In it, Niagara 2 (first called "Rough and Ready") was housed. Later the building was sold and removed to Union Street to be converted into a store and tenement. The other structure was erected on Elm street, between Lawrence and White streets, in which Syphon 3 was housed. Later it was removed to the southerly side of Oak street. In 1850, a fourth hand-engine company was formed in South Lawrence under the name of the Tiger Fire Association. For its quarters, a building, similar to the others, was erected at the corner of Turnpike and Crosby streets.

The site of the present fire department headquarters, or close to it, on Lowell street, has been marked by an engine house since the very early days of the department. The original fire station in this location stood on part of the site of the Central firehouse. It was occupied by the Hook and Ladder, City Hose and Lawrence Protective companies, the last named being disbanded in 1853. In 1854, the building was removed to Amesbury street, in the rear of the First Baptist church, where it remained until 1864. Then it was removed to a lot near the corner of Concord and Franklin streets, when it was enlarged and used for fire purposes until the present brick firehouse was erected there.

Prior to 1860, none of the engine houses were provided with hose towers worthy to be termed such. They were occasionally heated by box stoves in cold weather, and were provided with small bell towers. The first hook and ladder truck purchased by the town was a crude affair of light construction, with a small number of ladders of medium length, a few hooks, axes and lanterns. The City Hose carriage was a two-wheel affair, capable of carrying 500 feet of hose and manned by a company of 10 members. Later a five-wheel carriage was substituted, and its name was changed to Eagle Hose Company which organization ceased to exist in 1870.

The construction of the first brick firehouse, at the corner of Haverhill and White streets, long since known as the Old Battery building, was authorized in June 1856. The following September the old wooden house on Oak street was sold, and hand Engine 3's company moved into the new quarters. This house was later also occupied by the Bonney Light Battery which was organized in 1865, at the close of the Civil War, and named for Mayor Bonney; hence the name of Old Battery building. For many years, the house has not been used by the fire department, and the Bonney Light Battery long ago went out of existence. The building is now used as a storehouse by the Public Property department, besides being a polling place for Precinct 8. The old brick fire house at the corner of South Broadway and Crosby street, occupied by Engine No. 3 and Chemical No. 3, was built in 1869, and the one on Garden street, occupied by Engine No. 2, in 1871. The old brick house at the corner of Franklin and Concord streets, occupied by Ladder No. 4, was constructed in 1876.

The newer houses, all of brick, were constructed as follows: Engine 4's, Oxford street, in 1910; Central fire station, Lowell street, in 1907; Combination 6's, Howard street, in 1896; Combination 7's, Park street, in 1896; Combination 8's, Ames street, in 1900; Combination 9's; Bailey street, in 1908.

At the time of the Pemberton mill disaster, January 10, 1860, the necessity for a more adequate system of fire protection was brought home with telling force, and the city government purchased the Pacific No. I from the Amoskeag Manufacturing Company of Manchester, N. H., it being the fifteenth steam fire engine made by that concern. This steamer was placed in service in Lawrence on July 6, 1860, and was first located in the Old Battery building. It was transferred to Lowell street when the former brick house there was built. After 11 years of regular service, the old Pacific was set aside as a reserve steamer, and nine years later it was sold for one quarter of its original cost.

Atlantic No. 2 steam fire engine, built for the purpose of exhibiting it at the world's fair in London, England, in 1861, was purchased by the City of Lawrence on March 6, 1862, the inducements offered for its shipment across the Atlantic not being regarded as sufficient. This steamer was temporarily located in the house on Lowell street, being later removed to Garden street. In June 1862, the steamer known as Tiger 3 was purchased from the Amoskeag Company, and located in the house on South Broadway. Both these engines were replaced by larger and more modern types in 1889.

Essex 4 steam fire engine was secured by the city on September 24, 1864, and placed in the old firehouse on Morton street. In 1889, it was replaced by the steamer now in use at the new house of Engine 4 on Oxford street. Washington steam engine No. 5, now known as Engine 5, was purchased in 1870, and placed in service in April of the following year. This steamer responds to second alarms today. It is located at the Central fire station.

The Franklin hook and ladder truck at the Concord street house was secured on February 16, 1875. The double tank chemical at Engine 3's house was placed in service on March 30, 1880. It was located at the Lowell street headquarters until 1886 when the protective wagon was installed there and the chemical engine removed to the Soth Broadway house. The aerial ladder truck at the Central fire station was purchased in 1889. The water tower, also located at the Lowell street headquarters, was secured in 1905. The various other pieces of apparatus have been provided as the need appeared.

Today the department equipment comprises 50 trained horses, four steamers, four hose wagons, four combination hose and chemical wagons, one protective wagon, one double tank chemical, four hook and ladder trucks, a water tower, chief's and deputy chief's wagons, besides nine supply and exercise wagons. The personnel includes a chief, deputy chief, 11 captains, nine lieutenants, 69 permanent men, 60 call men and 100 substitutes. There are nine engine houses, including the seven-run central station, one of the largest of its kind in the country.

The Firemen's Relief Association, organized in 1878, is still in existence and in a flourishing condition.

An animate reminder of the hand-tub days, and a distinguished member of the Lawrence fire department, is Charles W. Foster, engine man at the Central fire station, who is the oldest fireman in the United States, if not the oldest in the world, in active service. He has been connected with the department for over 66 years, having joined it in 1851. He is 83 years old, but despite his age, he reports regularly every day at the firehouse. For 30 years, he has run the old Washington 5 steamer.

The town fire department was organized on June 12, 1847, established by legislative enactment the following year. At first fire, wardens were chosen. Two years later the system was changed, and a fire chief was elected. In June, 1891, the department was reorganized by an act of the Legislature, and a board of three engineers, a chief and two assistants, the former to be permanent and the other two "call" commanders, was provided for. These were named by the Mayor and confirmed by the Board of Aldermen. When the new city charter, or commission form of government, went into effect January 1, 1912, it provided for the abolishment of the board of fire engineers. Early that year Alderman Cornelius F. Lynch, the first director of public safety, designated Chief Dennis E. Carey as chief, and Francis J. Morris, then a captain in command of Combination 8's company, as deputy fire chief. Both have continued to hold those positions.

Prior to 1869, the fire alarms were given by ringing small bells on the several engine houses, except in case of a fire of considerable magnitude when the City Hall and corporation bells were rung. In the early days frequently much confusion prevailed in locating the fires, as there were no signal boxes as there are today. The sources of water supply, too, were limited and the apparatus was crude. In July 1869, the first fire alarm telegraph system was introduced. It comprised 14 boxes and three bell strikers, which were installed at an expense of $8,000. This system was gradually enlarged and improved upon until 1909 when the present modern Game well system, including what is called the fast and slow time method, was provided at a cost of $22,000. There are 139 signal boxes.

The next step toward modernizing the Lawrence fire department will be the installation of automobile equipment, which has been persistently advocated and which must eventually materialize.

THE POLICE DEPARTMENT

In the early days of Lawrence, every one was too busy to be concerned about criminal doings, but, as the town began to grow, evils cropped out and the need of some law-enforcing department was felt.

At the first town meeting, 10 constables were appointed, and of these 10 men Gilman F. Sanborn, Nathaniel Ambrose, and James D. Herrick were successively at the head of the town police.

Not until Lawrence was incorporated as, a city was a regular police department organized. From the founding of the city till 1888, the police were subject to annual change as went the fates of politics, but in 1887, a law was passed making the police force permanent. The growth of the department has kept pace with the development of the city. At the close of the year 1917 the force consisted of a city marshal, three assistant city marshals, one lieutenant, two sergeants, six inspectors, one clerk, one keeper of the lockup, a matron, one inspector of wires, 94 regular patrolmen and 29 reserves.

The first lockup was located near the corner of Turnpike (Broadway) and Common streets. In 1850, the selectmen discarded this lockup and established police headquarters in the basement of the Town (City) Hall. Cells were built in the arches supporting the vaults of the town clerk. At that time the chief of police had his office on the first floor of the hall where what is now the assessors office. Some time later, a public protest arose over the alleged unsanitary arrangement of the cells in the Town Hall, and they were abandoned after a new lockup was built on Common street, near the corner of Jackson street. It was constructed of wood after the plan of a cottage house, and contained eight cells. For a time a small wooden lockup was also maintained on Elm street between Lawrence and White streets.

These facilities served until 1867 when a brick station was erected on the site of the present headquarters at the corner of Common and Lawrence streets. This building was built despite sturdy opposition, and for many years, it was more than ample. In recent years, however, it had far outgrown its usefulness, and in 1914, the building was razed, and the present modern structure was constructed, being finished for occupancy the following year. It contains the most modern equipment and appliances for police work. It has a well-ventilated, well-lighted cell room, with 42 cells. Besides, there are well-arranged accommodations for both the administrative officers and the patrolmen. In the basement is a timely equipped emergency aid room.

The present District Court which occupies the second floor of the police station building was established by an act of the Legislature in 1914. It has jurisdiction in civil cases from Lawrence, Methuen and the Andovers, and concurrent jurisdiction with the trial justices in criminal matters from the same district. It is the outgrowth of the Lawrence police court, instituted by legislative enactment in 1848. Prior to this, justice had been administered by Trial Justice Joseph Couch. The first judge of police court appointed was William Stevens who resigned in 1876 after serving 28 years, total blindness making his retirement necessary. He was succeeded in 1878 by Nathan W. Harmon, in the meantime Associate Justice William H. P. Wright having served. Ill health caused Judge Harmon to resign nine years later, and the late Hon. Andrew C. Stone was his successor. Judge Jeremiah J. Mahoney, the present presiding justice, was next in line, his appointment to succeed Judge Stone being made in 1905 by Governor Douglas.

The efficiency of the police department was greatly increased by the installation of the police signal system in 1894. This system has been perfected in many respects since its adoption and the police system generally has been modernized in accordance with the very latest ideas. The horse drawn patrol and ambulance was replaced in 1917 by automobile equipment.

There is the dark side of police annals that concerns crime, its commission and consequences, into which we do not intend to delve, as we do not think it is necessary for the completion of the aims of this book. It is not our intention to drag forth family skeletons or to hold up to the present generation scandals that should be best left forgotten. But, at the same time, we do not wish to leave the impression that Lawrence has been free from sensational happenings of this nature.

A complete sketch of the activities of the Lawrence Police Department, from the days of- the old-fashioned lockups to the present with its well equipped system, would show that the city, although on the whole a peaceful, law-abiding community, has had its share of crime. In detection of crime and the protection of life and property, however, the police department of Lawrence has a record which will compare favorably with that of any other city in the country. Competent police chiefs and alert, capable inspectors and patrolmen have built up a service full of commendable achievement. There have been cases where criminals have escaped apprehension, but very few as compared to the number of successful prosecutions.

CITY'S LIGHTING SYSTEM

The lighting system of Lawrence will compare favorably with that of any other city of its size in the country. Plenty of lights of the arc variety and the incandescent are so well distributed on all the thoroughfares that on the darkest night there is no trouble in finding one's way in the most remote neighborhoods, while on the principal thoroughfares, where the most powerful arcs are used, there is hardly a stretch that the luminating rays of the street lamps do not penetrate.

The public of today is so accustomed to good lighting facilities, that there is little reflection on the vast improvement in the system during the last 50 years. It is only when a bad storm puts a circuit out of commission and a section is plunged into darkness that one realizes what conditions must have been in the early days.

Before the introduction of electricity and its general adoption by the public, in conjunction with gas, the gas lighting companies had a keen competitor in kerosene as an illuminant. At that time the city was lighted by both oil and gas lamps, and the service was feeble as compared to the modern lighting system of today. The lamps were few and, consequently, the distribution was such as to make the lights appear as widely separated dots in the blanket of darkness. In time the oil lamps lost their popularity, and gas was used almost universally.

The street department had charge of the street lighting in those days, and a force of lamp lighters was employed to light the lamps and keep the globes clean, while police officers were always provided with matches for the purpose of igniting lamps that had gone out or been overlooked by the lamp lighters. The policemen had also the duty of turning off the lights, and at 11 o'clock all lights, except those on the principal streets, were extinguished. The latter burned all night. When the moon shone brightly the lights were not lit, a bit of economy that is not practiced in these days of modern lighting methods. Prowlers, after 11 o'clock, were always in danger of arrest.

In 1880 the first electric lights were installed in the city, large arcs being placed on the common. The Lawrence Electric Light Company had begun to manufacture electricity in the old fish line mill building of the Essex Company, now a part of the Farwell Bleachery plant, and provided service chiefly for street lighting. This was the beginning of the present extensive system, Lawrence's streets being now lighted by electricity exclusively.

Today the city spends over $61,000 a year for street lighting, an amount that is constantly growing as the service is extended. There are distributed over the numerous thoroughfares 1240 lights, of which 642 are incandescent, and 598 of the arc variety. The lamps are well divided, being placed to the best advantage. On the principal streets high powered arc lights are used, while on the residential thoroughfares there are both arc and the less luminous incandescent.

As soon as electricity became a serviceable medium and the inventions made for its perfection became of commercial value, the majority of the old-line gas companies combined their gas business with that of the new discovery. In this movement the Lawrence Gas Company was among the first, having at once seen the advantage of such a departure. The concern from the start has aimed to improve its service, and it has been ever ready to adopt innovations tending to that end. A vast amount of capital invested in this line of commercial activity stands out nowhere with greater prominence than in Lawrence, where since 1848 this company has given a service which has worked for public and private good.

The story of the development of the city's lighting system is in reality the history of the growth of the Lawrence Gas Company which concern serves the adjacent towns of Methuen, Andover and North Andover, as well as Lawrence. The company is a Massachusetts corporation with a capital of $2,500,000. Bonds to the extent of $300,000 have been issued.

The gas works on Marston street were established in 1848 by the Essex Company, the Bay State Mills and the Atlantic Mills, for the purpose of supplying light to those corporations. In 1849 a number of Boston capitalists bought the works and incorporated the business under the name, Lawrence Gas Company. Henry G. Webber who was its first manager served in that capacity until 1853, when George D. Cabot was made manager. In 1884, after 31 years of service, Mr. Cabot resigned, and C. J. R. Humphreys, the present efficient head of the concern, succeeded him.

The company has had a steady growth almost from the beginning. It started with works, capable of making and supplying to its customers about 20,000 cubic feet of gas per day. Today, with its immense, modern plant and tremendous gas holders it is able to distribute 2,500,000 cubic feet of gas each day. In 1905 about 275,000,000 cubic feet of gas was consumed in Lawrence and vicinity. In 1917 over 576,000,000 cubic feet was supplied.

In 1887 the Lawrence Gas Company bought out the Lawrence Electric Light Company. In 1890 it acquired the plant of the Edison Electric Illuminating Company, located on Common street. Under the energetic management of the Gas Company, in educating the people to the use of electricity for various purposes, the old plants soon became inadequate, and the equipment was enlarged and improved.

In 1900 the demand for electricity for commercial and manufacturing purposes had grown to such an extent that a new plant was built and equipped on the south side of the river, the company still maintaining and operating the Common street station as it does to this day, chiefly as a distributing station. The plant was built of sufficient size to take care of increasing business for years to come, and has been of special service to a great many manufacturing plants locating here, many of which depend wholly upon electricity for power to operate their machinery equipments. This plant is equipped with waterpower machinery of about 2500 horsepower, and with steam turbines of 8,200 horsepower.

In the beginning, when gas (then of inferior quality) was used commercially, the price per 1000 cubic feet was $4.00. Today, with a modern plant and appliances strictly first class, gas is supplied to the people at the price of 85 cents per 1000 cubic feet. At first gas was used exclusively for lighting; now it is used for a number of useful purposes, principally for lighting, cooking, and power, many gas engines being operated by its application. It also supplies heat. Of late years, however, gas has come to be regarded as an indispensable adjunct to the household, for cooking purposes. In 1892 less than 40 gas ranges were in use in Lawrence. Today, there are few families without one. During the more recent years gas has come into general use for heating water in houses, so doing away with the waterfront of the coal range, a great convenience, especially in hot weather. So rapidly has the Lawrence Gas Company kept pace with the great growth of the city that there is no part of the community that is not served by the company's service pipes and lines.

A large portion of the office floor of the company's building on Essex street is used as a show room for gas stoves and gas and electrical appliances. Several years ago the company acquired the old property of the Young Men's Christian Association on Appleton street, which is occupied by its appliance department.

The officers of the company are: President, N. H. Emmons; vice president, C. J. R. Humphreys; treasurer, R. W. Emmons, 2nd; clerk, H. R. Peverly; directors, Walter Coulson, Franklin Butler, C. J. R. Humphreys, Nathaniel H. Emmons, R. W. Emmons 2nd, Frank Brewster and Alfred Bowditch

John H. Tarbox School

Lawrence Schools

Development of the Public School System

Probably no better illustration of the rapidity of the growth of Lawrence can be found than in the development of the public school system of the city. From the very beginning there has been a constant growth of the school plant, the demand for accommodations becoming larger and steadier as the population mounted; the building up of the educational facilities has kept pace with the growth of the community, though the increase in the number of pupils in the last several years has been so extraordinary that it has been a most difficult problem to provide suitable accommodations.

The importance of the school system in municipal affairs may be noted in the amount appropriated each year for its maintenance, the appropriation being nearly a third of the entire sum apportioned for all city departments. Fortunately, the needs of the school department have usually had precedence over those of other departments, in the consideration of municipal governments.

One may comprehend the extent of the school plant of Lawrence in the following data, based on figures for the school year ended in 1917:

Number of school buildings: Primary, 23: grammar, 8: high, 1. Total, 32.
Besides these, there are several portable school buildings and rented accommodations to take care of the overflow in the elementary grades.
Number of classrooms: Elementary, 258; high, 23. Total, 281.
Number of pupils in day schools: Elementary, 9,108; high, 1,117. Total, 10,225.
Number of teachers in day schools: Elementary, 316: high, 41. Total, 357.
Number of pupils in evening schools: Elementary. 1,189: high, 538. Total. 1,727.
Number of teachers in evening schools : Elementary, 42 : high, 30. Total, 72.

Total cost of maintaining department, including evening schools: $411,991.13.

Cost to the city per pupil for education a year: $42.10.

Value of school buildings and land, including new central Oliver grammar school: Estimated at $1,500,000.

In the list of class rooms are included the accommodations for the afternoon sessions at the High school, these sessions being necessary to provide for the great overflow in the day High school. It might be stated here that the city has appropriated $50,000 for the purchase of adjoining property west of the High school building, with the view of constructing a large addition to the present plant. It is expected that the near future will see the work of construction under way.

The story of the development of the present system of public schools is interesting. In 1845, when the Essex Company commenced operations here, there were three one-story district school houses, two in the Methuen portion of the territory now included in the city area, and one south of the river, in the Andover section. They were crude affairs, uncomfortable and unattractive. One was located on Tower Hill, the second at the intersection of what are now Prospect and East Haverhill streets, and the third on the south side, near the intersection of the Lowell road and the Turnpike (South Broadway). There were summer and winter terms of a few weeks' duration. In 1846, the Essex Company erected a schoolhouse between Haverhill and Tremont streets, where a school was opened under the direction of the Methuen school committee, on November 7th, by Nathaniel Ambrose as teacher. He commenced with 25 scholars, but before the expiration of the first year, the roll included 150 scholars.

When Lawrence was incorporated as a town, the following were named a school committee: James D. Herrick, Dan Weed and William D. Lamb, M. D. To these men was entrusted the founding of the present school system. At their second meeting they voted that one male and five female teachers be employed, Mr. Ambrose as male teacher in the Essex Company's house. Miss Robinson for the Durant district. Miss Ford for the Tower Hill district. Miss Brown and Miss Abbott for the Free Will Baptist Vestry and Miss Odell on the south side of the river. During this year, a story and a half schoolhouse was built on Jackson street, where the Unitarian church now stands, and a similar one upon the Lowell road on the south side of the river.

Concerning the work of this original committee, the school committee of 1848 had this record: "They erected the school house on the south side with a view to the future; and it will answer its purpose for an indefinite period. On this side (the North) of the river we were put in possession of

102

the Prospect street, the Jackson street and the Haverhill street school houses, as property of the town; and of the Hampshire street house, as the property of the Essex Company, rented by the town. All of these buildings contained a single room, with the exception of the Jackson street and Southside schools which were of two rooms each.

Early in the year 1848 the school committee, after consultation with Hon. Horace Mann and other distinguished educators, adopted a continuous system of public instruction wherein the primary school is introductory to the middle, the middle to the grammar, the grammar to the high, and the high to the college or the actual pursuits of life. And that plan is in vogue today, although much improved in the method of application.

The first grammar school on the north side (later named the Oliver) was opened in April 1848, in the Jackson street house, and was moved into the original Oliver school building upon its completion near the close of the same year. Another grammar school was established about the same time in the new Southside building. The Lawrence High school was organized January 31, 1849. On that day, a class of seventeen members was admitted, without strict regard for qualification. Provisions were made for them in the front room of the lower floor of the old Oliver High school house, where the High school was located until the original High school building was erected.

When Lawrence was created a city in 1853, the following were elected school committeemen: Hon. Charles S. Storrow, mayor and chairman; Henry K. Oliver, James D. Herrick, William Stevens, Ivan Stevens, Enoch Pratt and L. W. Wright, the mayor and one representative from each ward. The new city was in possession of ten school buildings, including the Oliver, containing also the Oliver high school; the Newbury street, the Oak street, the Amesbury street, the Cross street and the Prospect street schools. All of these buildings were located on the sites occupied by buildings of the same names today, and all during the past 64 years have been greatly remodeled, except the Oak street and the old Oliver grammar school buildings which were razed to make room for the new central Oliver grammar school. The other early-day schoolhouses long ago proved inadequate and were abandoned. The original High school building, which after the opening of the new and more commodious structure on Lawrence street was used only as the headquarters of the school authorities and as an annex of the evening schools, was totally destroyed by fire December 6, 1910. The building had been constructed in 1867, and it was beautiful in architectural design.

In the year 1892, a notable revolution was inaugurated in the architecture and construction of the school buildings of Lawrence. In that year, the City Council authorized the erection of the John R. Rollins grammar school on Howard street, Prospect Hill. This handsome brick building, completed in 1893, contains ten class rooms, a large hall, rooms for teachers and master, a library, and every modern convenience. Its lighting, heating and ventilation equipment is one of the best obtainable. Its approximate cost was $70,000. Other buildings followed, in general construction similar to the Rollins, the number of class rooms ranging from ten to sixteen. In 1895, the John K. Tarbox grammar school on Alder street was erected at an approximate cost of $60,000. A few years ago a large addition was made to this building, at an expense of $60,000. The Emily G. Wetherbee grammar school on Newton street was built in 1897 at an approximate cost of $95,000; the new High school in 1901, at a cost of about $250,000; the Alexander B. Bruce grammar school on Ames street. Tower Hill, in 1902, about $100,000; the Gilbert E. Hood grammar school on Park street, in 1905, about $150,000; the John Breen grammar school, in 1911, about $135,000.

In June, 1915, the construction of the new central (Oliver) grammar school was started, and the building was completed in the fall of 1917, at an estimated cost of $210,000. The structure is the last word in schoolhouse construction. It contains 36 class rooms, besides an assembly hall, four manual training and domestic science rooms, teachers' rooms, etc. It also contains a fine suite of offices for the school department. The building occupies the sites of the original Oliver grammar. Oak street and old High school buildings, and extends from Haverhill street to Oak street, with a frontage of 152 feet on Haverhill street.

The Packard school was named for Rev. George Packard, first rector of the Grace church; the Oliver for Gen. Henry K. Oliver, former mayor and superintendent of schools; the Harrington for Rev. Henry F. Harrington, first pastor of the Unitarian church; the Walton for George A. Walton, first principal of the Oliver school; the Storrow for Hon. Charles S. Storrow, first mayor of the city; the Saunders for Hon. Daniel Saunders, known as the founder of the city; the Rollins for Hon. John R. Rollins, a member of the school board for 30 years; the Tarbox for Hon. John K. Tarbox, another highly respected citizen; the Hood for Gilbert E. Hood, donor of the Hood prizes and former superintendent of schools; the Bruce and the Breen for former mayors of the city, Hon. Alexander B. Bruce and Hon. John Breen. The other schools received their names from the streets on which they are located.

From its earliest inception the educational advancement of the city has kept pace with her material progress. Changes in courses of study and in methods of instruction have been made as the advantage became apparent, and the best features of the new education have been incorporated into the school system. Besides the regular subjects, music, drawing, and sewing are taught in the various grades under the supervision of special teachers, and in connection with the work of the High school, a four years' course in manual training is maintained.

Eight years constitute the elementary course of study, below the High school, the first three years of which are spent in the primary schools. The grammar grade course covers five years, though the first two grades of the course are commonly referred to as "middle" grades. In 1917, there were 511 graduates from the grammar schools, the largest number in the history of the city. Departmental work has been established in all the grammar schools, and here a firm foundation is laid for the higher education to come. Each school is under the control of an experienced master.

The High school curriculum is one of the broadest and strongest in the state. Courses in 27 distinct subjects are offered, the study of English and Literature being more than exceptionally prominent. It is probable that more thorough work in Literature is done in Lawrence than elsewhere in the state. Good training is also given in the sciences, languages, and commercial subjects, besides the course in manual training. Promotion is by subject, pupils being classified according to their capacity, and four, five or even six years may be spent there before graduation. The great majority, however, complete the course in four years. The school has earned such an excellent reputation among the colleges that it has been accorded a place upon the privileged list by those colleges which accept certificates in lieu of examinations. In 1917 there were 164 graduates. Based on the figures for 1917, the High school costs about $60,000 a year for its maintenance. Of this amount, the sum of $44,980 goes for salaries alone. The expenditure per pupil is $53.54 year.

Occupying a unique place among the schools, and doing most vital work, is the Lawrence Practice School which since 1905 has occupied the Gilbert E. Hood schoolhouse. For many years prior to the establishment of the Normal school at Lowell, and for a few years subsequent to that, Lawrence maintained its own independent training school. To it, graduates of our High school or other High schools were admitted after examination, and graduated for teaching after a course of a year and a half. In 1901 an agreement was reached between the city and the commonwealth, by which the Training school (as it was then called) was incorporated into the State Normal school system as a school for observation and practice. Lender this agreement, graduates of our High school took a two years' course of academic work at Lowell, during which they spent one period of three months in practice teaching in the Hood school. After graduation from Lowell, residents of Lawrence were entitled to take up a supplementary course of practice teaching, five months in duration, after which they became eligible to teach in the elementary schools of the city. In 1900, the term of undergraduate practice was eliminated. Graduates of Massachusetts Normal schools are now required to spend a period of five months practice teaching in the Hood school before they are eligible to appointment.

In addition to the day schools, Lawrence has a great system of evening schools, one of the largest in the state. This valuable and now indispensable adjunct of the school department was first inaugurated in the winter of 1859-60. A committee of the board of advice to the city missionary, consisting of Rev. George Packard and Hon. Charles S. Storrow, petitioned the City Council in 1859 for an appropriation to assist them in establishing an evening school. They reported that the city missionary would act as principal of the school, and that he was able to obtain teachers who would gratuitously and cheerful give the necessary time for the instruction of the pupils. They proposed to use the cast off furniture of the regular school department and to secure some convenient room where the school could be held.

The City Council gave them the munificent sum of $100. Quarters were secured in Odd Fellows hall which was then located at the southwesterly corner of Common and Hampshire streets. The room rent amounted to about $50, and that and the cost of supplies caused an expense of about $216 the first term, part of which was met by the aid of proceeds from several benefit entertainments. It was necessary to ask the City Council for $41 more to meet the deficit.

More than 200 scholars were taught that first winter, who from want or neglect of early privileges needed and desired the instruction such as the school gave. The school, thus begun, prospered and increased greatly in attendance as the years went by, and the first quarters became so crowded in 1863 that a request was made for the use of a portion of the basement of the City Hall. A room, 25 feet wide and extending the length of the basement on the north side, was fitted up. With the exception of two or three small portions cut off from this room for other purposes, it is still in a condition similar to that as at first finished, and it is now occupied by the city grocery. In May 1870, the school committee took charge of the school and accommodations for the girls were provided in the Oliver grammar school building. The boys, for a time, remained in the old quarters in the basement of the City Hall. Later, the disturbances and interruptions, in the use of this room for caucuses and elections and in connection with the performances in the hall, became so great that the school was not held there after the winter of 1876-77, accommodations for the boys also being found in one of the school buildings.

106

The evening schools are now maintained three evenings in the week from October until March. During the term ended in 1917, there were employed 72 teachers, including a supervisor. The total expense, excluding costs of heating and lighting which are very considerable items, amounted to $16,950.54. The elementary evening schools in 1881 occupied eight rooms in the Oliver and Packard school buildings. The record does not give the number attending. The committee spent $1,700 for evening schools that year. In 1882, the evening High school had 18 pupils. Besides the High school, four other buildings are now occupied by the evening schools. During the school year ending in March 1917, there were 177 pupils enrolled, of which number 538 attended the evening High school. In 1916 there were 132 evening High school pupils awarded diplomas after completing the three years' course. In 1917 the four-year course went into effect and there was, consequently, no graduation this year.

The course of studies in the evening High school is nearly as good as that offered in the day school, there being little difference except in the amount of time given the various subjects. Many young men and women, who have been compelled to take up the task of earning a livelihood upon reaching the working age, avail themselves of the opportunity afforded thereby for advanced education. In the High school building, but distinct in organization, are the advanced evening grammar school classes, doing work parallel to that of the 6th, 7th, and 8th grades of the day schools. Pupils completing the work of the eighth grade class are given certificates of advancement and are entitled to entrance to the regular High school course. In the basement of the building, occupying the quarters of the manual training department, is located the evening drawing school. Here well-filled classes of men are nightly at work during the evening school season. The courses, architectural and mechanical, are in charge of veteran instructors of the day High school.

A new and interesting feature of the evening school system is the Naturalization school, the first of its kind in the country. In January 1914, this department was opened in the High school building, on Tuesday and Friday evenings, for men desiring to make preparation to become naturalized citizens and for foreigners over 21 years of age wishing to learn the English language or to improve their knowledge of it by further study. The school was organized by Cornelius F. Sullivan, the master of the Oliver school, and he is assisted in the experiment by several experienced teachers. The success of the project thus far has been gratifying, and the school has come to be regarded as a permanent institution. It has proved of great assistance in the work of naturalization and has been an incentive to many aliens to become citizens. At the end of the term, the certificates of naturalization are publicly awarded, with appropriate exercises, to those who have qualified therefore through the course of instruction offered by the school.

Lawrence was the first city to avail itself of the commonwealth's invitation to open an independent industrial evening school, half of the expense of maintenance to be paid from the state treasury. Under the management of a local board of trustees, a fine training is imparted in mechanical, textile and domestic science subjects. During the term ending in May 1917, there were over 1,500 pupils enrolled, and there were 54 instructors, including a principal. The city's share of the cost of maintenance was about $10,000. The evening trade extension work covers a wide field. It gives those employed during the day an opportunity of advancing themselves along their lines of work. While this school is wholly independent of the public school system, it may be properly included in the story of the educational opportunities which Lawrence so lavishly offers to every individual, young or old, who is ambitious to improve his mind or increase his earning power.

The Parochial Schools

The parochial schools are regarded as a valuable aid in the educational work of the city. Excellent training is imparted in all the desirable educational subjects up to and including the grammar grades in all of these schools, while St. Mary's High School enables the girls to complete their education or preparation for college and advanced study, in an atmosphere whose religious influence helps greatly in the development of sound moral character.

Eleven well-equipped school buildings provide accommodations for the 5,878 parochial school pupils. Based on the estimated cost per pupil of $41.20 a year for maintaining the public schools for the school year ending in 191 7, the maintenance of the parochial schools, which are supported by the Catholic parishes, saves the City of Lawrence the sum of nearly a quarter of a million dollars a year. This sum does not include the interest on the capital invested in school buildings.

The parochial school system had its beginning here in the St. Mary's schools, the first parochial schools established in this city, although there had been in the early days a small private school conducted by Catholic laymen. In August 1859, five Sisters of the Notre Dame were brought to Lawrence by Rev. James O'Donnell, Sister Constance who died July 1, 1878, being the superior. An ordinary dwelling house, No. 346 Oak street, was given them for a residence, in which, with additions made at two different times, they remained for, nearly 35 years. On September 5, following, St. Mary's school for girls was opened under their teaching. They commenced with 200 pupils in three departments, viz., primary, intermediate and grammar, with accommodations on the first floor of what, for over a score of years, was known as the "Girls School", in a wooden building on Haverhill street, since removed, and which was situated about half way between the present stone school building (then St. Mary's church) and the new convent.

Ten years after that beginning, Father Edge opened a school for boys in old "St. James' Hall", also since removed, but then standing at the corner of Haverhill and White streets. This, also numbering about 200 pupils at the start, was placed in charge of the same sisters who were allowed for some years to teach the boys until they had received their first communion. Both schools grew rapidly and soon the buildings became inadequate. On September 19, 1880, Father Gilmore had the stone building which since the erection of the new edifice had been known as "St. Mary's Old Church", transformed into a school and hall. The exterior of this building- now occupied by the boys' department of the school, and in which are located the quarters of the Catholic Young Men's Association, organized in 1886, has been but slightly changed in appearance.

In accordance with their rules, the Sisters of Notre Dame were obliged to relinquish the teaching of all but the youngest of the boys in St. Mary's schools, so in 1889, Rev. James T. O'Reilly secured the services of the Xaverian Brothers to take charge of the older ones. As a residence for them, he remodeled the old parochial house of the Immaculate Conception church on White street.

On December 20, 1893, the Sisters moved into the new convent at the corner of Haverhill and Hampshire streets, upon the completion of that handsome and commodious structure. The convent is one of the finest of its kind in the state and cost about $48,000. The old convent on Oak street has been replaced by a modernly constructed brick school building of 16 classrooms. This is occupied exclusively by girls. The stone building has 11 classrooms.

During the term ended in June 1917, St. Mary's schools were attended by 2,103 pupils. In the high school for girls, there were 141 pupils, and at the commencement exercises, 25 were awarded diplomas. In conjunction with the schools on Haverhill street, St. Mary's parish also supports St. Rita's school for boys and girls. This is also in charge of the Sisters of Notre Dame. It has about 500 pupils. The Assumption school for boys and girls, in charge of Sisters of St. Domenic, is connected with St. Mary's schools. It has 80 pupils.

A remarkable feature in the development of St. Mary's schools, and which is a forceful demonstration of the influence of the parochial school system, is the annual May Procession, held in honor of the Blessed Virgin. This institution was established in the early days of the parish, and it has grown bigger and more attractive each year. This year, 1918, fully 3,500 children took part.

Other parishes, following the lead of St. Mary's, have established schools, all of which have become important factors in the educational work of the church. Besides St. Mary's Schools, there are —St. Anne's (for boys), in charge of Marist Brothers, and St. Joseph's (for girls), in charge of Sisters of Good Shepherd; 1,793 pupils. St. Laurence's (for boys and girls), in charge of Sisters of Notre Dame, 321 pupils. St. Patrick's (for boys and girls), in charge of Sisters of Charity; 551 pupils. Sacred Heart (for boys and girls), in charge of Sisters of Holy Union of Sacred Heart; 539 pupils. Holy Rosary (for Italian boys and girls), in charge of Sisters of Notre Dame, 346 pupils. Holy Trinity (for Polish boys and girls), in charge of Felician Sisters of St. Francis; 225 pupils.

GRACE EPISCOPAL CHURCH

CHURCH HISTORY

An All-wise Providence has put it into the hearts of all His rational creatures to worship, and it was only natural that the first comers to the "new city" should have their thoughts turned religiously. Church history in Lawrence really began with the founding of the town. Religion has always been a most potent factor in the life of the community. Its importance today is evidenced in the great number of houses of worship here.

The development of the religious organizations has kept pace with the growth of the town and the city. There are now established in Lawrence 43 churches and 10 smaller organizations, making in all 53 religious bodies. The 43 churches are included in 12 distinct denominations.

The leading religious sects made almost simultaneous beginning in Lawrence, although 15 years before the founding of the town, on May 12, 1832, a church was duly organized in that part of Methuen now North Lawrence, in the old Prospect Hill school house. It was called "The First Protestant Episcopal Church of Methuen". Several months later, it became known as "Mount Zion Church". An effort was made to have constructed a church building on the old Methuen Orthodox church site on Clover Hill, but the movement failed, and during the four or five years that this church existed services were held in the old Prospect Hill school house, in the old brick school house on Howe street at Grosvenor's Corner, and in a hall at Methuen village. The first Christmas service ever celebrated in this locality was held by this church. The communion service ware in use by this church served at Grace church in the early years of its organization, and was afterward loaned to the Lawrence street church for use at the first communion of members thereof.

The importance of Lawrence as a field for religious teaching was fully comprehended by Catholic leaders, and they sent here, as pioneer workers for the church, men of large capacity and untiring energy.

We cannot fix with certainty the exact date when pioneers of this faith held first service here. Mass was probably first offered in Lawrence by Father McDermott of Lowell in the dwelling of Michael Murphy on Newton street in South Lawrence, in December, 1845, or early in January, 1846.

In April, 1846, Rev. Charles French commenced ministering to Catholics in Lawrence. He was the first clergyman of any denomination to actually purchase land for a church building. In a few months, a modest wooden edifice was erected upon Chestnut street at the corner of White street, where regular services were held and quite a large school was maintained. About 35 percent, of the population of Lawrence in 1848 was naturally Catholic in religious tendency. Today this denomination predominates.

Father French died in January, 1851, being succeeded by Rev. James H. D. Taaffe, during whose pastorate, in 1854, the brick church (Immaculate Conception) was built. In 1861, the fine-toned bell was placed in the tower, the first church bell to sound in the city.

The first building dedicated to religious worship in the city by Protestant worshipers was erected by Grace Episcopal Church on the lot near the corner of Jackson and Common streets, just north of the present stone edifice. It was a chapel of wood. Divine service was held in the building in October, 1846, and it was consecrated the following November. Later it was removed to Garden street and used as a vestry until, torn down to make room for the new and commodious brick chapel there erected.

The church edifice of stone was built in 1851, and consecrated in May, 1852. The building was enlarged in 1896. From the first gathering of this pioneer church until his death in 1876, the Rev. Dr. George Packard was rector of the church and parish. The present rector is Rev. Arthur Wheelock Moulton.

The Methodists, Congregationalists, Baptists, Unitarians, and Universalists, were also pioneers in the religious life of the community, all having become established here prior to 1850.

In June 1846, the first Methodist preaching service in Lawrence was held at the house of Charles Barnes, No. 5 Turnpike street (Broadway). The Essex Mission (so called) was organized June 1, 1846. Two months later, the Methodists moved across the street into the attic of an unfinished building which was called "Concert Hall". The church building at the corner of Haverhill and Hampshire streets was dedicated February 20, 1848. In 1911, this society, the First Methodist Episcopal church, consolidated with the Garden street Methodist Episcopal church, forming the Central Methodist church which now occupies the new attractive stone edifice on Haverhill street just east of Lawrence street. The Garden Street M. E. Church was for many years located in the brick structure at the corner of Garden and Newbury streets.

The Merrimack Congregational Society (so called) was organized August 1, 1846, but the name was changed to the Lawrence Street Congregational Church the following year, and January 5, 1847, meetings were begun in a small wooden building at the corner of Haverhill and Lawrence streets. On October 11, 1848, the old wooden church which for so many years occupied this site was dedicated. This structure was totally destroyed by fire in 1912, and was replaced by the present handsome stone edifice which was dedicated in May 1915.

The pioneer Baptist organization was the First Free Baptist church which was organized January 17, 1847, although services were first held by this sect in the boarding house of Timothy Osgood on Turnpike street (Broadway) in April, 1846. The church worshiped in a small chapel at the corner of Haverhill and White streets. This property was sold in 1857; the building was cut in two and made into two dwelling houses. The present church building, at the corner of Common and Pemberton streets, was dedicated April 21, 1857.

The First Baptist church had its beginning in the spring of 1847. Services were held irregularly in private homes or school houses until June, 1847, when a permanent church organization, the new body taking the name of the Amesbury Street Baptist Church. A temporary building was erected on a lot in the rear of the site of the present structure. But, this was soon found to be inadequate, and the Essex Company gave the lot of land at the corner of Haverhill and Amesbury streets, where the society commenced the work of building the church it now occupies, which was completed and dedicated October 20, 1850.

On August 30, 1847, the Unitarian church was organized. The first meetings were held in the Odd Fellows hall on Hampshire street, and later in a chapel which had been erected for that purpose. In May 1850, the old wooden church building at the corner of Jackson and Haverhill streets was dedicated, the tower and spire of which was destroyed by fire August 12, 1859, and had not been replaced. This structure was torn down in 1916 and a much smaller building erected.

On November 15, 1847, the First Universalist Society was organized and the first meetings held in a school house on the southerly side of Haverhill street near where the Battery building now stands. Meetings were afterwards held in Bridgman hall, on Oak street, and later in Lawrence hall (since known as Music hall) on Common street. In 1852 a church edifice was erected on Haverhill street, and in 1865 the building was remodeled and enlarged, and a spire added, forming the present structure.

In touching on the pioneer churches, mention should be made of the Central Congregational Church, since merged in the Trinity Congregational Church. This society was organized December 25, 1849, meetings were held in the City Hall from that date until August 5, 1854, when a new church at the corner of Essex and Appleton streets was dedicated. Here regular services were held until August 12, 1859, when the structure was totally destroyed by fire. In the fall of the same year the society commenced work on the stone church (now Trinity church) fronting the common on Haverhill street, which was dedicated June 1, 1860. On June 28, 1883, the Central and Eliot Congregational churches were consolidated, and the name changed to Trinity Congregational Church. The Eliot Congregational society had been organized September 28, 1865, by some members of the Lawrence street and Central churches. Services were held in the City Hall and Grace church until September 6, 1866, when the brick church building at the corner of Appleton and Methuen streets was dedicated. For a number of years this structure was the home of the Young Men's Christian Association. It is now occupied by the appliance department of the Lawrence Gas Company.

St. Mary's Catholic Church, another pioneer, had its beginning in November 1848, when Rev. James O'Donnell came to Lawrence and celebrated mass in old Merrimack hall at the corner of Jackson and Common streets. He secured the central site now occupied by St. Mary's granite school building on Haverhill street. Here on the first Sunday in January 1849, it held service in an unfinished rough church edifice constructed of wood. It was winter, the roof was open, and snow came down upon the congregation as they knelt; the pulpit was a pile of shingles. In 1851, the granite church building went up, over and about the little chapel before its removal. This structure is a part of the present stone school building.

In August 1859, Father O'Donnell introduced the Sisters of Notre Dame who established the parochial school that has developed to such great proportions. Father O'Donnell was the real founder of St. Mary's church, although the corner stone of the present magnificent edifice (the largest and most imposing in the city, and one of the best specimens of Gothic architecture in the country) was laid on August 19, 1866, during the pastorate of Rev. Louis M. Edge. While in Philadelphia arranging for raising the cross on the new St. Mary's church, Father Edge was thrown from a carriage, and death resulted on February 24, 1870.

The present St. Mary's church was completed under the direction of Father Galberry and was dedicated September 3, 1871. The parochial residence on Haverhill street, occupied by Augustinian Fathers who now have charge of all the English-speaking Catholic churches on the north side of the Merrimack River, was completed October 5, 1873. The chime of bells in St. Mary's church tower was placed in position December 12, 1884.

Rev. James T. O'Reilly, the present pastor, came to Lawrence in 1886. His indefatigable energy and business acumen have brought the parish to a most remarkable state of development. Father O'Reilly was interested in promoting the organization of nearly every non-English speaking Catholic parish of the city. St. Mary's Parish over which he has jurisdiction, includes St. Mary's, Immaculate Conception, St. Augustine's and Assumption of Mary churches. Other religious organizations in the city were established in the following order:

United Presbyterian: Organized in June. 1854. Church edifice on Concord street, now occupied by the Armenian Congregational church, built in 1870. Society moved into the old Haverhill Street Methodist Episcopal Church building, corner of Haverhill and Hampshire streets, on October 1, 1911, following the merging of that church in the present Central Methodist Episcopal church.

Second Baptist: Organized September 6, 1860. Present building on Common street erected in 1874.

St. John's Episcopal: Organized May 14, 1866. For many years located on Bradford street in the building now occupied by the Lithuanian Catholic church. Corner stone of present edifice on Broadway laid on October 11, 1903.

South Congregational: Organized May 13, 1868. Although a Sunday School was established in 1852. Present church building erected in 1896.

St. Patrick's (Catholic): Parish formed in 1868. First church building of wood, built on site of present substantial structure, was dedicated March 17, 1870. Corner stone of brick edifice on South Broadway laid in 1881 and building was dedicated June 17, 1894.

Parker Street Methodist Episcopal: Organized September 16, 1870. Present edifice on Parker street dedicated in 1875.

Advent Christian : Society had its beginning in 1860. Church organized in November, 1870. Edifice on Lowell street dedicated in 1899.

United Congregational: Lowell Street. Organized as Primitive Methodist church in 1871. Name changed to Tower Hill Congregational in 1877, and since March 2, 1886, has been called the United Congregational. Church building erected and occupied in 1872.

St. Anne's (French Catholic): Parish formed in December 1871. Construction of old church on Haverhill street commenced in 1873. Completed and dedicated in 1883. In the meantime, mass was said in the basement of the building. First service in commodious edifice on Franklin street held January 7, 1906.

St. Laurence's (Catholic): Old structure at the corner of Essex and Union streets, now occupied by the Holy Rosary church (Italian Catholic), was dedicated as St. Laurence O'Toole's church July 12, 1873. Present brick edifice at the junction of Newbury and East Haverhill streets erected in 1903.

Riverside Congregational: Water street. Sunday school established in April, 1862. Church organized as Union Evangelical church in Tune, 1875. Became a Congregational Church March 9, 1878.

German Methodist Episcopal: Vine street. Organized in 1878. Church dedicated December 11, 1881.

St. Augustine's (Catholic): Church building on Water street completed and first mass celebrated there on Christmas Day, 1878.

German Presbyterian : East Haverhill street. Had its beginning in 1872. Church building dedicated December 12, 1875. Organized as a Presbyterian church in 1879. There had been a split in the congregation in 1878, members of Methodist inclination forming the German Methodist Episcopal church.

St. Mark's Methodist Episcopal: First known as the Bodwell street Methodist Episcopal church. Organized in December, 1879. Name changed to St. Mark's Methodist Episcopal church in 1890. Edifice at the corner of Essex and Margin streets dedicated May 22, 1890.

St. Paul's Methodist Episcopal: Wyman street. Organized December 30, 1885, as the Arlington Union Church in a building known as the Lake street chapel. Became a Methodist Episcopal Church April 30, 1891.

Religious Society of Friends: Established May 12, 1886. First service in the meetinghouse on Avon street in March 1896.

Church of Assumption of Mary (German Catholic): Parish formed in 1887, and present edifice on Lawrence street erected the same year.

Congregation of Sons of Israel (Jewish): Organized October 3, 1894. Synagogue on Concord street built in 1913.

First Church of Christ (Scientist): Sunday school established in 1887. Church organized in March, 1896. Edifice on Green street dedicated in August, 1896.

St. Joseph's Syrian (Greek Catholic Rite): Parish formed by Rev. James T. O'Reilly of St. Mary's in 1898. First worshiped in St. Mary's stone school building. Church on Oak street dedicated in 1905.

Sacred Heart (French Catholic): Parish formed in 1899. Established in basement of proposed church building on Groton street in 1915.

Wood Memorial Free Baptist : Sunday school established in 1898. First service held in church building on Coolidge street in November, 1899.

Congregation of Anshea Sfard (Jewish): Organized April 6, 1900. Synagogue on Concord street built in the fall of 1907.

St. Anthony's Syrian Maronite (Catholic) : Parish formed in May, 1902. First worshiped in St. Mary's stone school building. Church on Elm street dedicated in 1906.

St. Francis (Lithuanian Catholic) : Parish formed in 1903 by Rev. James T. O'Reilly of St. Mary's. Building on Bradford street, formerly occupied by St. John's Episcopal church, bought the same year and congregation became established there.

Holy Trinity (Polish Catholic): Parish formed in December, 1904. First worshiped in the basement of the Holy Rosary (Italian) church. Church on Avon street dedicated February 5, 1905.

Sts. Peter and Paul (Portuguese Catholic) : Parish formed by Rev. James T. O'Reilly of St. Mary's in 1905. First worshiped in the basement of the Immaculate Conception church. Edifice on Chestnut street dedicated in 1907.

St. Augustine's Episcopal : Established as a mission of Grace church in 1905 when the chapel was built at the corner of South Union and Boxford streets. Became a separate parish in 1907, and in 1910 occupied the basement of the proposed church.

Franco-American Methodist Episcopal: Organized October 20, 1907. Moved to building on Water street in 1914.

Church of Holy Rosary (Italian Catholic): Parish formed March 4, 1908, when congregation became established in old St. Laurence's church building at the corner of Essex and Union streets.

Salem Street Primitive Methodist: Organized as a mission station in September, 1915. and became established in the present building on Salem street the same year.

Bethel Armenian Congregational: Started as a mission of the Lawrence Street Congregational church about 1902. Organized as a church in 1916. Became established the same year in the building on Concord street, formerly occupied by the United Presbyterian church. Besides the above mentioned, there is a number of smaller religious organizations established in the city, including: Armenian National Apostolic Church, First Spiritual Church, Lighthouse Mission, Lithuanian National Catholic Church, St. George Syrian Greek Orthodox Church, St. John Baptist Russian Greek Catholic Church, Salvation Army, Spiritualist Temple, Swedish Lutheran Church, Syrian Protestant Church.

Y. W. C. A. AND Y. M. C. A.

Besides the churches there is a number of semi-religious organizations identified with the moral uplift of the community, notable among which are the Young Women's Christian Association and the Young Men's Christian Association. Both associations provide fine facilities for physical and mental development and comfort, in addition to the religious instruction which is carried on through bible classes.

The new Y. M. C. A. building is one of the attractive structures of the city. In 1909, during a whirlwind campaign of ten days $169,000 was raised by popular subscription for this building. Besides all the usual equipment and activities of a Y. M. C. A., there is a large swimming pool. The Y. M. C. A. was organized in 1876, and reorganized in 1893. It was incorporated January 14, 1880. The early Y. M. C. A. of 1856 did not survive the hard times of that period and the Arlington Y. M. C. A. was merged in the present organization. The Y. W. C. A., for young women, was organized June 6, 1892. The aim of the organization is to do spiritual work among young women, recognizing at the same time their intellectual, social, and physical needs. The association has had a steady growth, and it is especially helpful to young women who have no home ties here.

SOCIAL AND FRATERNAL ORGANIZATIONS

Probably no city in the country, of its size, has more social, fraternal and such organizations than Lawrence. There are altogether about 300 of these societies or clubs which are a prominent factor in the life of the city. Many of them hold valuable realty and are established in their own buildings.

The first fraternal organization here was United Brothers Lodge of the Independent Order of Odd Fellows, which was instituted May 28, 1847, the building on the southeast corner of Hampshire and Common streets. It is the parent lodge of Odd Fellows in Lawrence. The members held meetings in that hall for several years, after which they removed to larger quarters on the north side of Essex street about midway between Lawrence and Pemberton streets. Here the lodge was located until the completion of the Odd Fellows building in 1874. The organization has had a steady, healthy growth. Today it is one of the most firmly established of the several branches of the order in the city.

Another early fraternal organization was Grecian Lodge of Masons. It was chartered December 14, 1825, to be held in Methuen. It continued there until 1838, when the charter was surrendered to the Grand Lodge. After the incorporation of the Town of Lawrence, several of the old members petitioned the grand lodge for a restoration of the charter, which petition was granted December 27, 1847. Its first meetings were held in a hall at the corner of Essex and Amesbury streets. In 1872 it moved, with all the other Masonic bodies, to the Saunders block, its present location.

Lawrence Encampment, I. O. O. F., was also here before the incorporation of the city. It was instituted March 15, 1853, existed until July 1, 1857, when, for the lack of support, it surrendered its charter. The encampment was re-instituted October 15, 1874. Its growth at first was slow, but it is now a flourishing branch of the order.

Today there are 96 secret or strictly fraternal organizations, representing 37 distinct orders, in Lawrence. There are nearly 200 social and various other kinds of organizations which are active in the social, moral, intellectual, and physical welfare of the community. It might be stated that, besides these, there are 31 labor unions. Every nationality and creed have their representative societies, although the greater number of the organizations have no distinction as to race or sect, and all are working for the public weal.

LAWRENCE BAR ASSOCIATION

The Lawrence Bar Association represents the law fraternity of the city. Some of the keenest legal minds in the state have been and are still identified with the organization. It has furnished four judges of the Superior Court, Judges Edgar J. Sherman, Charles U. Bell, Charles A. DeCourcy and Louis S. Cox. Judge DeCourcy is now a justice of the Supreme Court of Massachusetts. It has also provided a judge of Probate Court, Judge Harry R. Dow. Members of it have been prominent in municipal, county, state and national affairs, as well as in the courts of law.

Although there has been an organization, of some kind, of local members of the bar since about the beginning of the city, it was not until January 11, 1905, that the present incorporated association was organized. This organization was brought about by a movement for a suitable law library in Lawrence, the need of which was felt by the local fraternity. The association has been instrumental in having established at the county court house one of the finest law libraries in the state, for the upkeep of which the County of Essex contributes a certain sum each year.

The first officers of the incorporated association were: President, William S. Knox; vice president, William J. Bradley; treasurer, J. P. Kane; secretary, John C. Sanborn, Jr.; executive committee, Newton P. Frye, Harry R. Dow and John J. Donovan. Today it has a membership of 70, including men reputedly well versed in every branch of law. The present officers comprise: President, Walter Coulson; vice president, John P. S. Mahoney; treasurer, Matthew A. Cregg, secretary, Daniel A. Arundel.

Lawrence has always had big men in the law profession. Among the most prominent of the earlier years, and who are still remembered for their accomplishments, were John K. Tarbox who had served as mayor, member of Congress and insurance commissioner; Elbridge T. Burley who had a state-wide reputation as a lawyer, and especially in the later years of his career as an authority on the law of wills; William S. Knox, a notable criminal lawyer, who for eight years represented this district in Congress; and then, there was Daniel Saunders who passed away April 19, 1917, at the ripe old age of 96 years. Mr. Saunders at the time of his death was the oldest living alumnus of Harvard Law School. He was a man of wonderful vitality, and his keen mind stayed with him to the last. He was still in harness up to the time of the illness which resulted in his death.

Responses to Country's Calls

Lawrence in the Civil War

Lawrence has a war record of which any community might well be proud. Her responses to the country's calls have been quick and generous, and many of her sons have been sacrificed in the defense of the nation's integrity and honor.

For several years prior to 1861, Lawrence had maintained two well organized and disciplined companies in the State Militia. These companies were among the first to offer their services when the Rebellion reared its head. Early in January, 1861, and long before the blow fell upon Fort Sumpter, the Lawrence companies, together with the others composing the Sixth Regiment, tendered their services to the Governor whenever they might be needed. This was the first offer of organized troops for the defense of the national government. Lawrence blood was the first to be spilled in that famous passage of the Sixth Massachusetts Regiment through Baltimore on April 19, 1861, when Sumner H. Needham, a citizen of Lawrence and a member of Company L gave his life for his country.

Statistics show that Lawrence did her full duty in the Civil War, and from 1861 to 1865 furnished 2,617 volunteers and drafted men, a surplus of 224 above all calls made upon her. This was a little less than one-seventh of the population which in 1861 was but 18,000; of this quota, 255 were killed in battle or died of wounds.

As in the epoch days of the Civil War, so in a later generation did Lawrence acquit herself, at the outbreak of the Spanish-American War. Her sons were among the first to volunteer. Although the city furnished many men to the regular army, the navy and other volunteer organizations, the part which Lawrence took in the brief but glorious campaign of '98 must be largely confined to her two representative infantry organizations, viz. Company F of the 9th, and Company L of the 8th Regt. Infantry, M.V.M. On May 4, 1898, Company F left for the state campgrounds at South Framingham. On the following day Company L departed, joining Company F at the muster field. Battery C of the Field Artillery was not called, as the national government needed no volunteer light batteries then.

Both infantry companies were mustered into the service of the United States on May 10 and were duly ordered south. Company L was sent to Chicamauga, Ga., and Company F to Camp Alger, Dunn Loring, Va. The 9th Massachusetts, which was brigaded with two Michigan regiments, the 33d and the 34th, experienced the vicissitudes of a siege in the trenches around Santiago de Cuba, and afterward the dreaded fevers of a tropical climate. It left Camp Alger on June 24, and on July 1 reached Siboney, some seven miles east of Morro Castle. The regiment had hardly disembarked when they were ordered to the front. After an all night tramp over a tortuous trail they arrived at the battleground, to the accompaniment of whistling mausers and screaming shrapnel. With the rest of the regiment. Company F was assigned by General Shafter to General Kent's division, and General Bates' brigade with the 3d and 20th regular infantry. It took a position at the extreme left of the line. On July 17 it witnessed the surrender of Santiago.

Company F left Cuba the latter part of August, sailing on the "Alleghaney" for Montauk Point. During the voyage, on August 28, Stephen J. Ryan, for whom the local camp of Spanish War Veterans is named, died of heart failure which was super-induced by malaria. His body was consigned to the deep off Cape Hatteras, making one of the fifteen ghastly milestones that marked the route of the transport from Santiago Bay to the Sound. A portion of the company arrived in Lawrence at midnight September 8. The rest were left behind, some in hospitals at Santiago and Montauk and others scattered from New York to Boston, victims of malaria. The company was furloughed for two months, and was mustered out of the United States service November 26, 1898, having served six months and lost four of its members from the effects of tropical fevers.

Longing for a taste of actual warfare and chafing under the humdrum routine of a rigid camp life. Company L spent several months at Chicamauga, guarding against typhoid fever. On July 18 Harvey A. Dunn, a member of the company, succumbed to the disease, the first Lawrence volunteer to die in his country's service. In January, 1899, the 8th Regiment was ordered to Matanzas, Cuba, on provost duty. The last of April it was sent home and mustered out, having completed a year in the service of the United States.

When trouble with Mexico threatened in 1916, the Lawrence militia units readily responded to the call. Companies F and L of the 9th and 8th infantry, respectively, and Battery C of the Field Artillery joining the troops assembled on the Mexican border. The local boys left the city in June. They returned the following October, looking a picture of health, a fine example of the results of present-day military sanitation. Not a man was lost through disease, and, since the imbroglio with Mexico did not reach a very serious stage, none died in action.

In 1917, Lawrence, with the rest of the country, faced a most serious crisis in her history, when on April 6, the United States declared a state of war with Germany and the nation became involved in the great European conflict.

LAWRENCE IN THE WORLD WAR

In the World War, Lawrence achieved, and, at this writing, is still achieving a record for service, which will compare favorably with that of any other community of her size in the country. In every activity for a successful prosecution of the war, the city has responded nobly, and she is prepared to go the limit for the cause.

With the declaration of war against Germany on April 6, 1917, and the plunging of the United States into the great European conflict, Lawrence quickly rallied to the support of; the nation in her fight, that the world might be made safe for Democracy. In men, money and labor the city has contributed generously and wholeheartedly. Already 32 young men from Lawrence, in the forces of the United States and the armies of the Allies, have made the supreme sacrifice. These martyrs to the cause of Democracy have, with few exceptions, been killed in action, or have died of wounds received while on the firing lines.

The first step for the cause, and the forerunner of the call to arms, was the formation, on April 2, 1917, of a Public Safety Committee, which followed the appointment by legislative act of a State Committee on Public Safety that contemplated adjuncts in the different cities and large towns of the commonwealth. The local committee was composed of 45 members, divided into nine sub-committees.

At that time, with the sudden entrance of our country into the World War, with stories of plots threatening the safety of our manufacturing and producing sections, the committee devoted itself, first of all, with other cities, towards perfecting measures that would conduce as far as possible to a continuance of public safety and the maintenance of order. Funds were raised by public subscription to meet the expenses of the committee, and later the municipality took up the support of the organization, appropriations of money being made for the purpose as the necessity presented itself. This money was expended to relieve conditions growing out of the war. Every precaution was taken against the activity of enemy propagandists.

123

Under the order of the President, Lawrence conducted her selective draft registration on June 5, 1917, without expense to the Federal government. No disorder accompanied this first important step in the movement for the mobilization of the manpower of the country.

LAWRENCE BOYS WHO HAVE MADE THE SUPREME SACRIFICE

Apitz, Oswald E., U. S. Regular Army
Ashkexazy, Joseph D., U. S. Regular Army
Beevers, Frank, U. S. Marine Corps
Berwick, Thomas, British Army
Bodkin, John, American National Army
Booth, John, British Army
Cate, Thomas J., U. S. Aviation Corps
Cranston, John, Canadian Army
Damphouse, Joseph, Canadian Army
Fallon, Thomas J., American National Army
Fyfe, Charles G., Headquarters Co., 102nd F. A.
Gaudette, Gerry, Canadian Army
Gutherie, William J. Company L. 104th Infantry
Hewett, Alfred, Canadian Army
Hutcheson, Elwood C., American National Army
*Kaplan, Samuel, Company F, 101st Infantry
Kellett, John, British Army
Kenney, Everett R., Battery C, 102nd F. A.
Lynch, Felix, Canadian Army
McDonald, Warren, U. S. Navy
McGillen, Daniel, Canadian Army
Martin, Charles A., U. S. Navy
Morgan, Fred, British Army
O'Commor, Frank, U. S. Regular Army
Peel, Robert, Company F, 101st Infantry
**Ravich, Joseph, U. S. Regular Army
Rogers, Thomas, British Army
Russll, Ernest, U. S. Regular Army
Sweeney, John J., Company F. 101st Infantry
Townsend, Benjamin, British Army
Vaudreuil, Arthur, Company L. 103rd Infantry
Welch, John, Canadian Army

*First Lawrence soldier with the United States forces to be killed in action (died February 26, 1918).

**First Lawrence boy with the United States forces to die in service (victim of appendicitis at Fort Slocum. N. Y. December 21, 1917).

While the draft was going on, four local units of the National Guard were sent to training camps, where they were merged into new regiments, and subsequently sent to France to take their places in the fighting lines on the western battle front. These units were Battery C, 1st Field Artillery; Company L, 8th Massachusetts Infantry; Company F, 9th Massachusetts Infantry, and Headquarters Company, Field Artillery. They arrived at the front line trenches early in February 1918. Battery C fired its first shell into the German lines on February 8th.

Drafted men were sent to cantonments, as the National Guard companies were sent overseas, until after one year of the declaration of war Lawrence had given all told 3,550 men to the army and navy forces of the United States. Of this number about 3,000 were volunteers. Besides, a great number of Lawrence young men had enlisted in the armies of England, France and Italy. Officially, the city aided in the recruiting of residents of British allegiance. From Lawrence, 610 of such joined the British colors.

Unstinted was the response of Lawrence to the many calls for money to back up at home the sacrifices her soldiers were in part making across seas. Three Liberty Loans, asked for by the National government, were oversubscribed far beyond the quotas named. The third loan drive in Lawrence was the most remarkable success. While the amount subscribed was smaller than in the second loan drive, in which the corporations bought heavily of bonds, the number of subscribers was more than doubled. In the third loan drive, there were 31,000 subscribers, a little less than one-third of the city's population. In two Red Cross drives for funds, Lawrence gave generously. Likewise did the city respond in the raising of money to support the Y. M. C. A., Knights of Columbus and several other organizations in their activities for the moral and physical comforts of our soldiers, and the succor of the suffering people of war-ridden Europe.

The chairmen of the organizations in charge of the major movements for the raising of money, and the amounts raised were as follows: First Liberty Loan, Fred H. Eaton, $3,387,100; second Liberty Loan, Albert I. Couch, $6,368,000; third Liberty Loan George Fred Russell, $4,600,000; first American Red Cross War Fund, Leonard E. Bennink, $32,000; second American Red Cross War Fund, George Fred Russell, $138,867; Y. M. C. A. Red Triangle War Fund, George Fred Russell, $104,792; Knights of Columbus War Fund, James H. Bride, $46,000. During a drive for membership in the American Red Cross 21,353 joined the organization in Lawrence. George Fred Russell was also chairman of the local committee in charge of this movement.

The Draft Exemption Boards comprised: Division 1.: H. Christopher Chubb, chairman; Fred E. Twiss, Dr. Granville S. Allen.; Division 2: Wilbur E. Rowell, chairman; Clinton O. Andrews, Dr. George W. Dow. Division 3: John Hendry. chairman; Nathaniel E. Rankin, Dr. John J. O'Sullivan. On the District Board of Appeals Lawrence was represented by Matthew A. Cregg.

Appeals for soldiers' benefits were met in innumerable cases by the people of Lawrence. Schoolchildren, societies, churches, and individuals joined in the work of knitting and sending comforts of many kinds to the soldiers in camps, while the boys in active service across the Atlantic were not forgotten. Three score calls of a smaller nature were all generously responded to. When disaster overtook Halifax, Lawrence officially had a relief committee appointed, and, besides sending clothing, forwarded a large money contribution to the stricken Nova Scotia city.

There has been from among the poorest to the wealthiest in the city a spirit to aid in every way to a winning of the war, and a kindred spirit to accept with cheer the burdens that the war of necessity imposed.

The municipality, in honor of the Lawrence boys in the service, erected on the common a handsome large tablet bearing the names of those who have joined the colors. This so-called service roll was dedicated with appropriate exercises on Patriots' Day, April 19, 1918. After the war, it is intended to replace this memorial by a more permanent monument.

Lawrence early realized that food would be an important item in the prosecution of the war, and she increased the production of food supplies by preparing land, free of cost, for tillage in both city and suburbs. In all, 720 such garden plots were prepared in the summer of 1917. These aggregated 98 acres, and the yield was bountiful. A fuel committee was organized to regulate the fuel supply. Steps were taken to conserve the supply, and many difficulties, caused by inadequate transportation facilities, were mitigated.

With the regular companies of the National Guard in the service, home protection was assured by the forming of a company of the Massachusetts State Guard, which was equipped partially by the state and partially by the city. This organization has regular drills at the State armory, and has become practically another contribution from Lawrence to the needs of the war. An emergency police force of 1000 men has been formed, consisting of nine companies, all officered, assigned to stations,

SOLDIERS AND SAILORS MONUMENT

and under a chief. This force also meets and drills regularly. It has been equipped for any required action, but it is to be called into service only in case an emergency might arise which would cause the police authorities to believe that its assistance was needed.

Volunteer enlistments are still going on, selective draftees still going away to join the colors, and with no faultfinding or attempt at backsliding. Lawrence is behind the President 100,000 strong, ready to make any sacrifice for our country's cause. All hope for an early peace, but it must be peace with honor, and with assurance that the principles which gave America her birth and happiness shall not perish from the earth.

Lawrence Common

Public Buildings and Institutions

The Lawrence Common

Few communities lay claim to a public park more beautiful than the Lawrence Common. This reservation, located in the very heart of the city, and comprising 17½ acres, was deeded to the people of Lawrence in 1848, by the Essex Company, the deed being dated October 1, of that year. Traversing the common, in every direction, are broad paths, lined with stately elm and maple trees which enclose expansive grass plots, set off with attractive flowerbeds. The last report of the Park Department gives the number of trees on the reservation as 421.

The common was originally, in the greater part of its area, a sand heap. The high ground was sown occasionally with buckwheat which was ploughed in as a fertilizer. At one time, near the northeastern corner, two acres were set out with cabbages. The eastern section, along Jackson street, was an alder swamp with a brook running through it. The willows in the southeastern corner, the last of which were removed several years ago, were some of the original trees that grew up by the wall which was one of the boundary lines, of the Gage farm that stretched away to the eastward. One of these willow trees, cut down in 1899, had 69 rings in the trunk, denoting an age of 69 years.

In 1874-75, the old fence which enclosed the park was removed, and the granite curbing was provided. The present concrete water-basin, or artificial pond, built in 1914, replaced the original goldfish pond for which ground was broken in August 1857.

The Soldiers and Sailors' monument was erected on the common in 1881. The initiatory steps for this purpose were taken by Post 39 of the Grand Army of the Republic in September 1879, when $500 was contributed by the Civil War veterans. This action was followed by a meeting of citizens on November 13, when a committee was appointed to consider the matter. This committee reported to a large assemblage of people on November 24, recommending that a monument of granite be placed in some central position on the common, and that contributions be solicited in small sums in order that the monument might literally be the people's memorial to the deceased soldiers and sailors.

129

An association was at once formed under the name of "The Monument Association". Its officers were : President, Robert H. Tewksbury; vice presidents, John R. Rollins and Thomas Cornelie; secretary, Frank O. Kendall; trustees to receive and invest funds, Mayor James R. Simpson, Hezekiah Plummer, Waldo L. Abbott, Joseph Shattuck, Frederick E. Clarke, James S. Hutchinson, Byron Truell, John Hart, Edmund R. Hayden. Subsequently a society of women was organized in aid of the association, and active work was commenced on the project.

The several corporations, by their agents and treasurers, contributed $3,000. The schoolchildren, through the efforts of Capt. Horatio G. Herrick, by a penny and dime contribution, raised over $200. A concert by the Ladies' Choral Union, under the direction of Reuben Merrill, added about $200 more, and the remainder was contributed by the people generally, in the mills, workshops, stores, municipal departments, etc., the Grand Army members raising their donation to $700. The total cost of the monument was $11,111.75, the total number of subscribers being 9,136, and in this list, the names of three Chinese residents appear.

The crowning figure of the monument, representing "Union", was designed by David Richards. The figure was cut from Concord granite by Theodore M. Perry, at the Quincy granite works. The shield bears the legend of the Lawrence municipal seal, "Industria", and the emblematic bee. On the buttresses at the base of the column stand three figures in bronze. The first representing an infantry soldier, nearly a duplicate of one in Albany, N. Y., was designed and modeled by Henry Ellicott of New York. The other two, one representing a sailor and the other a dismounted cavalry officer, were modeled by William R. O'Donovan at the foundry of the general designer of the monument, Maurice J. Power, in New York where all were cast.

The monument bears the following inscriptions:
"ERECTED IN 1881
By the People of Lawrence
In Honor of Those Who
Served in the Army and Navy,
1861—1865"
"In Memory of Brave Men,
Whose Sacrifice and Death
PRESERVED THE UNION"

Three bronze tablets contain the names of those who died in service or were killed in battle. They number 255.

The monument was dedicated on the evening of November 2, 1881, amid a brilliant display of fireworks and calcium lights. It was accepted in behalf of the city by the Mayor, Hon. Henry K. Webster, who delivered an appropriate address.

As one of the results of the great Flag Day demonstration on October 12, 191 2, following the big strike earlier in the year, Lawrence has a permanent and elaborate flagstaff on the common, the gift of Joseph Shattuck. This flagstaff replaced a less costly one which was destroyed in a storm of hurricane proportions that swept through the city on the night of August 4, 1910, entailing considerable damage, especially on the common where a number of large trees were uprooted.

The gift was offered to the city on October 18, 1912, and on December 18 Mr. Shattuck wrote a second letter to the government, stating that he would deposit with the city treasurer a check for $4,000, the money to be expended upon the flagstaff, its base and approaches, and another check for $1,000 in the Essex Savings Bank in the name of the City of Lawrence, the income only to be drawn by the city treasurer and to be used for the perpetual replacement of flags for said staff or any other erected in its place.

The city government accepted the gift on December 23, 1912. On January 6, 1913, the following commission was appointed to carry out the deed of the gift: Rev. George E. Lovejoy. Joseph McCarthy, James D. Home, Fred H. Eaton, William T. Kimball, Michael S. O'Brien, James R. Menzie and Alderman Alfred Bradbury, the last named being director of public property and parks. Alderman Bradbury was elected chairman, and Mr. Kimball, secretary of the commission.

The commission, after investigating the qualifications of architects of countrywide reputation, finally decided unanimously upon R. Clipston Sturgis of Boston to furnish the design. It was the desire of the commission to have the memorial flagstaff dedicated on October 12, 1913, the first anniversary of the memorable Flag Day parade, but circumstances compelled a postponement, and it was not until the observance of Patriots' Day on Monday, April 20, 1914, that the unveiling and dedicatory exercises were held.

Prior to the ceremonies there was a great civic and military parade in which thousands participated. The procession terminated on the common where, amid the booming of cannon and the crashing of bands, the cheers of the multitude and the grateful beating of thousands of hearts, the memorial was uncovered by little Dorothy Shattuck, daughter of the late Joseph Shattuck, then president of the Third National Bank of Springfield, and granddaughter of the donor. John Campbell, commander of Needham Post, 39, G. A. R., and John H, Gilman, past junior vice-commander of General Lawton Post, 146, G. A. R., raised the first flag to fly from the staff head. Alderman Bradbury presented the gift, in behalf of its donor, and Mayor Michael A. Scanlon delivered the speech of acceptance.

A tablet at the base of the flagstaff bears this inscription:

The gift of Joseph Shattuck, to the people of Lawrence, as a perpetual remembrance of October 11, 1912, when 32,000 men, women, and children of the city marched under the flag for God and Country.

The granite base is surmounted by one of bronze, symbolic of the City of Lawrence and its industries. This base is supported by four cogwheels. The first band is ornamented by threads. On the four corners are wound spindles from which the thread leads to smaller spindles and is then transformed to cloth. What represent four folds of cloth are spread on the four sides, and on these are inscribed appropriate quotations from ancient and modern authors.

Above these inscriptions, the next band is composed of shuttles. Up to this point, the design is symbolic of the industries of Lawrence. Further above are designed flowers and fruits, symbolic of the joy and pleasure of living, and the fruits of industry. On the staff, itself, are carved arrows, symbolizing war. They are bound together with laurel. At the very pinnacle of the staff stands the emblem of peace, with her hand outstretched, symbolic of the blessing of our industrial community.

The present bandstand on the common was built in June 1904, replacing the old structure which for so many years occupied a site near the location of the Shattuck flagstaff.

The public sanitary station, located in the same section, was completed and opened to the public December 30, 1907.

Besides the common, the city's park system includes parks and playsteads in every ward, which are of great benefit in keeping the children off the streets and in providing breathing spots.

Note: As a recognition of the nearly 3,600 young men from Lawrence, who had entered the service of the United States during the first year of the war against Germany, a handsome service roll, bearing their names, was erected on the common, near the Soldiers' and Sailors' monument. This was dedicated with patriotic exercises on April 19, 1918. The celebration included a great parade through the city's streets.

THE PLAYGROUND MOVEMENT

Lawrence had its playgrounds and recreation spots way back in 1848, when the Essex Company, deeded the present Common to the city. But it was not until 1912 that the Municipal Department of Parks, under Alderman Michael S. O'Brien who was elected a member of the first City Council under the commission form of government and served as Director of Public Property and Parks, installed for the first time in the city's history a system of supervised play and public recreation.

Before proceeding, however, with a brief story of the playground movement in Lawrence it might be well to look back a little. The Essex Company, following its liberal gift of the Common, from time to time deeded other tracts of land to the city, which are now favorite breathing spots, and, incidentally, it might be added, made possible the development of the playground movement. There is Storrow Park, a reservation of 10 acres on the highlands of Prospect Hill, in Ward One, which was deeded to Lawrence December 3, 1853. By a deed dated November 19, 1873, the Essex Company made another gift of a tract of land, containing seven acres and closed on three sides by low ridges lying in Ward Five south of Bodwell street, which is known as "The Amphitheatre", or Bodwell Park. The conditions of this grant required that the city appropriate at least $200 a year for a term of 10 years in improving and embellishing the grounds, and forever keep the same as a public park. In addition to these gifts, the Essex Company laid out as a public park a beautiful reservation of 11½ acres, extending easterly from South Union street in Ward Six and known as Union Park. The public park on Hampshire street, familiarly known as "The Jail Common", is another gift from the Essex Company, besides the small Stockton Park at the junction of South Union street and Winthrop avenue. All of these parks were given outright to the city and are today valuable assets.

As has been stated, the supervised playground movement was begun in Lawrence early in the summer of 1912, the first cost being borne by the city with some financial assistance from private citizens who were interested in bringing it about. For the purpose of experimentation, only four stations were established that year. The principal playground was located on the Common where an average of 500 children of both sexes were accommodated daily. The other experimental stations were located at the Tarbox school playstead, Union Park and on land leased for the purpose from the Essex Company off Rowe street and along the Merrimack River. Expert men and women instructors were employed, and the boys and girls were not only afforded instruction in helpful physi-

133

cal exercises but other educational features were introduced, especially for the girls who were taught basketry, needlework, and the like. These playgrounds are equipped with paraphernalia for amusement and muscular exercise.

The physiological value of the supervised playgrounds was instantly recognized as a powerful influence for good, and the idea met with popular favor in Lawrence with the result that each succeeding year has seen new activity in this line. There are now 17 public parks and playsteads in the city, containing 164.67 acres. This number includes *Riverside Park.

The Public Library

The Franklin Library which was the nucleus of the present Lawrence Public Library was incorporated in April 1847. Capt. Charles H. Bigelow, the engineer under whose direction the dam was built, was its first president.

Hon. Abbott Lawrence donated $1,000 to it, to be expended in the purchase of such books that would "tend to create mechanics, good Christians and good patriots", and at his death, in 1855, Mr. Lawrence bequeathed an additional $5,000 to the institution.

The Franklin Library Association was the solitary literary society in Lawrence for many years. The "Lawrence Athenaeum" sustained a course of lectures for two seasons, and the "Lawrence Lyceum" a course for one or two seasons, but both were finally merged into the Franklin Library Association. A course of 12 lectures was sustained for several years by this organization.

In 1872, the library and funds of the association were turned over to the city by definite arrangement, and the Free Public Library, aided by the White Fund, was successfully established. Library and reading room found immediate favor with the people. Circulation books reached an almost unprecedented average; patrons outgrew accommodations, and, in three years from the first opening, the library was removed from the Saunders block to spacious rooms in the new Odd Fellows block.

The present library building at the corner of Hampshire and Haverhill streets was opened to the public in 1892. Originally, it cost $50,000, but in 1902, it was enlarged at an additional cost of $37,300.86. Today it has 70,475 volumes (including 7000 volumes turned over in 1895 from a library conducted by the Pacific mills), a valuable reference department and as modern facilities as any institution in a city the size of Lawrence in the country. On August 1, 1898, a branch library was opened on South Broadway, and this gives good service to the people of South Lawrence.

The land upon which the library building stands is a plot saved from the original White tract. The main library building was given to the city by Mrs. Nathaniel G. White and her daughter, Miss Elizabeth W. White. While there is a similarity of names the donors were not related to Judge Daniel Appleton White who made possible the White Fund which provides for a course of lectures annually and defrays the cost of other educational enterprises.

The White Fund has given thousands of dollars toward the maintenance of the public library, besides having provided the land on which the building is located. The present librarian is William A. Walsh.

Judge Daniel Appleton White, whose name is so familiar with educational matters in Lawrence, was born in June 1776, in an old farmhouse which stood on the site of the present high school at the corner of Haverhill and Lawrence streets. He was graduated from Harvard College in 1797. For many years he was judge of probate in Essex county, residing in Salem, where he was first president of the Essex Institute. He also served one term in Congress, while a resident of Salem.

Judge White's old homestead, with the lands lying between the Merrimack and Spicket rivers and Appleton and Franklin streets, was first conveyed in January, 1845, by a conditional deed, to the Water Power Association. The first conveyance by Judge White embraced all his holdings without restriction. He soon afterwards became aware that provisions in old deeds required that part of the lands should be reserved as a family burial ground. In consequence of this, at his earnest solicitation, the associates in taking their absolute deed, dated March 28, 1845, relinquished their claims to a lot of about six acres, nearly in the centre of the tract they had purchased. It was provided, however, that these six acres should be restricted as to use, or reserved as a public or private burial ground. Immediately after the organization of the Essex Company, the associates conveyed to that company all the land they had purchased; consequently their deed contained the reservations and restrictions.

Judge White seemed to have had little enjoyment in the possession of the property, constantly increasing taxes becoming a burden. There was no income from the property; sanitary considerations prevented its use for a cemetery; no one would purchase any part of it in the condition in which the title then stood. It became evident that the land could only be utilized by joint action of both Judge White and the Essex Company. There were upon the land but three graves (still undisturbed, near the corner of Hampshire and Concord streets, surrounded by dwellings), occupying together a space not larger than an ordinary burial lot. This left nearly six acres of unoccupied land in the heart of the city. Joint action of the two parties might have given to this land a value of many thousands of dollars, to be divided between them. Happily, at the suggestion of Judge White, he and the Essex Company, joined in devoting this property to a purpose which would benefit, not a class or a single generation, but all who might dwell in Lawrence in time to come. The indenture conveying the land to trustees, with power to sell and invest proceeds in a fund, for a purpose clearly stated, is a model of precise wording and clearness in detail, so far as it relates to the character of the lectures and use of the fund for that purpose The language is that of Judge White.

The original proposition of Judge White, as explained in his letter of June 19, 1852, to Treasurer Storrow of the Essex Company, proposed simply the establishment of an annual course of lectures, the special subjects being those first specified in the indenture or deed of trust. Being confident that the value of the land and the sum that would eventually be derived from it would far exceed the expectations of Judge White, Mr. Storrow suggested that, while the original object which he had in mind should first be fully provided for, precisely as Judge White intended, it might be well to allow the trustees to select other methods for promoting morality and education, especially to authorize liberal appropriations from the income in aid of a free library and provide for the gift of a building site for such an institution. Thus originated the White Fund, and thus Lawrence obtained valuable help for its public library.

WHITE FUND AND LECTURES

In, 1852 Hon. Daniel A. White of Salem, and a native of one of the pioneer farms that had occupied the site of Lawrence, gave a large tract of land extending from the vicinity of Amesbury street westerly, and now intersected by Haverhill, Bradford and Concord streets, the proceeds from the sale of which were to be devoted for educational purposes, including a free course of six lectures each year for the industrial classes of Lawrence. The income was to be known as the White Fund. Trustees were appointed under a deed of trust to carry out the provisions of the gift, and the original trustees were Charles S. Storrow, Nathaniel G. White, and Henry K. Oliver. It was suggested by Judge White, the trustees seeing fit, that a lot of land be reserved for a public library building. The intentions of the donor were carried out, and the proceeds, derived from the sale of the land, formed the nucleus of the proposed fund. The White Fund lectures were established in 1864 and have since continued from year to year. The lot of land whereon the Public Library building stands was reserved as intended. The introductory lecture of the White Fund course was by Dr. James Walker, president of Harvard University. Among the other lecturers of that year were Ralph Waldo Emerson and Oliver

Wendell Holmes. It has been the aim of the trustees to secure the very best talent obtainable, and the courses have been of a high degree of excellence. The subjects are varied, and there is something interesting and instructive for all. Beginning with the establishment of the Public Library in 1872 the White Fund has made an annual appropriation, usually of $1,000, for the purchase of books and pictures for the library. The proceeds from the fund, greatly exceeding the amount required for the lectures, and the language of the indenture being broad in its scope, the trustees have been enabled to use a part of the proceeds for a number of purposes tending to the moral and intellectual uplift of the inhabitants of the city. Among other notable undertakings for which the income of the fund has been used was the survey of the housing conditions of Lawrence, made in 1911. This survey was the means of bringing about a great improvement in the building and sanitary regulations of the city. Besides the three original trustees mentioned, George D. Cabot, James H. Eaton, Charles U. Bell, Wilbur E. Rowell, Walter E. Parker, and *Charles G. Saunders have acted as trustees of the White Fund, the last three named serving at present.

Post Office

The Post Office, located in a handsome sandstone structure at the corner of Broadway and Essex street, was established under the name of "Merrimack" on September 7, 1846. The present building was occupied in 1905, and provides excellent facilities for the enormous amount of business of the office. The parcel post and postal savings departments, recent additions to the service, have become important branches. In 1917 the postal savings department had deposits of about $200,000. In the handling of the mail, there are 33 clerks and 52 carriers regularly employed.

County Court House

At first, the people of Lawrence were obliged to travel either to Salem or Newburyport when concerned with matters having to do with the superior court. After the Town House or City Hall was, built quarters were provided for the court, and then known as the court of common pleas, in the audience hall of the building. Later sessions of the court were held in old Lawrence hall (Music hall), but this was inadequate and in 1858, the first county court house was erected, the Essex Company giving the land, the city providing the foundation and the Essex county commissioners

---

Charles G. Saunders died Feb. 19, 1918. On June 24, 1918, Irving Sargent was appointed to succeed him.

erecting the building. James K. Barker, who was mayor of the city in 1861, was the architect. In the fire which destroyed the United States hotel in 1859, this building which stood at the corner of Common and Appleton streets, about on the site of the present courthouse, was ruined. It was rebuilt in 1860. In 1900, the Lawrence Bar Association inaugurated a movement for larger quarters and finally the legislature authorized the expenditure of $100,000 for an addition. George G. Adams was selected as architect, and J. N. Peterson & Co. of Salem was awarded the contract. Another $100,000 was required to finish the addition and when it was completed the appearance of the original portion was so much at variance with the newly constructed part that an additional $50,000 was set aside to provide the handsome, commodious court house that is in use today. The building furnishes accommodations for a superior criminal, a superior civil and a probate court, a registry of deeds, a law library, besides offices for various county officials, grand jury and petit jury rooms, etc. The law library is the finest in New England, outside of Boston. It has 13,000 volumes. The structure is fireproof, built of brick with freestone trimmings.

House of Correction

The Jail or House of Correction was built in 1853, and has since been very much enlarged by additions and improvements. The original structure cost $100,000. The building, located on Auburn street, is built of stone and is imposing in appearance. The main portion is octagon in shape with wings extending north, east and west. It has 116 cells with accommodations for about 180 prisoners. The town purchased the site for $2,000, and also an acre of land, in front of the building, laid out as a park, for $1,280.

Couty Training School

The Essex County Training School, located off Marston street, was established as a county school in 1891. It was first opened as an industrial school for refractory boys by the City of Lawrence in 1860, and became known as the Lawrence Reform School in 1870. In 1891, the county took over the school and later it became known as the Essex County Training School. Only truants and those who have committed school offences are admitted. There are several well-appointed buildings and also extensive grounds. Besides the common school instruction, attention is given to trade subjects and practical gardening is taught. In 1917, the inmates included 132 boys and six girls.

STATE ARMORY

The State Armory, on Amesbury street, was opened in 1893, when the large brick structure was completed and the local units of the State Militia took up quarters there. In the building are officers' and company rooms, drill and gun sheds, shooting gallery, mess hall, and other necessary accommodations. In 1913, an annex to the Lawrence armory was built for the battery on the Lowell road in Methuen. It is of brick construction, and includes assembly, company, and officers' rooms, gun shed and stable, besides having .an extensive drill field. The annex was established for outdoor drilling, and it was the first of its kind in the state.

POOR FARM AND MUNICIPAL HOSPITAL

The Poor Farm and Municipal Hospital, officially known as the Lawrence Almshouse and Almshouse Hospital, are located on Marston street. The institution includes several roomy buildings, and it has a large acreage of cultivatable land. The Almshouse was opened by the town on February 20, 1849, when seven persons were admitted. It now averages 130 inmates. Provisions are also made for the care of indigent people in the hospital department where there are four wards, with 33 beds, for their accommodation. In 1912, a movement was started for the establishment of a hospital section free from the stigma of pauperism. Fourteen rooms in this portion are now fitted up with 24 beds for private patients. The hospital has since been called the Municipal Hospital, having been known prior to then as the "Cottage" Hospital. It has a resident physician, a surgical staff and twelve nurses, and it is well equipped for the treatment of all kinds of medical and surgical cases. In addition to the medical service at the hospital, the Charities Department of the city employs six ward physicians who treat the outdoor poor in need of such attention.

ISOLATION HOSPITAL

The Isolation Hospital, located off Marston street, is used by the Health Department in cases of highly contagious and infectious diseases. It has two wards and nine rooms, and can accommodate as many as 27 people. When it was established, in 1902, smallpox epidemics were not uncommon, and the local institution was prepared for the proper isolation of Lawrence cases. For several years past there has been little occasion to use the hospital.

TUBERCULOUS HOSPITAL

The Tuberculosis Hospital on Chickering street was established by the city in 1909. Prior to that time provisions were made for tuberculosis cases in the day camp at the General Hospital. The patients used to stay at the camp during the day and went to their homes at night. Through the efforts of the Anti-Tuberculosis League, the hospital was established. In 1917, the Municipal Health Department took over the Tuberculosis Dispensary, maintained by the league, and this is now conducted in connection with the Tuberculosis Hospital. The institution occupies a commodious building, situated on sandy ground and having a southern exposure. There are plenty of windows so arranged that patients get all the fresh air and sun possible. It has four wards with 22 beds each, and has averaged 75 patients. There are in attendance a superintendent and seven nurses, besides two visiting doctors.

DENTAL CLINIC

In April 1917, the Health Department established a Dental Clinic, well equipped for the examination and treatment of children with defective teeth. Two dentists are regularly employed in connection with the work which also includes visits to the schools and instructions on the care of the teeth. This is an adjunct to the system of medical inspection carried on in the schools, in which the services of six physicians, one for each ward of the city, are employed.

THE PEOPLE'S FORUM

One of the popular and instructive institutions in the winter life of Lawrence is the People's Forum. The purpose of this activity is a free and sane discussion of the questions of the day with the view of breaking down the walls of prejudice and engendering a regard for one another's opinion. A great employer of labor once said, after listening to an expression of the views of the other side in what had become a bitter industrial dispute, that most of the misunderstanding in life was due to failure to show proper respect and regard for the other fellow's opinion. In creating an opportunity for an interchange of opinions, the Forum is of great benefit. No church, political combination or "ism" controls it. It brings together people of different nations and creeds, from all the walks of life, and it is regarded as having a broadening influence on the minds of many. Capable lecturers and good selection of subjects have made the meetings attractive. The Forum was established January 31, 1915, by a number of public-spirited citizens. Its chairman from the beginning has been Leonard E. Bennink to whose commendable zeal and indefatigable energy is largely due the success of the project.

THE ORPHAN ASYLUM

The Orphan Asylum and Home for Invalids, known as the Protectorate of Mary Immaculate, on Maple street, was the first purely charitable institution permanently established and located in Lawrence. The house was opened by the Sisters of Charity, or the "Gray Nuns", on January 29, 1868. In recent years, large additions have been made to the original building. The inmates include 221 boys and girls, besides 22 aged women who at this writing are cared for by the sacrificing nuns. There are 19 sisters in charge of the institution. Everything possible is being done for the moral, intellectual, and physical development of the children. A system of education is maintained which enables them to finish the grammar school course at the asylum. When the boys reach the age of 12 years, good homes for them are found outside the institution. The girls may stay as long as they wish. An excellent course in domestic science is given. On January 29, 1918, the asylum celebrated its golden jubilee, or fiftieth anniversary of its establishment. The receipts of the "Patriots' Tea", held April 19, of each year, are given toward the support of the institution.

LAWRENCE GENERAL HOSPITAL

The Lawrence General Hospital, a private institution but one of great benefit to the community, was established in 1883 in a building erected for the purpose on Methuen street. In 1902, the hospital moved to the present ideal location on the summit of Prospect Hill, away from the hum of industry about the old location. The institution is one of the best equipped of its size in the state. It has 137 beds, with wards for acute medical and surgical cases, a maternity ward, a children's ward and an isolation ward for diphtheria and scarlet fever, with a staff of 27 physicians and surgeons and a large corps of trained nurses, besides an ambulance service; also connected with it is a training school for nurses. The institution is partly supported by contributions and donations. The proceeds from the annual May Breakfast, begun in 1876 and primarily conducted in support of the Children's Nursery and Home, are given in aid of the hospital which also has received many bequests. The Children's Home referred to was abandoned in 1912, when the property on Howard street was purchased by the Ruth Verein and devoted to the use of the German Old Folks Home.

LAWRENCE HOME FOR THE AGED

The Lawrence Home for Aged is located in a handsome brick structure on top of Clover Hill, built in 1909 on land donated by Edward F. Searles, Methuen's millionaire philanthropist. Spacious grounds surround the home, and together with the great elm trees and beautiful flowerbeds add much to the attractiveness of the place. The home was incorporated in 1897. It was for many years situated in South Lawrence and had been familiarly known as the Wood Home, named for its first benefactors. It has 28 inmates. It is supported mostly by gifts from charitable people.

LAWRENCE CITY MISSION

The Lawrence City Mission, located on Jackson street, was organized in 1859, and incorporated in June 1876. The purposes of the mission are to relieve distress, to prevent unwise giving, to encourage independence, to protect children, and to study social problems. Rev. Clark Carter is the missionary in charge. The foundation of the present evening school system was laid by the Lawrence City Mission.

The Arlington Day Nursery, a nursery and permanent home for children whose parents are unable to give them care; the Asrath Noshim, for the purpose of financially aiding the poor and needy of the Jewish race; the German Ruth Society, a home for destitute men and women, and the Lawrence Boys' Club, for promoting good citizenship and morality, and providing a vacation centre, physical instruction and manual training, are included among the local charitable corporations, listed by the State Board of Charity. Besides these, there are a number of public benefit organizations working for the physical, mental, and moral improvement of the community, outside of the regularly recognized institutions.

Public Transportation

Street Railways

The growth and development of communities is largely dependent upon their transportation facilities. Usually the expansion of the former follows the extension of the latter. This is especially true in the case of street railways which are more closely identified with the communities they serve than are the steam roads.

The street railways have been a potent factor in the development of Lawrence and outlying districts. By making travel easy and rapid, they have brought all sections into closer touch, and incidentally have been of great benefit in encouraging building, lessening congestion and increasing property valuation, besides being a big help to general business.

Not only is every neighborhood in the city, with the adjoining towns, penetrated by the street railways, but the country for hundreds of miles about is traversed by the various lines. Nowhere in the United States is there a section so thoroughly netted with trolley lines as that of eastern Massachusetts and Lawrence occupies a position where it is an important centre from which lines radiate in all directions and from which one may travel by trolley to practically any point in New England. Furthermore, if one were so disposed, he could go by trolley from Lawrence into New York state or Pennsylvania.

The days of the old stagecoach are not so far back but that they are well remembered by many of Lawrence's citizens today. It seems hardly possible that that period of slow and uncomfortable travel is within a lifetime. Yet, notwithstanding the great state of development attained by the street railways, 50 years ago stagecoaches were driven between Lawrence, Methuen, Andover, and Lowell.

The Bay State

The Bay State road here is the outgrowth of the pioneer street railway in this locality. From a little horse road the Lawrence division of the Boston & Northern Street Railway, formerly the Merrimack Valley Horse Railroad and now known as the Bay State Street Railway, has become a network of 50 miles of track upon which are run over 75 cars. The entire system has about 960 miles of trackage.

The first company to operate a street railway in Lawrence was organized August 13, 1867. The corporation was formed with the following officers: President, William A. Russell; treasurer, James H. Eaton; secretary, Charles E. Goss; board of directors, William A. Russell, A. W. Stearns, George A. Fuller, William R. Spalding, Charles E. Goss; superintendent, Stephen Dockham. Ground was broken for the first line October 21, 1867, work being begun at the woolen mill in Methuen. When, on Christmas Day, 1867, two horse cars were run on Essex street from the depot to the Everett mills, it was made a day of general rejoicing. Everybody turned out and struggled for a chance to ride on those cars with the result that the first day's collection amounted to $130. The following day the first car was run to Methuen.

In the autumn of 1868 the road was extended to the Machine shop, North Andover. In 1876 the tracks were again extended by what was then called the South Lawrence branch, running to the depot. In 1887 the Newbury, East Haverhill, and Berkeley streets line was built. The Belt line was constructed the same year, made necessary by the burning of the Union Street Bridge and cutting off of North Andover on the old location. The tracks on Water and Lawrence streets were built in 1888. Extension of local lines, one after another, gradually followed until it was deemed wise to experiment in wider fields, so that in 1893 a line was extended to Haverhill, and the next year to Lowell, thus connecting these three great factory cities of the Merrimack valley. Andover was connected before this, in 1891. The Middleton, Danvers, & Salem line of the Lawrence division was opened in 1902.

From the early days of the old horse cars there has been a reaching out by the management of this road for improvements. The most marked improvement in equipment came when the radical change from horse to electricity as motive power was made in 1890 and 1891. Attempts have been made several times to secure a franchise locally to carry freight by the operation of a so-called trolley express, but up to the present writing the City Government has deemed it advisable to refuse the petition of the street railway company.

The road was moderately successful until a few years preceding 1918 when the expenses had increased in such proportion and the receipts had declined to such extent that the company went into the hands of a receiver. The decrease in the receipts was largely due to the competition of the so-called "Jitneys", automobiles which gave quicker transportation, whose routes of travel were more mobile, and which could be more readily adapted to the demands of the public. To meet the increased cost of operation and the falling off in revenue, the Public Service Commission approved an increase in fares on the street railway of one cent for every five-cent fare. At this writing— the road is still in the hands of a receiver.

THE MASSACHUSETTS NORTH EASTERN

Although the Massachusetts Northeastern Street Railway, formerly known as the Southern New Hampshire, has a smaller amount of trackage in the city than has the Bay State, the company has extensive lines through the surrounding country. The local terminal of the road is at Hampshire and Essex streets, from which it runs into southern New Hampshire and Haverhill. Its lines run through much open country which, until the heavy rails of this fast growing corporation were laid, was sparsely inhabited.

Between its interurban and transfer points this road courses through largely private land, and the speed attained by the high-powered trolley cars is exceeded in few places in the country.

From the Hampshire street terminus cars run to Haverhill direct and via Point A in Salem, N. H., also to Lowell and Pelham, Nashua, Hudson and Goffs Falls, N. H., where connections can be made for Manchester, N. H.

Canobie Lake Park, one of the most beautiful inland pleasure resorts in this section of the country, and which is owned by the Massachusetts Northeastern, is in the radius of these lines. It was opened to the public in 1903.

The first franchise granted this road in Lawrence was in 1899, when on December 26th of that year the Municipal Council gave the Lawrence & Methuen Street Railway Company the privilege of laying a track on Hampshire and Centre streets. The Lawrence & Methuen road was later absorbed by the Southern New Hampshire.

The power station from which the various lines of the Massachusetts Northeastern are operated is located at Portsmouth, N. H. The main offices of the company are in Haverhill. David A. Belden of Haverhill is the president of the road and Franklin Woodman of Haverhill, its general manager.

Practically all streets in Lawrence, traversed by trolley cars, are paved with granite blocks, and as these thoroughfares are kept well cleaned and sprinkled in the open season there is little annoyance from dust. Both street railways have franchises granted by the municipal government for an indefinite period.

Besides the street railway transportation facilities, there is the steam railroad, Lawrence being on the main line of the Portland division of the Boston & Maine system. There are 150 passenger trains coming into and leaving the city daily. The demand for freighting facilities can be imagined from the fact that Lawrence is the third city in Massachusetts in value of general manufactured products.

The Central Bridge

No public improvement, undertaken in the history of the city, has been more fraught with difficulties than has the building of the Central Bridge. The project has followed a pathway strewn with obstacles, and it has been only with the greatest effort that some of these were surmounted. The construction of the bridge has been merged in bitter controversy at times, and it has been used as a political football with which men have ridden in and out of office.

There have been some who contended that there was no need of so costly a structure; that more careful deliberation in the matter of construction plans, and contracts, and of property damage, would have saved the city many thousands of dollars. However, when the bridge was built it was constructed with an eye to the future, and there is no denying the permanency of its construction, nor its massive beauty. The bridge stands today, one of the finest of its kind in the country.

The cost of the entire Central bridge project can only be conjectured at this writing, for while the main bridge is completed there are yet the canal bridge approaches to be built, besides the laying out of new highways, leading to the main structure, with further land damages. The cost of the improvement, as it is, may be estimated as a little over $1,000,000, which includes over $500,000 for damages to mill property seized in laying out the site. In this estimate is figured the sum of $100,000 in which the County of Essex is bound to reimburse the city upon the completion of the project, as its share of the expense. The first cost may be further reduced, as it is proposed to lease the electric railway privileges over the bridge and also to rent the wire conduits, but there is no means of knowing, at this time, how much revenue will be derived from these sources. It has been predicted that the cost of the entire project, including the river bridge, canal bridges, and improvement of highway approaches, will reach close to $1,500,000, although it is probable that the total expense wall fall far short of that figure.

146

The Central bridge is a reinforced concrete structure, 1,500 feet long by 80 feet wide, spanning the Merrimack River at the foot of Amesbury street, approximately 460 feet south of Essex street, the principal business thoroughfare in Lawrence. With the extensions over the canals, which traverse at right angles at either extremity, the entire structure will measure 1,750 feet.

The design involves 200 feet of retaining wall of the counterfoot type, with earth fills, at each end of the bridge. There are six 107 feet three-centered reinforced concrete arch spans of the open spandel type, six 44 feet segmented arch rib spans and one temporary 90 feet concrete arch span. This last mentioned span was built in such a manner that it can readily be replaced with a double leaf bascule draw span, whenever the Merrimack River is open for navigation. In the original design no provision was made for navigation, but legislation subsequent to the signing of the contract necessitated the erection of two large abutment piers to provide for the future installation of a bascule span in the middle of the river channel.

The deepest foundation, that laid for the southerly bascule pier, is sunk 53 feet below water, making the height of this pier 98 feet and 6 inches, which, to give some idea of its immensity, is about as high as the Bay State building, the highest building in Lawrence.

The roadway over the full length of the structure is 56 feet wide between curbs, one foot wider than Essex street. Provision is made for two electric railway tracks. The sidewalks are 12 feet wide, three feet narrower than those on Essex street. A reinforced concrete balustrade of ornamental design extends the full length, intercepted at regular intervals by lampposts which are also constructed of reinforced concrete and made high enough to support the span wires carrying the trolley wires. Provision has been made to light the structure by attaching to each of the 26 lamp posts a four-light cluster phosphor bronze fixture. Each lamp is of 200-candle power. As a "white way", the bridge will be unsurpassed by anything of that nature to be seen in this locality. Thirty-six 3½x3½ terra cotta conduits have been provided beneath the easterly sidewalk for carrying wires. The streetcar rails are 110 pound, nine inch grooved girder rails laid on creosoted ties, flush with the paved highway surface.

Indeed, the Central Bridge is modern in every detail, spacious and imposing, and artistic in design. What is most satisfying of all is the fact that it is built for all time, capable of carrying the very heaviest traffic and requiring hardly any expenditures for repairs.

The commission in charge of the construction of the bridge comprised John J. Donovan, chairman; John O. Battershill, secretary; Joseph J. Flynn,

John A. Brackett and Otto Parthum, with City Solicitor Daniel J. Murphy as counsel. The engineer was Benjamin H. Davis of New York. The commission was appointed by Mayor John T. Cahill on January 23, 1911. The first excavation for the bridge was made on October 1, 1914, and the first concrete was laid on October 20 of that year. The structure was completed on March 20, 1918.

The construction of the bridges over the North and South canals, approaches to the Central bridge, is at this writing going on, under the direction of the City Council, the Central Bridge Commission having completed its duties with the completion of the main bridge.

The Essex Company, according to its charter, being obliged to construct and maintain "sufficient" bridges where new highways are laid out over the canals, and there being a disagreement as to the character of the structures the company should build, a compromise was reached whereby the Essex Company agreed to pay $40,000 toward the cost of the canal bridges upon the condition that the city construct the bridges and that the company be released from the obligation of maintaining them. An agreement was drawn up to that effect, and it was ratified by the State Legislature of 1917. The plans provide for two concrete structures whose architectural lines shall be in keeping with those of the Central Bridge. They were drawn by B. H. Davis, the Central bridge engineer, who is under contract to supervise the construction.

LAWRENCE'S INDUSTRIES

American Woolen Companyrican Woolen Company which employs more people than any other industrial unit in New England, and which is the largest manufacturer in the world of carded woolen and worsted cloths (men's wear), had its beginning in Lawrence where are located its largest plants, including the mammoth Wood Mills. This great corporation was conceived by William M. Wood, the present head, who has become a striking character in modern industry.

Soon after the late Frederick Ayer had, on September 12, 1885, acquired the Washington Mills, Mr. Wood became connected with the plant, as a road salesman for worsted fabrics. In recognition of his ability and enterprise he was later given the management of these mills which he directed so well that a heavy indebtedness was discharged, and the concern was established as one of the most prosperous woolen organizations in the country.

The Washington Mills weathered the difficulties of the Gorman-Wilson tariff of 1894-97, which proved disastrous for many textile-manufacturing concerns. About this time Mr. Wood who had gained much prestige as a captain of industry, and won the confidence of capital, was besought to interest himself in other undertakings. He and his associates acquired, one by one, a group of woolen mills, nearly all of which had suffered from tariff adversity. With the Washington Mills as a nucleus, the American Woolen Company was incorporated March 29, 1899, Mr. Ayer becoming president and Mr. Wood, treasurer. The directorate included men who had distinguished themselves in the industrial and mercantile lines, and who in the early days gave solidity and prestige to the corporation. Later Mr. Ayer resigned the presidency, and Mr. Wood succeeded him. William H. Dwelly is now treasurer.

The American Woolen Company is, in the location of its plants, almost exclusively a New England creation, for only two of these plants, the Fulton Mills, at Fulton, N. Y., and the Bradford Mills, at Louisville, Ky., are outside of New England's boundaries. The other mills range across New England from Maine to Connecticut, the greatest of them, as stated, being located in Lawrence which has become, next to Philadelphia, the largest woolen manufacturing community in the United States. Besides the 50 or more mills which the corporation has purchased, it built the Wood Worsted Mills and the Ayer Mills in Lawrence. The two latter plants, with the Washington Mills and the Prospect Hill, comprise the factories of the concern here. Most of the old mills acquired have been enlarged, and the equipment of all has been improved. Its Assabet Mills at Maynard are the largest carded woolen, as the Wood Mills are the largest worsted plant in existence.

It has been stated that the company each year turns out enough cloth to belt the earth and in addition to festoon the United States from New York to San Francisco. It has a product not only great in bulk but remarkably diversified. It makes a specialty of uniform cloth for the United States Army and Navy, and has introduced some of the most durable and useful fabrics worn by the soldiers and sailors of the government. The production for general wear includes kerseys, friezes, meltons, thibets, wool and worsted, plain and fancy over coatings, covert cloth, broadcloths, mercerized cloths, Venetians, granites and vicunas, piece-dye and mixed-dye clay diagonals, unfinished worsteds, fancy weave piece dyes and mixtures, serges, wool and worsted cheviots, all grades of worsted and wool fancy trouserings and suitings, wool and worsted cross-dye and resist-dye fabrics, and rain cloths, plain and fancy. Yarns for practically all purposes are also manufactured.

The corporation has introduced a number of commendable ideas for the convenience and comfort of its operatives. It has constructed villages of modern dwellings for them in Lawrence and Maynard. Housing accommodations have been provided in nearly every city and town in which its mills are located. The houses in this city are attractive, and are rented at moderate prices. They occupy pleasant and wholesome sites near the south bank of the Merrimack River, opposite the city proper and yet close to the great mills whence the people draw their livelihood. Opposite the Wood Mills stands a large restaurant where good food is served at cost, and in the large mill building, 1100 feet in length, there are escalators to convey the workers quickly and easily to or from the various floors.

The American Woolen Company is an admirable example of the large, modern industrial organization. It represents, perhaps, about one-eighth of the total productive woolen machinery of the country. It has about 30,000 employees in all of its plants, and has 13,000 stockholders, many of whom are employees as well. The capital of the corporation is $60,000,000. It has paid without interruption a dividend of 7 percent, on its preferred stock. The assessed valuation of the property in Lawrence for 1917 was $9,039,400.

In disposing of its product the concern follows the policy of selling direct from the mills, instead of through commission houses.

THE PACIFIC MILL

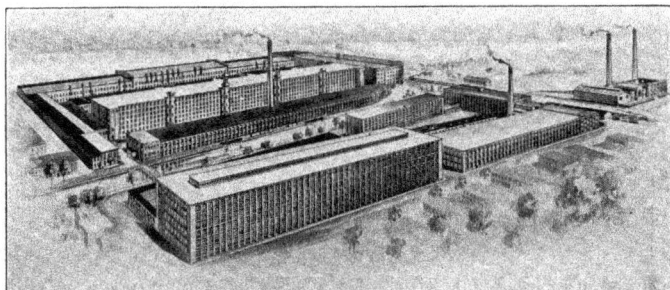

PACIFIC MILLS—COTTON DEPT.

The Pacific Mills, the main plant of which is located in Lawrence, are famed the world over for their fabrics. They have an unrivaled output of printed, dyed, and bleached cotton goods, and are also the largest manufacturers of cotton-warp and all-wool dress goods. So widely are the products of these mills known and used that the trademark "Pacific Mills" is not unfamiliar in Japan, China and other far-off Asiatic countries. The extent of the mills, in Lawrence, their marvelous equipment, the magnitude of their operations, and the perfection of their work excite the admiration and astonishment of all visitors.

The weekly payroll of the entire corporation, paid in silver dollars piled one upon another, would be more than twice the height of Washington Monument, or more than 1,110 feet. If its looms were placed end to end, they would make a continuous line over 24 miles in length. Its buildings have 177 acres of floor space. Over 135,000 tons of high-grade coal are burned in its boilers annually. Electricity enough is generated every day to run the entire street lighting of Boston and all the other cities and towns within 10 miles. The normal product of nearly 200,000 acres of cotton (or about 80,000 bales), and the wool from 2,366,383 sheep are woven every year. Over 330 miles of cloth are woven each day, or enough to reach from New York to Washington, D. C. (226 miles), and half way back again. Over 500 miles of cloth are finished and packed ready for shipment each day. The annual output of finished cloths would reach more than 5½ times around the world.

The Pacific Mills were incorporated in 1853 with a capital of $1,000,000, which was increased in 1855, 1858 and 1862 to $2,500,000. At the, present time the capital of the corporation is $15,000,000, including the main plant in Lawrence and the mills at Dover, N. H. and Columbia, S. C. The Pacific goods first appeared on the market in the fall of 1854. At that time, under a low tariff, English printed calicos and delaines came largely in competition with home products, causing a sharp contest for control of the trade, which was eventually won by the New England mills.

The original mills and print works were built under the supervision of the Essex Company. They were remodeled in 1882, and since then they have been enlarged and added to from time to time, until at present the local plant is one of the largest mill plants in the United States, with brick buildings, and a floor space of 135 acres. The main cotton mill building is 806 feet long by 72 feet wide, and seven stories in height. Weave sheds, yarn mills, dye houses, print works, and power plants spread over an immense area. The assessed valuation of the property of the corporation in Lawrence is $10,157,700, a little less than one-eighth of the city's entire valuation.

In 1901 the first dynamos for electric power were installed, water power and steam solely having been used for power before, and in 1907 the electrification of the whole plant was begun, with the erection of a large new power house.

The purchase of the Cocheco Manufacturing Company at Dover, N. H., January 26, 1909, was the first step toward external growth. The Cocheco mills, much older, were printers of cotton goods, and in that field were formidable competitors of the Pacific. They are now confined to the production of cotton cloths for printing, dyeing, and bleaching.

On June 29, 1911, the Hamilton Print Works at Lowell were purchased, and in 1915 the calico printing plant of the Merrimack Mills at Lowell was acquired, and the business moved to Lawrence.

Then a big, modern printing plant was constructed on a 17-acre tract on the riverbank below the Wood Mills, and there assembled the machinery from the old buildings at Lawrence, Dover, and Lowell. It has been in operation since 1913, and is reputed to be the largest print works in the world. It has 48 printing machines, besides a dyehouse and bleachery for dyeing, bleaching, and finishing cotton fabrics.

In 1910 there was built a six-story worsted yarn mill with a one-story weave shed, to accommodate the worsted department, more than 1,000 looms, with 16 acres of floor space.

The Hampton Mills department of the Pacific corporation, at Columbia, S. C, with 200,000 spindles and 4,800 looms, was acquired June 26, 1916. This department also makes cotton cloths for printing, dyeing, and bleaching.

The last addition in Lawrence was the purchase on March 31, 1913, of the Atlantic Cotton Mills, bought at auction. Thus was secured a valuable mill site which would allow further expansion for the main plant. Part of this property, on the approach to the new Central Bridge, was seized by the City of Lawrence.

The latest statistics of the Pacific corporation show 561,312 cotton and 92,880 worsted spindles, and 12,204 cotton and 3,435 worsted looms. The raw cotton consumed in a year is over 40,000,000 pounds, and the weekly output is about 5,000,000 yards of cotton cloth and 460,000 yards of worsted cloth. The floor space of all the buildings of the corporation is 177 acres, over a quarter of a square mile, and 6,500 males and 3,800 females are employed. The total annual payroll (in 1918) is over $7,500,000.

The mills at Lawrence employ 7,600, and the weekly payroll amounts to $136,000. There are in the local plant 214,448 cotton spindles, 92,880 worsted spindles, 3,833 cotton looms, and 3,435 worsted looms.

In cotton goods the Pacific turns out mousselines, percales, lawns, organdies, challies, draperies, flannelettes, suitings, satins and crepes; in worsted goods, poplins, alpacas, cashmeres, henriettas, serges, brocades, diagonals, voiles, taffetas and challies. All the printing is done at the local plant. To the Dover and Columbia mills are chiefly reserved the year-in and year-out cotton staples, while the product of the Lawrence mills is more varied.

The officials of the corporation are Robert F. Herrick, president; Edwin Farnhani Greene, treasurer. Walter E. Parker is the local agent and

153

manager of the great plant in Lawrence, and has occupied that position since January 1, 1887, coming here to take charge of the cotton department of the mills April 1, 1881.

THE ARLINGHTON MILLS

ARLINGTON MILLS.

To tell in full the story of the founding and development of the Arlington Mills, from the original small wooden structure, in which the concern was established, to the great system of mills now operated by the corporation, it would take a fair sized volume in itself.

The plant today is one of the city's greatest manufactories, giving employment to 6,500 operatives and its buildings covering a ground area of 20 acres. It has a floor space of 2,275,076 square feet. The area of its entire holdings, including yards, land and water, comprises 49 acres.

The corporation is capitalized for $8,000,000. The last valuation placed on the mills by the city assessors amounted to $4,620,050. It was the first corporation of any magnitude to adopt the system of weekly payments to its employees, a method now required by law.

These mills have every modern appliance necessary for the production of worsted men's wear and dress goods, worsted yarns and tops. They have the distinction of having introduced into this country the manufacture of black alpacas, mohairs, and brilliantines.

They are famous for the quality and variety of their yarns, there being numberless kinds of yarns made by these mills. Arlington fabrics are noted for their texture. Whether the weave be plain or fancy, the colors solid or combined in plaids, figures or stripes; whether the fabric be made of white yarn for subsequent piece dyeing, or yarn dyed in the wool or top, commonly designated as slub dyed; whether the width be 36 inches or 58 inches, or the weight 3 ounces or 16 ounces to the square yard, all these specialties are made as required by the trade.

When running to its full capacity, the Arlington has a weekly payroll of $115,000. It consumes about 1,000,000 pounds of wool a week. It produces each week 450,000 yards of worsted fabric and 275,000 pounds of worsted yarn of every description, all of which is now woven in its looms. The plant consists of a large number of separate buildings. It is equipped with 117,000 worsted spindles, 2,700 looms, 118 combs, and 150 cards.

The corporation had its beginning in 1865 when an act of incorporation was secured by Robert M. Bailey, Charles A. Lombard, Joseph Nickerson, and George C. Bosson who comprised the stockholders. They commenced business with a capital of $200,000, in the old Stevens piano case factory on the Spicket River. The original name of the concern was the "Arlington Woolen Mills", and the early products were only fancy shirting flannels and wool felted fabrics. In 1866 the plant, with machinery, was totally destroyed by fire, but it was rebuilt on a larger scale the following year when the capital was increased to $240,000.

The tariff of 1867 materially changed the conditions of the worsted goods trade, and the company at once turned all the facilities of its new plant to the production of women's worsted and cotton warp dress goods, the plant being well equipped with a variety of worsted machinery, including 160 looms. Many difficulties were encountered in establishing the new enterprise, and less determined men would have become disheartened and abandoned the venture. In 1869 the corporation became financially embarrassed, but the stockholders paid into the treasury the whole amount of the capital, $240,000. A change in the management was also made, by the election of Joseph Nickerson as president and William Whitman as treasurer and general manager. These men laid the solid financial foundation of the great plant, and to them and the present head, Franklin W. Hobbs, the corporation is largely indebted for its wonderful development.

In 1871 began the work of remodeling the plant and increasing the productive capacity, and since then there have been large additions of buildings and machinery. In 1875 the name "Arlington Mills" was adopted. By this time an enviable reputation for various special lines of goods had been built up, and the mohair, alpacas, and brilliantines manufactured by this company were known to the trade of the entire country. Thence the growth of the business was very rapid, but perfectly wholesome. Considerable more land in both Lawrence and Methuen was purchased. To keep pace with the demand for the products of the mills, it has been several times necessary to increase the capital stock for the purpose of enlarging the facilities for manufacturing, notwithstanding that a considerable portion of the yearly earnings are devoted to the improvement of the plant.

A noteworthy departure of the company was the erection in 1896 of a worsted top mill which is devoted exclusively to carding and combing wool for the use of the spinners. Another feature of the top mill business has been the construction of a solvent plant for removing grease from wool by the application of naphtha. This process is now recognized as effecting a considerable saving and is of material advantage to the quality of the product. The Arlington Mills own all rights to the process in the United States.

In the early history of the business, cotton spinning was introduced to accommodate its own looms and those dealing in this class of goods, and a specialty was made of prepared warps for the various kinds of dress materials. Until very recently the sale of cotton yarns was an important feature. In April 1917, the cotton business of the Arlington Mills was sold to the Acadia Mills.

In 1905 and 1906 the Arlington spent nearly a million dollars in the erection of several modern brick buildings. These, with the other buildings, spread over an immense area, the plant extending into the adjacent town of Methuen. The top mill, alone, is a huge structure. Its actual dimensions are 757 feet 8 inches in length by 109 feet 8 inches in width over all, with a wing 84 feet 8 inches long by 87 feet wide over all. The main building and wing have each four stories and basement. This mill is upon the site of a former group of dwellings which for years were the homes of operatives, and most of the newer structures extend over what was formerly Stevens pond. Among the later buildings erected are the large weave shed, a dye house, a finishing and warp dressing mill, and an up-to-date central power house.

Franklin W. Hobbs, the president of the Arlington Mills, has been connected with the plant since 1891. He held the office of treasurer until 1913, at which time he was succeeded in that office by Albert H. Chamberlain. John T. Mercer is the resident agent. A few years ago the treasurer's office was removed to Lawrence. The selling agents are William Whitman Company, Inc., with the main office at 78 Chauncy St., Boston, and branches in New York, Philadelphia, and Chicago.

EVERETT MILLS

The Everett Mills are among the plants that have brought fame to Lawrence as a textile centre. The fabrics of these mills have a country-wide reputation for quality and style. They include ginghams, shirtings, and denims. The ginghams are familiarly known as the "Everett Classics".

The

company was incorporated in 1860, its incorporators being James Dana, Samuel Batchelder and Charles W. Cortwright. The stone buildings of the original Machine Shop, erected by the Essex Company, were secured, and operations commenced that year.

Since then, the plant has been greatly enlarged and improved. The equipment has been kept abreast of the times, so that today the manufacturing facilities will compare favorably with those of any other plant of its kind in the country. Its buildings spread over an area of 17 acres. In 1909-10 a mammoth brick mill was added, which is said to be the largest cotton mill under one roof in existence. This structure extends a great distance along Union street. It has six stories, and there are 12 acres of floor space within its walls.

The assessed valuation of the property of the corporation for 1917 was $1,833,750.

The Everett Mills consume a quarter of a million pounds of raw cotton every week, and the production per week amounts to 1,170,000 yards of cotton goods. There are 143,296 spindles and 4,680 looms in operation. The plant gives employment to 2,000 people. The weekly payroll is $34,000.

The capital of the corporation is $2,100,000. The officers are Herbert W. Sears, president and Fred C. McDuffie, treasurer. The agent of the mills is James I. Milliken.

The Acadia Mills, formerly the cotton department of the Arlington Mills, were established in April 1917, with a capital of $2,000,000. They are located in both Lawrence and Methuen.

When the Arlington Mills' cotton department was sold to the Acadia Corporation, it was explained that the cause of the action of the parent corporation was the result of the changes that have taken place in the development of the worsted industry and the changes and growth of the business of the Arlington Mills. Early in the history of the latter corporation the cotton department was an adjunct of the worsted department, but in recent years it had ceased to be such, no portion of the product of the cotton plant being consumed by the worsted plant.

Such being the case, it was deemed advisable to separate these two distinct branches of the business, in order that each might be conducted independently along its special lines, and be developed with the highest possible degree of efficiency and economy. With this idea in view the Acadia Mills came into being, and they take their place as a very promising factor in the Whitman system of textile corporations.

The plant consists of five brick mill-construction manufacturing buildings, together with the necessary storehouses, engine and boiler houses, repair shops, etc. The buildings cover a ground area of 192,522 square feet. The floor space, in square feet, is divided as follows: Manufacturing, 495,942; storage, 146,190; miscellaneous, 17,442; total, 659,574.

The concern manufactures combed cotton yarns, mercerized, bleached, and dyed. It makes a very high quality of combed yarns. It also makes a specialty of high-grade mercerized yarns. Mercerizing is a big feature of the business. The process adds lustre to a cotton yarn, strengthens it, and makes it resemble silk. The Arlington Corporation was a pioneer in this process of manufacture, which has been developed to an extraordinary degree of efficiency in the Acadia plant.

The yarns are delivered to the trade in skeins, cones, tubes, quiller cops and warps. The finished product per week amounts to 200,000 pounds. In raw material, 120,000 pounds of cotton are used every week, and 125,000 pounds of yarn are received for finishing processes. There are 1,100 operatives employed, and the weekly payroll amounts to $20,000.

The officers of the corporation are William Whitman, president, and Ernest N. Hood, treasurer. William A. Pedler is the agent of the mills. The selling agents are the William Whitman Co., Inc., with offices in Boston, New York, Philadelphia, and Chicago.

Monomac Spinning Company

The Monomac Spinning Company was established by William Whitman in 1910 for the manufacture of French spun worsted and merino yarns. William Whitman is president, Ernest N. Hood, treasurer, and Walter M. Hastings, agent. The company was incorporated in 1913. The capitalization is $1,200,000.

The plant is of modern mill-construction, the buildings occupying about 72,000 square feet of land on South Union street. The property owned by the corporation contains seven and one half acres. The actual floor space in the mill is five and three quarters acres.

The mill produces about 3,000,000 pounds of merino and worsted yarn on the French System yearly. The product is sold through William Whitman Company, Inc. The business has been very successful from the start, and in 1915 arrangements were made to increase the machinery by 50%.

The company employs 350 operatives, and has a weekly payroll of approximately $7500. The employees of the company work in very healthful surroundings. The plant is clean and sanitary. Fresh air is forced into the mill, and is heated in winter and cooled in summer to maintain an even temperature throughout the year. Since the war started the unused land in the yard has been plowed and fertilized for the use of the operatives. This has resulted in many attractive vegetable gardens.

The power plant consists of a Cooper-Corliss condensing engine of 1450 horsepower with rope drive and a boiler plant of four Heine boilers. A cooling pond 200x125 feet is maintained for condenser purposes.

Katma Mill

One of the newest of the factories of the Whitman Corporation, and one of the busiest of Lawrence's industrial plants, is the Katama Mill on South Union street. The development of this plant has been remarkable. In less than two years its capital stock has been tripled, as has been its productive capacity. Its product, duck fabric, is shipped all over the United States, and has a national reputation for quality and durability.

The concern was established in 1916, with a capital stock of $500,000. In July of that year the plant started up with 124 looms. Today it has 338 looms in operation, and recently the capital stock was increased to $1,500,000. The capacity of the mill is 185.000 pounds a week. Over 300 operatives are employed. The weekly payroll averages $5,000. The plant consists of a large factory building and a storehouse. There are 111.000 square feet of manufacturing space, and 21,600 square feet of storage room. The assessed valuation for 1917 was $214,000.

The principal product is tire duck which is woven from the best-combed Sea Island yarns that are noted for their durability. This fabric is used in the manufacture of high-grade automobile tires. For several months the mill has also been engaged in the production of special material for the United States government. This work has so taxed the facilities of the plant, that a section of the storehouse is being used for manufacturing purposes, extra looms having been set up there, in order to keep up with the deliveries.

The mill is modern in every respect. The lighting and ventilation are of the best. It is equipped with the latest machinery, and many new practical ideas are in use in its operation. A notable improvement is the absence of belting and shafting. Every loom has an individual motor. Thus is the danger of accident minimized. By this scheme there is also avoided the necessity of shutting down an entire room when any difficulty occurs with the power, as is the case with ordinary equipment. Another feature worthy of mention is a trolley system that is used for moving the heavy rolls of yarn and fabric. This suspended railway extends over the whole plant. It is a great improvement over the old trucking method. An Allis Chalmers turbine engine of 1,000 horsepower generates the electricity required for the operation of the plant.

The officers of the corporation are William Whitman, president, and Walter C. Ballard, treasurer. John W. Alexander is the agent.

Wright Manufacturing Company

A manufacturing concern which has a wide reputation for the quality of its product is the Wright Manufacturing Company, located on Island street. The company manufactures cotton and mohair braids.

In 1854, Algernon S. Wright, an overseer in the Atlantic cotton mills, with Artemus W. Stearns and Dr. Alfred J. French, formed a partnership for the manufacture of woolen yarn, and leased a mill for the purpose. Later the project was abandoned, and, at Mr. Stearns' suggestion, the mill was equipped with suitable machinery for making braids. Fifty braid machines were installed. From the beginning the enterprise has had marked success. The growth of the business was rapid, and the number of machines has been increased to keep up with the demands upon the capacity of the plant.

In 1873, the company was incorporated with a capital of $60,000, and organized by the choice of Dr. French as president, and A. W. Stearns as treasurer. A. S. Wright was superintendent of the plant.

At first the production was confined to cotton and alpaca braids for skirts and men's wear. Later the company introduced the manufacture of mohair braids, and, by processes of its own invention, it was able to produce the finest grades on the market, and at prices that defied competition. In recent years the manufacture of skirt braids and braids for men's wear was discontinued, owing to the change of styles, and the production of various military and trimming braids taken up.

Today the concern turns out a great many kinds of braids for uniforms, awnings, shoelaces, and cloth bindings, ranging from fine mohair silk down to the common cotton yarn variety. A big feature of the business is the manufacture of various kinds of braids for the shoe trade. The company makes a specialty of a patented braided article used in button shoes, which is sold to 95 percent, of the shoe factories of the country.

The plant was purchased from the Stearns estate in 1910 by a company of which Richard Ward is the president and treasurer, besides having the controlling interest. Many improvements have since been made in the facilities, and the production has been greatly increased.

The concern occupies a four-story frame building, 250 feet long, fronting on Island street. There are about 30,000 square feet of manufacturing space. The output is about 20,000 gross yardage a week. The plant has 1,800 braid machines, and when running to its full capacity employs 300 people.

CHAMPION-INTERNATIONAL COMPANY

In the Champion-International Company Lawrence has one of the largest coated paper manufacturing concerns in the world. The company makes a specialty of high-grade surface coated papers which are used by many of the leading periodicals in the country.

This concern is the outgrowth of an industry established in Lawrence in the early 50's by William Russell and his sons. The business was incorporated in 1864, under the name of the Russell Paper Company. In 1898 it became a part of the International Paper Company.

In 1902 the present company was formed by the purchase of the Champion Card and Paper Company's mill at East Pepperell, Mass., and the repurchase of the paper and pulp mills from the International Paper Co. At the same time a large coating mill was built in Lawrence.

Not only is the concern one of the largest of its kind in the world, but it is one of the finest equipped. The newest and best methods and equipment for paper manufacturing are used by it, and to it is accredited the introduction of many progressive ideas into the papermaking industry.

These mills have had an important part in the development of the industry. They were pioneers in the introduction of the use of ground wood pulp in the manufacture of newspaper, and later in the introduction of soda and sulphite pulp in the manufacture of the higher grades of paper. It was in these mills that, when the sulphite pulp process was on the point of being abandoned for want of a suitable acid-proof lining, with which to line the receptacles in which the process of reducing the wood to pulp was carried on, such a lining was developed. This lining was universally adopted, both here and abroad, and is in use today in every successful sulphite pulp mill.

The capacity production of the plant a week is 100 tons. The employees number 600, and the weekly payroll amounts to $12,000.

Worthy of special note is the fact that the Russell family has been identified with the business since its inception. Hon. William A. Russell who for many years was in control was prominently identified with municipal, state, and national affairs. For several years he represented this district in Congress.

The present head of the concern, George Fred Russell, is the third generation in its management. Extensive improvements have been made in the plant since he became president and general manager.

The company is capitalized for $650,000. The assessed valuation of the property in Lawrence for 1917 was $540,550. The treasurer is P. A. Hammond.

THE GEORGE KUNHARDT CORPORATION

One of the most steadily operated of the city's manufacturing plants is The George E. Kunhardt Corporation which has an excellent reputation for the quality and texture of its fabrics.

This concern was established in 1886 when George E. Kunhardt purchased the plant, owned by the Lawrence Woolen Company and familiarly known as the Perry Mill. The Lawrence Woolen Company had been incorporated in 1864, during the Civil War, its projector and principal founder being Capt. O. H. Perry. The company had a struggle trying to keep the plant in operation, due to depression in the woolen industry, and when Mr. Kunhardt took over the mill it was shut down.

Since, the development of the plant has been remarkable the original buildings have been remodeled and the old machinery replaced by new. For some time the firm name was Philips & Kunhardt, but in 1895 Mr. Phillips was obliged to retire on account of ill health.

Under Mr. Kunhardt's management large additions have been made and the capacity of the mills has been greatly increased. The concern manufactures men's wear woolens and worsteds, and uniform cloths. Its woolen fabrics, especially, are in much demand, the company having established an enviable reputation for this class of goods. The weekly output of the plant is 40,000 yards. In raw material, every week the mills consume on an average of 50,000 pounds of scoured wool. There are 700 operatives employed, and the weekly payroll amounts to $15,000.

The officers of the corporation are George E. Kunhardt, president; James Hoyt Knapp, vice-president; Joseph W. Booth, treasurer and agent. The capital is $2,000,000. George Richardson is the superintendent of the mills.

PLYMOUTH MILLS

One of the busiest of Lawrence's industrial plants is the Plymouth Mills which manufacture fiber rugs and matting. The concern was established in 1906. The capital is $325,000. Its development has been rapid, and recently a large modern brick factory building was added to the plant in order to meet the increasing demand upon its facilities. The plant covers a ground area of 80,000 square feet. It has a floor space of 240,000 square feet. In raw material it uses each week 100,000 pounds of wool, cotton, jute, and paper, and its finished product per week amounts to 75,000 square yards. There are 300 employees. The weekly payroll amounts to $5,500. The assessed valuation of the property for 1917 was $269,100. The agent of the mills is H. A. S. Read.

About the others of the larger manufacturing plants the following data is given:

LAWRENCE DUCK CO.: Established in 1853; manufactures cotton duck; weekly output, 100,000 pounds; employees, 600; weekly payroll, $9,500; assessed valuation of property for 1917, $395,150. This concern has made sails for all of the America yacht cup defenders.

UNITED STATES WORSTED CO.: Established in 1908; manufactures worsted and woolen men's wear and dress goods; weekly output, 140,000 yards; employees, 1,500; weekly payroll, $27,000; assessed valuation of property for 1917, $796,150.

PEMBERTON COMPANY: Established in 1853 (present corporation formed in 1860 after the fall of the original mill); manufactures cotton goods and flannels, tickings, awnings and shirtings; weekly output, 70,000 pounds; employees, 600; weekly payroll, $7,500; assessed valuation of property for 1917, $431,100.

WALWORTH BROS., INC.: Established in 1895; manufactures dress goods and men's wear; weekly output, 18,700 yards; employees, 275; weekly payroll, $3,500; assessed valuation of property for 1917, $90,000.

ARCHIBALD WHEEL CO.: Established in 1871; manufactures vehicle wheels of all kinds for both horse-drawn and motor vehicles, also steam fire engine, gun carriage, caisson and limber wheels; weekly output, varies from 4,000 automobile wheels to 1,000 of larger and more expensive types; employees, 127 in Lawrence plant, 46 at Guilford, Conn., 150 in southern mill getting material; weekly payroll, local plant $3,000, Guilford $850, South $2,000. This concern is one of the very largest of its kind in the country.

A. G. WALTON & CO., INC.: Established in 1916; manufactures misses' and children's McKay shoes; weekly output, 35.000 pairs; employees, 600; weekly payroll, $10,000; assessed valuation of property for 1917, $119,000.

LEWIS SCOURING MILL: Established in 1870; wool scourers and carbonizers; weekly output 800,000 pounds. Employees, 475; weekly payroll, $11,000; assessed valuation of property for 1917, $232,650.

EMMONS LOOM HARNESS CO.: Established in 1866; largest manufacturers in the country of loom harness and reeds; weekly output, 12.000 shades of harness and 1200 reeds; employees, 200; weekly payroll, $3,500; assessed valuation of property for 1917, $84,100.

ALFRED KIMBALL SHOE CO.: Established in 1900; manufactures men's shoes; weekly output, 2,500 pairs; employees, 350; weekly payroll, $6,000; assessed valuation of property for 1917, $32,000.

FARWELL BLEACHERY: Established in 1886; incorporated to bleach, dye, mercerize, or otherwise finish cotton piece goods; weekly output, 1,000,000 yards; employees, 350; weekly payroll, $5,000; assessed valuation of property for 191 7, $283,500.

MERRIMACK PAPER CO.: Established in 1895; manufactures paper of all kinds; weekly output. 125 tons; employees, 275; weekly payroll, $5,000; assessed valuation of property for 1917 $295,400.

J. W. HORNE & SONS CO. :Established in 1871; manufactures paper mill machinery; each year produces paper-making machinery enough to equip four mills; employees, 120; weekly payroll, $3,000; assessed valuation of property for 1917, $201,200.

A great many smaller establishments, engaged in the manufacture of a large variety of products, including 20 machine shops and foundries, are located in the manufacturing sections of the city. Included among their products are woolen, worsted and cotton fabrics, yarns, paper, paper mill machinery, steam engines, pumps, mill supplies, carriages, fire department trucks, wagons and supplies, boilers, iron, brass, copper and tin, cement, stone and marble products, bobbins, spools, shuttles and wood products, rugs, chemicals, soaps.

Essex Savings Bank

The Essex Savings Bank, the largest bank in Essex County and the city's oldest savings institution, was incorporated March 15, 1847, and commenced business the following October in the rooms of the Bay State Bank, then located on the second floor of the old Bay State Bank building.

Charles S. Storrow was the first president and Nathaniel White, the first treasurer. Mr. Storrow served until i860, and was followed by George D. Cabot who in turn was succeeded by Joseph Shattuck in 1877. Mr.

Shattuck retired from the presidency in 1903, after twenty-six consecutive years of service, and Walter E. Parker, the present incumbent, was elected president.

Nathaniel White filled the office of treasurer until his death, which occurred September 12, 1866. He was regarded as one of the best financiers that Lawrence has ever known. James H. Eaton succeeded Mr. White as treasurer, serving in that capacity until his death, March 23, 1901. His recognized ability in matters of finance won for him an enviable reputation, and accounts in a great measure for the marvelous growth and prosperity of the institution during his service of 34 years. At his decease, Joseph Shattuck, Jr., was elected treasurer. He resigned in September 1902, to accept a similar position with the Springfield Institution of Savings, Springfield, Mass. Albert I. Couch was elected to succeed Mr. Shattuck as treasurer. He has since held the position, maintaining the high standard of efficiency set by his predecessors.

The Essex Savings Bank has never failed to compound the interest each April and October, and the 140 dividends already paid aggregate over $13,850,000. The rate of dividends has always been as high as sound conservative banking would warrant. The assets of the bank today are $15,600,000, and its business is steadily increasing. The rate paid on deposits for the year 1917 was $4\frac{1}{2}\%$.

The bank is located in its own building at the corner of Essex and Lawrence streets. Its quarters are roomy and attractive, and are well equipped for the handling of the enormous amount of business transacted. In 1917 they were considerably enlarged, being extended into a portion of the adjoining building which is also owned by the bank. The institution has by far the largest number of depositors, of any bank in the city.

THE BAY STATE NATIONAL BANK

The Bay State National Bank, the cities oldest and one of its most prominent financial institutions, and only national bank, received its charter February 10, 1847. On May 17, the same year, the bank organized with Charles S. Storrow, as president, and Nathaniel White, as cashier. The capital stock was fixed at $200,000, but it was rapidly increased to $500,000, making it at that time the largest bank in Essex County. Soon after the organization of the bank, a piece of land was deeded to the institution by the Essex Company, at the northeast corner of Essex and Lawrence streets, and a substantial structure was erected thereon, a portion of which was occupied by the bank for 57 years. The price paid for the first purchase of land was $1 per foot.

166

The original building was of brick, three stories in height, with banking rooms on the second floor. Here business was carried on for a period of 35 years, when the demand for a ground floor location became urgent. On April 17, 1861, two days before the gallant 6th Regiment marched through Baltimore, the directors voted $25,000 for the use of the Government. The bank became a federal institution in 1865. Early in the 70's, the adjoining property on Essex street was purchased, and in 1882, the two buildings were united and banking quarters were fitted up on the corner, just beneath the original ones. In 1899, the bank acquired the property of Marcus S. Dodge in the rear of its own. Plans were made for the razing of the old building and erection of the handsome eight-story structure now occupied.

In July 1905, the bank moved into its new quarters. A few years later, there was still another purchase of adjoining property, and in 1912, an addition was made to the building, increasing the frontage on Essex street to 76 feet. The structure extends to a depth of 206 feet on Lawrence street. The cost of construction was about $500,000.

The Bay State is the tallest building in the city. It is thoroughly up to the times in every way. The banking rooms are well equipped, and they are elaborately finished in Grecian marble with bronze and glass trimmings. There are six stores on the ground floor, besides the bank quarters. The second floor is largely devoted to mercantile purposes, while the upper floors are occupied by professional men, there being 230 offices.

The institution does a general banking business, including a finely equipped safe deposit department and savings department, also domestic and foreign exchange, etc. At the close of the year 1917, the capital stock was $375,000; its surplus, $225,000; its deposits, $2,200,000; its assets, $3,400,000.

LAWRENCE SAVINGS BANK

The Lawrence Savings Bank, the second savings institution to be established in Lawrence, and one of the city's most prosperous banks, was chartered by special act of the State Legislature on March 10, 1868, and commenced business on May 14 of that year. It was first located in the brick block at the northeast corner of Essex and Jackson streets, occupying the corner room on the second floor. Five years later it moved to offices on the second floor of the Schaake block, over the post office which was then located on the ground floor of that building. Here the bank remained until 1893 when its present location at 255 Essex street was purchased from the Pemberton National Bank which had decided to go out of business.

The institution has been fortunate in the calibre of the men who have directed it. The first president was Milton Bonney, a former mayor, who served the bank from 1868 to 1883. He was succeeded by Hezekiah Plummer, from 1883 to 1897; Frederick E. Clarke, 1897 to 1899; Robert H. Tewksbury, 1899 to 1910; Daniel Saunders, 1910 to 1917. Alvin E. Mack now holds that office. The first treasurer was William R. Spalding who served from 1868 to 1891. He was followed by his son, William W. Spalding, from 1891 to 1901; Albert L. Couch, 1901 to 1902. Lewis A. Foye became treasurer in 1902, and still holds the position.

The growth of the institution has kept pace with the development of the city. In 1911 when it became necessary to enlarge its quarters, the old building was torn down, and the erection of the present handsome structure started. On April 18, 1912, the new commodious, well-arranged banking rooms were opened to the public. The equipment is modern in every respect. The massive vault is both burglar and fireproof, is the largest in Lawrence and for safety and security is unsurpassed by none. The fixtures are in harmony with the prosperous atmosphere of the institution. In connection with the annual meeting on May 6, 1918, exercises commemorative of the 50th anniversary of the establishment of the bank were held.

On May 1, 1918, the bank's deposits amounted to $6,676,339, and its depositors numbered 15,179. Its guaranty fund and undivided profits account is $498,090. It has never paid less than four percent, dividends. It has $3,848,403 invested in first mortgages in Lawrence and vicinity, giving preference and every consideration to homebuilders in making its loans. It conducts school savings banks in the public schools of North Andover and Methuen.

BROADWAY SAVINGS BANK

The Broadway Savings Bank, the city's youngest savings institution, was established in 1872. Quarters were secured on the second floor of the Brechin block, corner of Broadway and Essex street. Here the bank was located until 1890 when it moved to the ground floor where it occupied rooms jointly with the Lawrence National Bank.

In 1905, at a cost of $60,000, the bank erected the building at 522 Essex street, in which it is now located. The banking quarters are attractive. They are equipped with all the latest desirable appliances for carrying on the business.

The first president of the bank was John Fallon, and the first treasurer, James Payne. The vice presidents were A. W. Stearns, J. A. Treat, Morris Knowles, H. C. Bacon, Thomas Scott, and Jacob Emerson, Jr. The original board of trustees was composed of Peter Smith, J. W. Smith, Peter Holihan. P. C. Kirk, D. M. Ayer, A. J. French, C. K. Pillsbury, P. G. Pillsbury, John Smith, F. L. Runals, S. W. Knight, D. C. Richardson, Jesse Glover, Patrick Murphy, James Payne, Daniel Hardy.

An interesting reminder of the establishment of the institution is in the possession of the bank in the form of a pass-book in which is credited the first deposit made on the opening day, May 1, 1872. The amount deposited was $10. One other deposit of $10 was made on this account in 1877. The total deposit of $20, with accrued interest and dividends, now amounts to $122.10, which is a good illustration of the way money accumulates when deposited in savings banks.

In April 1918, the assets of the institution were $6,000,000; surplus, $528,650; deposits, $5,381,000; number of depositors, 10,363. For more than a third of a century 4% in interest has been paid on deposits, with occasional extra dividends. The last dividend was ½% above the regular interest amount.

The treasurer of the bank is Clinton O. Andrews who succeeded Gilbert E. Hood upon the latter's death in 1905. For a number of years previously he was assistant treasurer.

The present officers are : President, William F. Rutter; vice president, W. E. Rowell; board of investment, W. F. Rutter, W. E. Rowell, A. S. Lang, L. E. Locke, G. W. Hamblett; board of trustees, C. O. Andrews, T. H. Bride, K. G. Colby. J. W. Cross, W. D. Currier, W. H. Gile, G. W. Hamblett, W. D. Hartshorne, L E. Home, A. S. Lang, L. E. Locke, F. L. Porter, W. E. Rowell, G. F. Russell, W. F. Rutter, G. L. Selden, H. L. Sherman, M. L. Shuttleworth, I. H. Stone, A. B. Sutherland, W. D. Twiss, Harry Wylde.

MERCHANTS TRUST COMPANY

The Merchants Trust Company which is an outgrowth of the consolidation of the Merchants, Lawrence and Pacific National Banks, was established March 6, 1911. At that time the Merchants National Bank consolidated with the Lawrence National Bank. In January, 1915, the Pacific National Bank was merged in the new organization. The consolidation of these three national banks resulted in the forming of one of the city's strongest and largest financial institutions. A remarkable feature of the organization is the strength of its board of directors which is composed of men prominent in the industrial and mercantile affairs of the city.

The Merchants National Bank, a remarkably successful institution, was incorporated March 4, 1889, with a capital of $100,000, and commenced doing business at 240 Essex street in the fall of that year. In 1890, it erected a handsome building at 264 Essex street, which was then the finest banking quarters in the city. The Lawrence National Bank was organized in February 1872, with a capital of $300,000, and began business in the Brechin block, corner of Essex street and Broadway, where a branch office of the Merchants Trust Company is now maintained. The Pacific National Bank was organized in January 1877, with a capital stock of $100,000.

When the Pacific National Bank was merged in the Merchants Trust Company, the latter moved into the quarters which had been occupied by the former at the corner of Appleton and Essex streets. Extensive improvements were made. The institution is equipped with the best facilities for the transaction of a general banking business. At the close of business May 10, 1918, the Merchants Trust Company had in deposits, $5,556,000; assets, $6,190,000; profit and loss, $85,000. The capital stock is $300,000, with a surplus of $150,000 paid in, making a working capital of $450,000.

The officers of the institution comprise President, George Fred Russell; vice presidents. Fred C. McDuffie, Langdon E. Locke, Byron Truell; treasurer, Henry L. Sherman; secretary and assistant treasurer, Arthur C. Dame; assistant treasurer, Arthur J. Crosby; board of directors, F. M. Andrew, C. O. Andrews, J. H. Bride, A. H. Chamberlain, D. Y. Costello, Y. W. Cross, M. J. Curran, W. D. Currier, A. B. Emmons, H. W. Field, Y. C. Forbes, L. A. Foye, W. H. Gile, G. W. Hamblet, W. D. Hartshorne, H. W. Home, J. E. Home, C. J. R. Humphreys, G. E. Kunhardt, L. E. Locke, Ashton Lee, F. C. McDuffie, G. E. Murray, W. E. Parker, F. L. Porter, W. E. Rowell, G. F. Russell,W. F. Rutter, G. H. Simonds, A. B. Sutherland, J. P. Sweeney, Byron Truell, C. W. Walworth, P. C. Wiggin, H. K. Webster, G. L. Wright.

ARLINGTON TRUST COMPANY

One of the progressive banking institutions of the city is the Arlington Trust Company which was chartered as the Arlington National Bank in 1890. It was first located at 265 Essex street. Later it absorbed the Pemberton National Bank. Shortly afterward, it secured the store of D. D. Mahony at the corner of Essex and Lawrence streets, its present location. The bank organized with a capital of $100,000. Its first president was Hon. William S. Knox, and its first cashier, Albert Butler. On October 15, 1910, the institution was incorporated as a trust company, with a capital stock of $200,000. Upon reorganization, Thomas M. Cogswell was elected president and James Houston, treasurer.

With the incorporation as a trust company, the bank was given a new lease of life, and its growth has since been rapid. Several years ago it purchased the building which it occupies, and it is expected that the near future will see a handsome, modern structure on the site, with roomier banking quarters.

The institution numbers among its steady clients a good share of the substantial manufacturers, merchants and professional men of Lawrence and suburbs. A wise spirit of liberality, tempered with conservatism, has been an attractive feature of its management.

It deals in loans, discounts and deposits, besides exchange and letters of credit. The best of the new thrift ideas are in vogue in its savings department. The banking section provides attractive conveniences. It is a custom now for women to have check accounts of their own at banks, and the Arlington has special facilities for handling business of this description. Another feature is the industrial department which has to do with small loans. The arrangement is such that the notes are redeemed through a weekly payment plan, thereby increasing the degree of security and at the same time making it easier for the borrower to meet the obligation.

At the close of 1917, this institution had in capital stock, $200,000; assets, $1,500,000; surplus, $23,081.58. The total deposits amounted to $1,437,820.52, including $859,637.69 in the banking department and $578,182.83 in the savings department.

The officers and directors comprise: John A. Brackett, president; Cornelius A. McCarthy, treasurer; James A. Brogan, Joseph Jackson, Edward I. Koffman, Cornelius F. Lynch, William H. Merrill, Daniel J. Murphy. Alfred Sager, Moses Shuttleworth, A. L. Siskind, Robert T. Todd, William H. Russell, David Brown, George A. Mellen and James F. Lanigan.

MERRIMACK CO-OPERATIVE BANK

The Merrimack Co-operative Bank, one of the fastest growing cooperative banks in the state, was organized March 21, 1892. The first president was John Breen, and the first treasurer, Cornehlius A. McCarthy who still holds the position. Quarters were secured at 263 Essex street, on the second floor. The bank was incorporated April 2, and began to do business April 28, 1892.

The most marked development in the growth of the bank occurred in the past five years, following the election of the incumbent president, John J. Hurley. In 1912 the assets were $111,000, and at the close of the year, 1917, they were $611,000, showing an increase of half a million dollars and nearly five times the amount gained in the preceding twenty years of existence. On December 31, 1917, there were 2,041 shareholders, representing 18,020 shares.

The bank continued to do business at 263 Essex street until April 1916, when the facilities became so cramped that a more commodious location was secured in the quarters formerly occupied by the Merchants National Bank, 264 Essex street. Here are provided modern banking facilities that place the Merrimack Co-operative Bank among the finest equipped in the state. Included in the advantages, over the old quarters, is a large fire and burglarproof vault, besides grille enclosures which have made it possible to handle the business with greater efficiency.

The institution loans money on first mortgages on real estate and on the shares of its members. Many hundreds of Lawrence people have built and paid for their homes through the monthly payment plan of this bank. Dividends have been paid regularly since the bank was incorporated, and have averaged 5¾ percent, per annum during that period.

Shares go on sale quarterly, in February, May, August, and November, and mature in 11 years and 10 months. A matured share is worth $200, the payments being $1.00 for each share per month and the profits amounting to about $58 per share upon maturity. No one member can hold over 40 shares. An attractive feature of the co-operative banking system is the compulsory saving idea which induces regularity in making deposits, and creates a habit of saving, that is most valuable, especially in cases of people who are not ordinarily inclined to be thrifty.

The board of directors is composed of : J. J. Hurley, president; T. J. Sullivan, vice president; C. A. McCarthy, treasurer; F. C. Harmon, E. P. White, M. J. Sullivan, J. A. Levek, J. P. Mulholland, James McDowell, M. A. Sullivan, T. J. Buckley, A. H. Rogers, J. H. McDonald, Frank Quinn, J. A. Brogan, E. A. Hart, J. J. Petroske, F. W. Boody, George Gelineau, C. H. Sugatt, M. B. Dorgan.

LAWRENCE TRUST COMPANY

The Lawrence Trust Company, the city's youngest banking institution, was incorporated July 19, 1910. It started doing business on November 23, of that year at 430 Essex street. Cornelius J. Corcoran, the present head of the bank, was elected the first president. Peter M. Macdonald was the first treasurer. The development of this institution has been remarkable. In less than five years after the commencement of business the bank outgrew the original quarters, and on June 15, 1915, it moved to its present location, corner of Essex and Hampshire streets.

The banking rooms are attractively finished in French marble with bronze and glass trimmings. The equipment is on most modern lines. The very latest methods and appliances for facilitating the handling of the business are in vogue. The institution was the first bank in the city to use bookkeeping machines which displace the ordinary individual bank ledgers. It was also the first in Lawrence to establish a Christmas Savings Club, a project which has since been generally adopted and which has proved very beneficial to the merchants. At the close of the last season the Lawrence Trust Company distributed, to the members of its Christmas Club $300,000, most of which went into the channels of trade.

This bank is reputed to be the originator of the scheme of selling Liberty bonds by the weekly payment plan. A recent innovation adopted by it was a departure from the regular banking hours. Under the new arrangement, the institution remains open until 6 p. m. each business day. Thus giving the people employed in the shops and the mills more opportunity to do business with the bank. Two shifts of clerks are used in carrying out the arrangement.

The institution does a general banking business, including commercial, savings, safe deposit, and industrial departments. The last named feature deals in small loans which are redeemed by a weekly payment plan. The capital stock of the bank is $100,000; the assets, $4,500,000; surplus, $80,070.67; deposits, $4,350,000. About two-thirds of the total deposits is in the savings department. There are 9,500 depositors in the savings department, and 1750 in the commercial department. In addition, the industrial department carries 4,600 accounts, including those in connection with the first and second Liberty Loans, besides over 6,600 accounts under the third Liberty Loan. There are 9,600 members in its Christmas club, and 1,000 in its Vacation club, the latter of which is another of the new thrift ideas.

MERCANTILE DEVELOPMENT

The mercantile development of Lawrence has kept pace with the rapid growth of the city. It is not much longer than an ordinary lifetime since Amos Pillsbury anchored his gondola at the north bank of the river just below the dam, then still in the process of construction, and began dealing in boots and shoes. From that, simple enterprise has sprung a system of mercantile establishments, which has made this city one of the most important trading centers in Essex County.

One of the first store blocks, extending from the Bay State building, at the corner of Essex and Lawrence streets, easterly along the main street to the corner of Pemberton street, known as City Block, is still with us, though the stores are greatly altered in appearance. The old fronts, with the poor equipment, small stocks and rural methods, have given way before the onrush of modern business, and, in general appearance and facilities, Lawrence's stores will compare favorably with those of any city of its size in the country.

Essex street, for a mile lined on both sides with attractive establishments, is one of the longest and busiest shopping thoroughfares in the county. On Saturday night, the principal shopping period, fully 15,000 people have been known to traverse the street. Lower Broadway is also popular with the great buying public, while of late years a large section of South Broadway has become a busy trade mart, dozens of business establishments having come into existence to meet the increasing shopping trade of the growing South Lawrence district.

Lip in the Arlington district, too, on upper Broadway are numerous shops. There is probably no greater variety, nor larger number of stores in the state, outside of Boston, and there are several emporiums that would do credit to much larger cities.

Lawrence is easily and quickly reached by several lines of electric railways and steam railroad. Like the arteries of the human system, these lines stretch out, through every part of the city and to the adjacent towns and nearby cities. Fast running cars bring into close connection with Lawrence the towns of Methuen, North Andover, Andover, Middleton and Salem, N. H., besides the cities of Lowell and Haverhill. Within easy distance of Lawrence's shopping centre are more than 150,000 people.

CHAMBER OF COMMERCE

The city's most remarkable progress has been made during the last twenty-seven years, and probably no organization has been more closely identified with that progress than the Lawrence Chamber of Commerce, or Board of Trade as it was originally known.

The Lawrence Board of Trade was organized February 8, 1888, with James H. Eaton as president, Charles A. DeCourcy as secretary, Arthur W. Dyer as treasurer, and about 75 members, including most of the mill agents and many of the business and professional men of the city. Today, the Lawrence Chamber of Commerce has 500 active members, representative of the industrial, mercantile, and professional life of the community.

The old Board of Trade was formed for the three-fold purpose of bringing to public notice the vital needs of the city, stimulating local trade and attracting new industries and business enterprises.

This commendable object was successfully adhered to through the 25 years of its existence, and it has been followed by the present Chamber of Commerce since the reorganization on June 1, 1913, only with a greater activity, made possible by the wider scope adopted.

The organization has assisted in attracting new enterprises to the city. In the way of advertising the advantages of Lawrence, an inestimable amount of good has been done. Statistical matter has been constantly sent abroad, telling of the marvelous growth of the city and the opportunities it offers for investment.

A notable enterprise in this direction was the sending, by the Chamber, of an industrial exhibit to the Panama-Pacific International Exposition at San Francisco in 1915. Many thousands of descriptive pamphlets were distributed in connection with the project, and Lawrence secured thereby invaluable publicity. Another feature of this undertaking was the sending of a special train to the Pacific coast, bearing 106 enthusiastic boomers for Lawrence. It is needless to say that 'the city was "put on the map" on this occasion, if it were not considered there before. The exhibit was given first prize.

Just prior to the reorganization of the Board of Trade as the Chamber of Commerce the Merchants Association, which had been organized in 1902, for the purpose of regulating the opening and closing hours of the stores, was merged in that body.

The Chamber has commodious quarters on the eighth floor of the Bay State building where there is on file a fund of information pertaining to the city's activities.

Deep Waterway Possibilities

A deep waterway to the sea would be a great contributing factor in the future development of Lawrence. Terminal and track facilities have not kept pace with the tremendous industrial expansion of the city in the past 20 years, and the need of improvement in freight transportation, such as would be afforded by river navigation, is keenly felt.

As far back as 1828, the Federal authorities saw the need of dredging the Merrimack River above tidewater, to encourage the building of seaport towns along its shores. From time to time in the years that have followed, it has been "resolved" and "reported" with occasional action that failed to fully produce the desired results.

In June 1848, the steamer "Lawrence" came up from Newburyport with a delegation from that place and adjoining towns. Since that time sundry efforts have been made to navigate the river, but with little success.

General Butler's effort in 1877 met with some success, and in 1879, E. M. Boynton made a marked advance in the project. Many obstructions were removed, boats built for transporting coal, lands leased of the Essex Company for a landing place and coal yard, and 22,000 tons of coal were delivered in Lawrence direct from Newburyport before winter set in that year. However, the channel at Mitchell's Falls proved to be neither deep enough nor wide enough to guarantee safe transportation, and interest waned.

The greatest stride in the various attempts to carry out this long cherished idea has been made in the last few years, and the progress attained was due to a large extent to the persistent, intelligent effort of Andrew B. Sutherland of Lawrence, who has been called the "father of the waterway" because of his activity in behalf of the project. With the able assistance of Judge Charles C. Paine of Hyannis, and Lewis R. Hovey of Haverhill, the other two members of the Merrimack Valley Waterway Board, he succeeded in 1917 in bringing the proposition to a point where the preliminary work for actual construction might have been started.

The approval of the project by the Board of Engineers of the United States Army had been secured, with the recommendation to Congress that the Federal government participate in the expense on a 50 percent, basis with the state of Massachusetts. The estimated cost at the time was $7,076,600, the cities and towns to be benefited to take care of all land damages, terminals, docks, etc. The State Legislature voted to co-operate in a financial way, but the bill was vetoed by Governor McCall on the ground that it was inexpedient at this time, notwithstanding the fact that it was pointed out that provision could be made whereby the legislation need not become effective until after the war.

The project proposes a navigable channel, 18 feet deep and 200 feet wide, from the sea to Lowell, a distance of 36 miles. There are on the banks of the river, in this short distance, four large cities and 12 towns, with a population of over 350,000, nearly 900 manufacturing establishments and about $250,000,000 of capital invested. The valley cities turn out annually manufactured products at a value of $350,000,000. Raw materials are imported at a value of $200,000,000.

The idea is not impracticable, and the undertaking does not seem so difficult when one considers the length of inland waterways elsewhere. New York is 20 miles by river to the sea. Mobile 40 miles, New Orleans 100, Baltimore 150, Philadelphia 100, London, Eng., 35, Liverpool, Eng., 20, and Manchester, Eng., 56 miles by river to the sea. The great Kiel Canal, completed in 1914, is 61 miles long and cost more than $65,000,000.

The Merrimack Valley has an annual commerce (not including lumber and merchandise) of $550,000,000. The valley's trade exceeds the foreign commerce of Boston. It exceeds the foreign commerce of any American seaport except New York, and that of any seaport in the western hemisphere except New York and Buenos Ayres. It is greater by $37,000,000 than the foreign trade of Manchester, England (where $100,000,000 has been spent in constructing a canal 36 miles long with an extensive system of docks). It exceeds by $66,000,000 the foreign trade of Glasgow, Scotland (where $55,000,000 has been spent in dredging and dock construction). It represents trade of almost two million dollars a day for every working day in the year.

America's keenest competitors in Europe are vastly extending their inland waterway systems, in order that after the war their commerce may be moved to and from ship sides at the lowest possible cost. There has been sufficient evidence of the inadequacy of the railroad accommodations, hereabouts to make it apparent that there is a great need of a deep waterway for the cities and towns of Merrimack Valley, and it is to be hoped that the efforts of those who have worked so hard to bring about a fulfillment of the project will yet be crowned with complete success.

BOARDING HOUSES
NORTH CANAL BAY STATE MILLS

MERRIMACK RIVER

Journalism In Lawrence

A newspaper-man was on the spot when the foundation of Lawrence was being laid, and newspaper enterprise has ever since been prominently identified with the development of the city. There have been many ventures in the local field of journalism, and most of them have been short lived. Newspapers are not made; they grow, and only the fittest survive.

The first newspaper in Lawrence was issued in October 1846, under the name of *The Merrimack Courier,* by J. F. C. Hayes who came here early in that year and set up a printing press in a partially completed building on Broadway. This paper, a weekly, was continued under the editorial management of Mr. Hayes, John A. Goodwin, Homer A. Cooke, Rev. Henry F. Harrington and Nathaniel Ambrose, a portion of the time as a tri-weekly, until soon after Lincoln's election in November, 1860, when the publication collapsed. In January 1847, *The Weekly Messenger,* published by Brown & Becket, was transferred to Lawrence from Exeter, N. H. It lasted about two years. Some time in the winter of 1847 or 1848, one or two copies of a paper were issued from *the Messenger* office, under the title of *The Engine,* by E. R. Wilkins. In the spring of 1848, a paper, called *The Herald,* by Amos H. Sampson, appeared, gave a few gasps and passed away. Immediately following *The Herald* came *The Vanguard,* by Fabyan & Douglass. *The Vanguard* was Democratic, and it was regarded as an able publication. The office was a joint stock concern, in which the publishers were very little interested, and subsequently the name was changed to *The Sentinel.* Under this title it had been edited by Harrison Douglass, B. F. Watson, George A. Gordon, Benjamin Bordman, John Ryan, John K. Tarbox, Abiel Morrison, and Jeremiah T.[sic], and Edward F. O'Sullivan. Only very recently this, the city's oldest weekly publication, gave up the ghost.

In 1856, a weekly paper, under the title of *The Home Review,* was issued here by J. F. C. Hayes. It was continued until *the Courier* came back into his hands, when it was merged in that paper. In 1855, the publication of *The Lawrence American,* by George W. Sargent and A. S. Bunker, began. The office, like that of *The Vanguard,* was a joint stock affair. It was owned by the members of the "Know-Nothing" party. Mr. Bunker sold his right to the paper to Mr. Sargent for $25, a few weeks after its commencement, and the latter conducted it alone for a time. Later George S. Merrill became associated with him, and finally succeeded him as sole editor. *The American* flourished as a "Know-Nothing" organ during the brief existence of the "Know-Nothing" party. When Mr. Merrill got control the policy was changed and, under his capable editorship. *The American* was a widely quoted Republican paper. In June 1892, William S. Jewett purchased the plant, and on August 1, 1893. He started *The Sun*, a morning daily, and later *The Sunday Sun*, a Sunday edition of both *the Daily American* and *the Sun*, from the same office. *The Sunday Sun* attained a large circulation. The present management, a stock concern, took over the plant in 1914. The daily Sun has since been discontinued, and the name of *the American*, the evening edition, changed to *the Sun-American*. The publications are now independent Democratic in political policy.

On December 1, 1860, the first daily paper in this city, *The Daily Journal*, was issued by Dockham & Place. It was continued for about two years as a daily, then became a tri-weekly, and in 1863 it was merged in *The American*. In the spring of 1867, *The Essex Eagle*, by Merrill & Wadsworth (Charles G. Merrill and Horace A. Wadsworth), was started, and was published weekly. Mr. Merrill soon retired and Mr. Wadsworth managed the paper alone, starting *the Daily Eagle* from the same office, July 20, 1868. *The Daily Eagle,* which in 1868 absorbed *The Essex Eagle*, is the oldest daily in the city, the *Daily American* being issued for the first time the next evening. With *the Eagle* there is now published daily *The Evening Tribune*, which was established in 1890, the first penny paper here. Their political policy is Democratic, and the Tribune has a large and influential circulation. In 1898, F. H. Hildreth and A. H. Rogers, under the firm name of Hildreth & Rogers, purchased *the Eagle* and *Tribune*. Upon the death of Mr. Hildreth in 1909, a stock company was formed, with Mr. Rogers as treasurer and general manager, and it took over the plant.

The Lawrence Journal, weekly, was started by Robert Bower, as a labor organ, in 1871, and was sold to Patrick Sweeney in 1877. It later became *the Sunday Register* which, after passing through several hands, suspended publication in 1913. There has been a number of later day publications which have gone out of existence, including *The Sunday Telegram, The Star,* and *The Daily News*.

The Sunday Telegram was established in 1884 by Winfield G. Merrill. Later George Goldsmith joined Mr. Merrill in the venture, and then became sole editor. With Harry Nice, Goldsmith began issuing *The Lawrence Telegram* daily on March 4, 1895, this publication taking the place of *the Sunday Telegram*. In 1896 it was rescued by John N. Cole, and under his supervision the paper was firmly established. In 1906, Kimball G. Colby purchased the controlling interest in the publication, further improving the plant and increasing the prestige of the paper. Today, The Telegram is one of the city's largest and most influential publications. Its political policy is Republican. All three daily newspaper plants are stock concerns. They are niodemly equipped, and not only is the local field thoroughly covered, but the news of the world is daily chronicled by the aid of wire services.

The Star, a weekly publication, was established by James E. Donoghue in 1893, and in 1900, *the Daily News* was started from the same office. Though *the Daily News* was a bright, newsy sheet, five years later it expired with *the Star.* There are several weeklies being published in the city today, including *The Leader, The Journal, The Critic, The Gazette, Anzeiger und Post* (German) and *Le Courier* (French). *The Leader* is devoted almost entirely to comment, very little straight news matter being carried.

DANIEL SAUNDERS, SR.

OLD LANDMARKS AND DESIGNATIONS

There are, in Lawrence today, few landmarks of the olden time, before the construction of the dam. Nearly all of them have been lost in the expansive development in which there has been little sentiment favoring the retention of reminders of the early days, that stood in the way of progress.

Norcross pond which received the drainage from the south side of Tower Hill, and which was used as a lumber dock into which logs were floated from the river to be cut into boards in the saw mill close by, is gone, though a remnant of the saw mill remains and is now part of the Gutterson & Gould property next to the Lawrence Boiler Works. Potter's pond away up on the slope of the hill near its top, where a big lump of ice probably got stranded, left behind by the melting glacier, has been used as a dump by the city's health department, and it has now entirely disappeared. Shanty pond on the opposite side of the river is preserved in the title of the main sewer draining the district. Gale's Hill was prominent in the west part of the city until it was carted into the swamps of Ward Five. General Gale had owned most of the hill, and had built an interesting octagonal concrete house on its top. Out of this hill came the sand for the first filter bed. One of the misfortunes of growing into a good-sized city, it may be said, is the loss of the old designations of localities. Stevens Village passed long ago; it is now the Arlington district. Stevens pond around which the village grew up, is practically gone, filled up and covered with buildings of the big Arlington Mills corporation. We never hear of the Paper Mill schoolhouse on the Atkinson road; it is now the Prospect street school. Nobody remembers that Adolphus Durant once made paper in a little old mill on the Spicket River, just east of East Haverhill street. The "Patch" (South Lawrence west of the B. & M. tracks) has gone; the "Plains" (Ward Three) likewise; West Parish road became Beacon street, and Barnard road is now known as Mt. Vernon street.

The old log dam upon the lower Spicket was carried away in the summer of 1878. It was an ancient affair, one of the few old landmarks. The current above the dam was sluggish, the course crooked. The breaking of this dam drained the usually deep river at this point, and revealed the foundations of a still older dam above it, of which there seems to be no account preserved either in records or traditions. It is said, however, that long ago there was a furnace at that point for smelting iron.

Where the library now stands was a pond in which boys used to swim. One man even committed suicide there by drowning.

The "Old Red Bridge" still holds its own, though it is not the red wooden bridge it used to be. The Lowell road, on the southside, used to run to Lowell, but Andover street as they call it now does not run to Andover. Lowell street does not run to Lowell, as strangers might think. It was not named for our rival city upstream, but for one of the early directors of the Essex Company. The "White Pups Bridge" is still with us, also "Bull Dog Field". Salem Turnpike has become Winthrop Avenue. Rumford street, named for Count Rumford, is now called Winter street. Turnpike street (originally Londonderry turnpike) was on September 2, 1868, given the name of Broadway.

There are numerous other old designations of localities which time and progress have changed. A number of old buildings, the last landmarks of the early days, are remembered by the older residents, but these have mostly disappeared.

The most notable landmark in Lawrence today is the ancient dwelling at the corner of Elm and East Haverhill streets. A portion of the old house had stood near the mouth of the Spicket River. It was removed to the present site when highways were laid out in the region, and it now stands, the only monument of the early pioneer days of which Lawrence can boast. The building has been much changed by successive repairs and alterations, but the foundations of the original portion are made as if to last forever. The chimney is of immense proportions, measuring 20 feet by 13 at the base. It was built, it is said, in 1738, although bricks have been, taken from the huge chimney marked 1688. They are laid in mortar, made by admixture of clay and chopped straw. The house was at first the dwelling of the Bodwell family, among the first of the pioneers in this section. In recent years, it was occupied by the late William B. Gallison and is, perhaps, better known to the present generation as the Gallison house.

There stands in the front yard of this house a noble elm tree which has braved the storms of over 100 years and still appears to be vigorous. It is said that Mrs. Bodwell employed a man to bring the tree, then a sapling, from the woods, and plant it in front of her door. The man was a soldier of the French War, and had just returned from the capture of Quebec. In return for his services, Mrs. Bodwell rewarded him with a quart of molasses.

What is known as the old Bailey house, now occupied by Mrs. Nellie E. Abbott, on the northeast corner of Andover and Parker streets, is one of the few landmarks of the pioneer days.

The old brick house of Daniel Saunders, founder of Lawrence, on the southwest corner of South Broadway and Andover street still stands, the last vestige of the Cross-roads settlement beyond the south end of Andover Bridge.

At the southeast corner of Ames street and Hudson avenue is what remains of the old Ames farm house, though removed from its original location. The old ferry house at Bodwell's Falls is still with us, but somewhat altered. It is located on the west side of Doyle street south of Water street.

The cemetery lot of Daniel Appleton White's family may be found in the rear of 32 and 34 Bradford street.

Den Rock Cemetery or Den Rock Park as it is known today, might be included among the notable of the few old landmarks that remain. The region around Den Rock was alive with weird stories in the old days, and men of today remember the superstition that still clung to the huge rock in their boyhood days. The Devil is said to have visited the place. With a frightful shriek waking the echoes, he was seen in a flash of lightning one stormy, dark night, sliding down a rent in the side of the rock. The place of his descent afterward became known as the Devil's Slide, and more than one boy has spoiled the seat of his pants trying to emulate the pastime of his satanic majesty, which gave this fissure in the rock its name.

There is a tale of a cave under the rock, where moonshiners had a still; where thieves stored their ill-gotten gains, and where counterfeiters plied their illegal trade. Boys have searched for this cave and men have wondered about it, but it is not known that any mortal eye has seen it.

The rock is one of the most picturesque features of this locality and the city is fortunate in owning it. The Park Commissioners took possession of it some years ago, and eventually, if it is not turned into a quarry, it may become a popular adjunct of the city's park system. Though the land around it was originally purchased for a cemetery, and some of it was laid out into avenues, and two or three lots sold to clinch the purpose, it never was used as a cemetery. So far as known, the only thing buried there was a dog. In the old days the Peters family had a brick yard at Den Rock, and to this day there have been burnt and distorted bricks found in the ground about the rock. These were not the work of the Evil One who amused himself by sliding down the rock in flashes of lightning on dismal nights, but were the result of the carelessness of a young Peters lad who fed the fires too freely.

DEN ROCK PARK

HISTORICAL REMNANTS

In this chapter are related what might be regarded as sidelights of history, incidents, dramatic and amusing, odd and whimsical, all of which may be found interesting. For want of a better caption, we call it, "Historical Remnants".

LAFAYETTE'S VISIT

A notable event in the pioneer days was the visit of General Lafayette who on June 20, 1825, passed through this section on his way from Boston to Concord, N. H. The general left Boston at 9 o'clock in the morning, with his suite, riding in an open barouche, drawn by four white horses. The route taken was through Charlestown, Medford, Reading, Andover, through the present Lawrence, and Methuen. He was met at the Andover line by a company of cavalry and escorted to Seminary Hill where the venerable Mr. Kneeland welcomed the honored guest. Several military companies here joined the cavalry and escorted him to Taylor's Hotel where he was welcomed by the faculty of the Institution. About 2 p. m. the distinguished party passed over Andover Bridge, now Broadway Bridge, in Lawrence, escorted by the Andover cavalry. At Methuen there was a welcome by the local militia and by one of the general's old light infantry soldiers, several of whom met him upon the route. At 3 p. m., at the state line, the cavalry delivered their guest to the staff of Governor Morrill of New Hampshire, the Granite State party arriving safely in Concord with their distinguished guest early the same evening. The only halt in Lawrence was to water the fine blooded horses at the Shawsheen corner well, and a short rest upon the old bridge where the picturesque rapids and pleasant scene attracted the attention of the noble Frenchman. All along the route, the people from the country about gathered to give welcome to Lafayette.

THE SHAWSHEEN PIGEON

The wild pigeon does not come directly into local life, but in the olden days, before Lawrence of today was dreamed of, the light lands of Shawsheen fields were extensive rye fields, and pigeons came in great flocks from far and near. The snaring and netting of this game became an occupation for old-time farmers of the region. The market for these birds was at Boston and Salem, and the Shawsheen pigeon was considered a dainty dish in those days.

A Corporation With a Soul

Some people say that corporations have no souls, but this could have hardly applied to the oldest corporation in this locality, the "Proprietors of Andover Bridge". At one time, the directors voted to allow all going from Andover to Methuen to church on Sunday to pass free of toll. The toll man was surprised at the religious interest attracting the Andover people to the north bank, but on inquiry could learn of no special awakening. Feeling that their liberality had been abused, they then voted to allow only those known to the toll man as churchgoers to pass free. This involved that official in dispute as to religious habits of travelers, and it was finally voted to charge saints and sinners alike, both Sundays and weekdays. The record shows, however, that the directors voted for several years to allow Adolphus Durant, Esq., with his family to go from Methuen to Andover to church free of toll. They also gave the reverend Dr. George Packard, the first rector of Grace church, free use of the bridge in his journeys to and from the parish.

An Old-Tyme Drink

Before lager beer became a New England beverage, "Flip" was an old-time drink, compounded of new rum and lemons (now civilized into punch). It was a favorite of the pioneers. Poor's Tavern and the Essex House, at Shawsheen corner, retailed great quantities of this beverage, for there gathered the merry-makers from a wide circle of the country. A glass of flip sold for four pence-ha' penny, a mug of ample size for nine pence and a full bowl of the fluid cost a shilling. New rum, the liquid base of the mixture, cost only 27 cents per gallon at the Newburyport distillery. There was substantial proof in the compounding and sale of this liquor by the glass, mug or bowl. On festive occasions, like military musters, trainings, election gatherings and horse races, flip was sometimes mixed in open rum barrels sawed in half; boys with pestles mashed the lemons, earning six to twelve cents per day.

Pioneer Race Track

The old Turnpike, from the rise at Shattuck street, near the Falls bridge, southward to Phillips Hill, was four rods wide without side-walks; this gave room for four parallel tracks or roadways and chance for races by nags of every gait, four abreast, with every kind of mount. On festival or public days the scene was an animating one. There were no elaborate rules and all sorts of horses and farm jockeys took part. There was little betting of money but a great deal of bragging, disputing and drinking. Wrestling was the old-time precursor of football, and this was also a popular pastime. Saturday afternoon seems to have been the time when nearly all farmers and workers took a half day off and found Shawsheen corner a place for games and great jollity. If moderns believe that old-time intoxicants were harmless or beneficial let them interview the oldest inhabitant whose memory goes back to the days when there were no laws regulating the sale of liquor and no disgrace attending the general use of it, and the illusion will be dispelled.

Junketing in the Old Days

Junketing is not a modern custom. The proprietors of the old Andover Bridge found solace at the Shawsheen corner taverns where their meetings were held. In the season of 1802, Benjamin Ames, the innkeeper at the old Essex House, charged 21 suppers, 19 pints of gin, 4½ mugs of toddy and 4 "beals of punch", with a liberal supply of brandy. The corporation paid 8 pounds, 14 shillings and one penny for these sustaining supplies. The great bill of liquors came when, in the summer of 1802, they rebuilt the bridge. John and Henry Poor, innkeepers at the Shawsheen, supplied the workmen with 111 gallons of N. E. and W. I. rum, and 142 lbs. of sugar for sweetening. The charge was made in many items, and $142 was paid out of the company's treasury therefore. No toddy or punch was supplied to laborers; they took rum straight or went dry. Laborers and mechanics then received 67 cents to $1.00 per day; a yoke of oxen could be hired for 84 cents per day. A night's lodging at the old Shawsheen tavern appears, from old bills, to have cost the traveler eight cents; a generous dinner, 25 cents; a week's board, $1.84.

An Inconsistent Reformer

There was trouble about the toll men at the Andover Bridge selling rum in the early days. A substantial citizen filed a remonstrance, stating that he sold the land on which the toll-house stood with the understanding that grog should never be sold thereon, and that said toll house was a flourishing grog-shop. In reading this protest one admires this old pioneer temperance reformer for a moment, but loses faith in him when reading further on in his complaint where he states that by reason of such

189

sale his own business as a seller of grog at the corner, half a mile beyond, had been ruined, and he had been compelled to close his house of entertainment. The proprietors appointed a committee to secure a toll man who would not sell grog.

THE OLD FIRE DOG

In the hand-tub days of the fire department, every company had its fire-dog. These four-footed "laddies" responded as faithfully as the men, and were sometimes of great assistance in the rescue of people from burning buildings. One, old "Jim Syphon", was a dog with a career. His exploits were many, and his happiest moments were when he was dashing ahead of the fire brigade. He had no particular respect for any one but firemen, and died about the time when the glory of the hand-tub began to wane.

THIS IS NO "FISH STORY"

In view of the fact that in the early days fishing was an important occupation of the inhabitants hereabouts, a reference to it may be interesting. It is no "fish story", we are told, in the usual sense but a true record, that Henry Noyes took, at the fishing pools of the river, near Falls Bridge, 20 shad at one dip of the hand net, and that Noyes and partner, on Sunday, June 3, 1850, took 676 shad, worth $67. It is recorded that, in the early summer of 1851, these old fishermen were taking 2,500 to 3,000 lamprey eels per day below the dam. It is evident that the fisheries of Lawrence have greatly declined in importance. Fishing rights once on the Merrimack had a marketable value and were bought and sold as valuable franchises. In the pioneer days prior to the dam, the Merrimack abounded in fish and was a popular resort for the dusky fishers of the Indian tribes as well as the early settlers. After the establishment of the town and the starting of the mills, a number of the inhabitants continued to secure a livelihood by fishing on the river. Some of the older residents still remember the remnants of the rude fish wharves that extended along the north bank of the river from the dam to the Essex County Training School.

THE HACKMAN AND THE GIANT

Among the amusing trials in the early court was the civil suit of a hackman against a 700 pound giant, exhibited in old Lawrence Hall. The hackman sued the exhibitors for breaking down his coach with the unusual load of physical greatness, and there was a counter suit for damage and delay caused by the breakage. Several interesting points of law were raised. Old citizens who remember some of the incidents that occurred in court in the old days have to laugh, for very funny happenings took place there, often to the distress of the dignity of the presiding justice.

SOME EARLY DESIGNATIONS

Before streets were consecutively numbered in Lawrence, certain localities were known by names that became household words. The region known as "The Plains" lay along the Spicket River to the north of Oak street. The "Patch" was the shanty settlement in South Lawrence west of Broadway. "The Swamp" was the lowland section of Ward Five. The "Corporation Reserve" was the open common that reached from Broadway to Union street, lying between Essex and Methuen streets, unencumbered by any but temporary wooden buildings for nearly twenty years. Merchants' Row was a line of modest brick stores west of Amesbury street. "City Block" included the old Bay State Bank building, on site of the present structure, and several stores to the eastward. The building at the corner of Essex and Appleton streets, directly in the rear of the City Hall, standing for years alone, was known as "The Empire House or Block".

INTELLECTUALLY TOO FULL

An amusing incident occurred at one of the Franklin Library lectures when Dr. Oliver Wendell Holmes spoke upon the subject of "Audiences". He described the various characters that make up a lecture audience, naming lastly "the man who goes out". He goes out, said the doctor, because he is intellectually full to the extent of his capacity to absorb; if he remains longer, he must necessarily run over, like, an overfilled goblet, for the rest of the evening. Just at this point, a tall hearer with a bland childlike expression arose, at the very front, and made for the door. The audience cheered him to the echo and he supposing something interesting had been said, gravely turned, and marched back to his seat, not intending to miss a good thing. For five minutes, the audience laughed at what had to be seen to be appreciated, and the jolly doctor lay over the great mahogany desk of the old City Hall stage in a paroxysm of laughter.

OLD COMMON POND

When ground was broken for the original pond on the common, August 11, 1857, at 7:30 a.m. a company of about 150 persons assembled with teams and spades and made an extensive excavation. General Oliver made a vigorous speech well spiced with Latin and Shakespearian quotations. There were other speakers, poems, etc., but all took a turn at shoveling in the excavation and were happy. The following October a "Pond Festival" was held at City Hall, to raise money for completing the excavation. Then there were more poems, speeches, and music. This pond was curbed and filled the following season (1858) and July 4th, 1859, the full force of the old reservoir on Prospect Hill sent a continuous stream into the air from the centre pipe to a height of 80 feet, to the great delight of visitors and small boys. For many years, the pond was a breeding place for a mixed species of fish, having the blended characteristics of the goldfish and the hornpout. They were fed and petted by children and visitors and led a lazy and luxurious life that proved enervating and destructive. They died from overfeeding and want of exercise. The luxuriant maple trees that encircle the spot were set in 1862-63 under the direction of Mayor W. H. P. Wright. There was much controversy and some bitterness in consequence of the location of this pond at a point east of the centre of the common. A few years ago, the old pond was replaced by the present wading pool.

"Black House" and "Know-Nothing" Riots.

In April 1847, a disturbance occurred at what was termed the "black house", a low resort on Water street. The row grew out of a report, industriously circulated by a woman that upon a certain night she saw a certain man knocked down, loaded upon a wheelbarrow and rolled off into the river. The man referred to chanced for a time to be missing, and great excitement followed upon the supposition that the story were true. Three days later the man returned safe and sound. Indignant that such a report should have grown out of nothing, a crowd assembled and nearly demolished the house. Several arrests were made but the parties were discharged with very light fines.

The riot of 1854 was of far more formidable character. On the one side were arrayed the Irish, commonly referred to in those days as foreigners, and on the other the "Know-Nothing" party. Like the trouble in 1847, that of 1854 was founded wholly upon falsehood. At that, it was based on a very meager matter, but to the receptive minds of blind and eager partisans, it was enough. It was reported that an Oak street Irishman had raised the American flag, union down. The "anti-foreigners" paraded the streets with bands and banners in the evening, shouting defiance to the "enemy". Men, since prominent in public office, joined the procession and took part in the fight that followed. On Common street, between Jackson and Newbury streets, the opposing forces met, when fists, stones, and even pistols were used. Fortunately, no one was killed though the house of the man who was said to have raised the flag was badly damaged. The city subsequently paid the bill. When the excitement was over, it developed that a so-called American had unconsciously offered the insult to the flag, it being raised union-down by mistake. As for a lack of respect for the flag among the Irish of the city, all doubt in that direction must have been removed during the war of the Rebellion when a great many of that race from Lawrence died and bled for the emblem. The names of a number of them may be found on the bronze tablets of the Soldiers' and Sailors' Monument on the common, martyrs to the country's cause.

THE ORANGE RIOT

The next riotous demonstration in the city, in which there was official feeing, occurred on July 12, 1875. On that day, the anniversary of the battle of the Boyne was celebrated by the (Orangemen of Lawrence by a picnic at Laurel Grove, in which they were joined by delegations from Lowell, Woburn, and Arlington. After the picnic, the Orangemen belonging here returned to the city on the Steamer City of Lawrence. They were met at the Water street landing with jeers and derision from several hundred persons who had assembled there. The Orangemen started down Essex street, followed by the crowd. Some stones were thrown, and near the Essex House, somebody tore regalia from one of the picnickers. The Orangemen flourished pistols, and for a time serious bloodshed threatened. Those with regalias sought shelter in the station house, and Mayor Tewksbury was sent for. The latter, with a detail of police officers, escorted the Orangemen to the house of the commander of the lodge on Prospect street. A guard was stationed there and no further disturbance took place. On the way to the house of the Orangemen's leader, however, two of the police officers were hit by stones hurled at them, and somebody in the crowd fired a pistol. The officers returned the fire. About a dozen shots in all were fired. Several persons were slightly injured. Since that time, the Orangemen have paraded here, but met with no opposition.

GENERAL OLIVER LOSES COAT TAIL

Lawrence has seen some turbulent elections, but very few that equaled in animation the last meeting of the electors of the town. B. F. Watson led the Democratic hosts. Early in the day, Mr. Watson made some motion intended to give advantage to his party and was declared out of order. Exasperated at his failure, he planted himself in the way to the polls and in a loud voice announced that "There shall be no voting here today", and called upon his friends to block the passage to the ballot box. The hall was filled with excited men who rushed to the point where Watson was standing. A party fight, on an extended scale, seemed almost unavoidable, when, above the din of angry tumult, the clear, calm voice of William R. Page, chairman of the selectmen, echoed through the hall: "Gentlemen, you will bring in your votes." Instantly General Oliver, agent of the Atlantic Mills, started, over the heads of the crowed, for the ballot box. After a severe struggle, he finally arrived at the object of his aim, minus his coattail. This incident operated like magic in allaying the disturbance. All parties regarded it as a joke worth laughing at, and order was far more easily restored than the coat tail.

THE CITY HALL PUMP

In the old days, everybody had a well or cistern, but a well today is considered almost a prize, so few are they. Probably the most notable of the old time pumps and the best remembered by some of us today was the City Hall pump in Pemberton street. Although the pump was removed some years ago, it is only within a very short time that the well was filled up and the platform removed. It fell a victim to modern ideas of public health preservation. It was a popular resort during the hot weather. Every warm day this well was pumped dry, for its water was sparkling and refreshing, and in great demand.

MANIA FOR WELLS HIT THE CITY

In the late 60's the advocates of temperance in Lawrence were especially active. Although the State had some kind of prohibitory liquor law, and the City had a liquor agent who dealt out such liquors as were legitimately called for, it is said that there were between 200 and 300 places in the city where intoxicants were sold illegally. Temperance societies flourished proportionately, claiming a total of a thousand adherents. Public meetings, several of them, were held every month in the churches and in the City Hall. The result of these meetings seemed to be the demand that many public wells be sunk throughout the city. One prominent citizen suggested that as many as six to a block were necessary. Dr. Packard, the venerable rector of Grace church, headed the petition praying that at least two be dug on the common, and one in Storrow Park. Others wanted wells dug in the cemetery. The City Council did provide some wells in answer to this demand, and those who could imagine themselves satisfied with water had a chance to work a pump handle. The last public pump to disappear was in the city park on Bodwell street. The State Board of

Health diminished the number by condemning most of the wells, but their condemnation did not always close them at once. The people clung to them with great pertinacity and it was with much reluctance in many instances that they were finally given up.

NOTICE TO THE DEAD

In 1859 the following peculiarly worded order passed the City Council: "That Aldermen Bryant and Norris be a committee to prepare a notice to the parties now occupying lots in the cemetery, unpaid for, and to cause such notice to be served on each party, requesting them to call for deeds of such lots and to settle for the same."

GOOD TIME AT CITY'S EXPENSE

In December 1856, both branches of the City Council voted $200 of the city's money for a farewell banquet to themselves and their friends to be served in Lawrence Hall. One hundred and fifty plates were to be laid and the price was to be $1.25 per plate. Some citizens petitioned the Supreme Judicial court for an injunction against this appropriation, which was secured.

OLD FIRE SIGNAL

August 3, 1868, before the fire alarm system was installed, the City Council provided that the fire bells should first strike or toll the number of the ward where the fire was, then ring rapidly for twenty seconds, then stop for about twenty seconds, and then repeat the operation continuously so long as the bells should ring. The City Hall bell was only to toll the number of the ward throughout the whole ringing.

SUN DIAL OWNED BY CITY

For some six or seven years, the city owned a sundial, although there is no record of it having been used. It was purchased in 1856 by the city government from the patentee for $100. During the years that the city had it in its possession, it remained in the safe connected with the city clerk's office, no effort having been made to test its value. What eventually became of it we have failed to learn. The dial was eighteen inches in diameter, and was said to be like those sold to the city of Portland and to the several Maine counties.

Compass Posts on the Common

On the easterly side of the Common, there are three stone posts in line, about 200 feet apart, nearly parallel with Jackson street. These define a true north and south line. The needle of the compass, as is quite generally known, points to the magnetic and not to the true north. The variation from the true north is now about twelve degrees, with an increasing variation westerly of about two and one-half minutes annually. These posts are of valuable assistance to nautical and civil engineers who come here to adjust their instruments. The placing of these markers was brought about by Gilbert E. Hood who as superintendent of schools sent a communication to the City Council in 1871 stating that the legislature of 1870 had provided that the county commissioners of each county should by means of stone posts establish a true north and south line in one or more places in the county. He represented that the common was the most suitable place for the establishment of such a line, and that it would be of great advantage to pupils in the High school. Upon petition of the City Council, the county commissioners placed the posts at their present location.

Distinguised Visitors in Lawrence

Lawrence has had many distinguished visitors, among them being: On November 14, 1847, Daniel Webster and his wife; September 8, 1849, Father Theobald Mathew, the distinguished Irish temperance reformer; in 1850, Horace Greeley, the famous journalist, who 25 years later lectured at City Hall on observations from his early visits; in February, 1853, Thomas Francis Meagher, the Irish patriot and afterwards a major general in the Union Army; in December, 1856, Senator Thomas H. Benton, for 30 years a member of the United States Senate; in 1860, Stephen A. Douglass, Lincoln's great opponent; in the spring of 1863, Gen. George B. McClellan, famous Union commander, and his wife; in August, 1865, Gen. U. S. Grant, commander- in-chief of the Union Armies, with his family and staff; December 21, 1877, Gen. James Shields; January 16, 1880, Charles Stewart Parnell, the Irish statesman; in 1889, President Harrison; in September. 1896, William J. Bryan, Democratic candidate for President and later erstwhile Secretary of State under President Wilson; January 2, 1897, Monsignor Martinelli, apostolic delegate to the United States, from Rome; August 26, 1902, President Roosevelt with members of his Cabinet. In the fall of 191 2, during the Presidential campaign, Lawrence had the distinction of receiving a President and an ex-President of the United States on the same day. In the morning ex-President

Roosevelt, Progressive candidate for President, visited the city, and in the afternoon President Taft, Republican candidate for re-election, came here and addressed a gathering of citizens on the common. A Chinese embassy, a Japanese embassy, and a company of naval officers and officials representing the Czar of all the Russias, have paid special visits to the city, inspecting the mammoth mills with great interest.

NOTES

In the spring of 1896 the Merrimack River rose out of its banks to a height of nine feet nine inches above the crest of the dam, three inches short of that reached during the great freshet of 1852. Little damage was done beyond the flooding of a number of cellars.

On February 1, 1898, occurred the greatest snowstorm in the city's history. In one night 36 inches of snow fell, and for a time business was completely paralyzed.

On June 1, 2 and 3, 1903, the semi-centennial of the founding of Lawrence as a city was celebrated. Imposing ceremonies were held, which were attended by Governor Bates and staff. A big feature was a great parade, representing all nationalities.

Hon. John J. Hurley
Mayor

ROBERT S. MALONEY, Alderman, and Director of Pubic Health and Charities. -Robert S. Maloney was born in Lawrence February 3, 1881. He attended the public schools. At the age of 13 years, he started to work in the Washington Mills. He took up the printer's trade at the old Telegram office in 1895, and he has since become 'prominently identified with that craft and the labor movement. He was the New England organizer for the International Typographical Union for five years. In 1907, he represented the American Federation of Labor as fraternal delegate at the convention of the Trades and Labor Congress of Canada, in Winnipeg, Manitoba. He was elected, as a Republican, to the Board of Aldermen, in 1909, and served as president of the board. In 19 12 he held office as Alderman and first Director of Public Health and Charities under the new city charter. During 1913, he engaged in the job printing business. In 1914, he was again elected Alderman and Director of Public Health and Charities, for a two-year term, at the expiration of which he was re-elected for 1917 and 1918. He served as President of the City Council in 1916, 1917 and 1918. Many notable improvements have been made in the Health and Charities Department during his administration. He has the record for tenure of office as Alderman.

JOHN A. FLANAGAN, Alderman, and Director of Public Property and Parks. - John A. Flanagan is a native of Charlottetown, Prince Edward Island. He was born February 14, 1865. He attended the parochial and public schools at Charlottetown, and upon leaving school he took up the trade of carpentering, with which he has been since identified. In 1884, he moved to Boston. He came to Lawrence from there in May 1896. For several years prior to his entering public office, he had been a building contractor. He was Assistant Superintendent of Public Property in 1905-1911. In 1913 and 1914, he served as Superintendent of Public Property and Inspector of Buildings. In 1914, he was elected Alderman and Director of Public Property and Parks, which office he has since held, being re-elected for a second two-year term in 1916. Alderman Flanagan has the care of all city buildings, parks, and playgrounds. Notable public improvements during his administration have been the construction of the new Oliver (Central Grammar School and the addition to the Tarbox Grammar School, over which he had supervision. The supervised playground movement has been largely developed since his induction into office, and the city's park system has been considerably extended. He is married and has two children.

JOHN F. FINNEGAN, Alderman, and Director of Engineering - John F. Finnegan is a native of Lawrence, being born here April 15, 1878. He attended the parochial and public schools of the city. Upon leaving school, he started to work in the mills, and later was employed in the meat and provision business. Fourteen years ago, he became connected with the Street Department, and has since served in various capacities in that municipal department, securing a wide range of experience. In the municipal elections of 1915, he was nominated and elected Alderman and Director of Engineering for a two-year term, and he was re-elected in 1917 for the years 1918 and 1919. A number of important improvements have been made in the Department of Engineering under his supervision, including the reconstruction of the east section of the old filter and the installation of the auxiliary water supply system on Phillips Hill. The latter improvement has fulfilled a crying need of several years standing. The granite block permanent pavement, for which Lawrence has become noted, has been extended by him in a number of thoroughfares. Alderman Finnegan has charge of the city's streets, sewerage, bridges, and water works. He is not married-

PETER CARR, Alderman and Director of Public Safety - Peter Carr was born in Ireland April 2, 1884. He came to Lawrence, with his parents, at the age of nine years. He attended the public schools, and the Lawrence Commercial School. For a number of years he was employed in the mills. He first appeared in the public eye in the fall of 1913 when he was elected, as a Democrat, to the State Legislature from the 6th Essex Representative District. He served as Representative in 1914 and 1915. He never missed a roll call, and was regarded as an active member of the House. He was deeply interested in labor legislation, being instrumental in having the amount of weekly allowance, under the Workingmen's Compensation Act, increased from one-half to two-thirds of the weekly wage of the applicant. He took a prominent part in the fights for the Merrimack Navigation and Salisbury Beach Reservation Bills. In 1916 and 1917, Mr. Carr engaged in the tea and coffee business- In December 1917, he was elected Alderman and Director of Public Safety for 1918 and 1919. In connection with his administration of the Police and Fire Departments, he has proposed a number of progressive ideas, including a well thought out plan for the motorizing of these departments. Alderman Carr is not married.

HON. JAMES R. TETLER, Senator – James R. Tetler was born in Lawrence August 26. 1877. Upon leaving the public schools, he became a plumber's apprentice, later attending the North End Plumbing Trade School, Boston, where he completed his training. He started in business for himself in 1904. He has been prominent in local politics. In 1903 and 1904, he was in the Common Council, and in 1909 and 1910, he served as a Representative. In 1913, he was elected to the State Senate. He was reelected for a fifth term as Senator in November 1917. Senator Tetler is regarded as an influential member of the upper branch of the Legislature. He has served on the most important committees. The Constitutional Amendment Bill, allowing the State to seize, by eminent domain, land at Salisbury Beach and return it to the people by lease or sale, was twice carried through the Senate by Senator Tetler, only to be defeated in the House the second year. To become law, it was necessary that the measure pass the Legislature two years consecutively. As chairman of the Merrimack Valley delegation, in 1917, he led the fight for the Merrimack River Navigation Bill which passed both branches of the Legislature, but which was vetoed by Governor McCall. Senator Tetler is married.

HON. MICHAEL F. PHELAN Congressman. – Michael F. Phelan was born in Lynn, Mass., October 22, 1875. He was educated in the public schools of Lynn, and Harvard University, receiving an A. B. degree in 1897 and an L. L. B. degree in 1900 from the latter institution. He took up the practice of law in Lynn. In 1905 and 1906, he served as a member of the Massachusetts House of Representatives. In the fall of 1912, he was elected, as a Democrat, from the 7th Massachusetts District, to the 63rd Congress, and in 1914 and 1916, he was re-elected to the 64th and 65th Congresses. He is an active member of the national legislative body, and is regarded as one of the best-informed men in Congress on matters bearing on financial legislation, particularly in relation to banking and currency. He was chairman of one of the sub-committees, which drew up the Federal Reserve Act that has put into the hands of the United States government the control of the banking system of the country, the first notable achievement of the Wilson administration. He also wrote and fathered the bill for the Rural Credits Law which passed Congress in 1916, and which has proven a great boon to the agricultural industry. Congressman Phelan is married and has three children.

HON. LOUIS S. COX. District Attorney. – Louis S. Cox was born in Manchester, N. H, November 22, 1874. Being graduated from the Manchester High School in 1892, he entered Dartmouth College where he received an A. B. degree in 1896. Studied for half of one term at Harvard Medical School. Then entered Boston University Law School. Given his degree in law and admitted to the bar in 1899. In January 1900, he came to Lawrence and became associated with Charles A. DeCourcy, now a Supreme Court Justice. Later became a partner in the law firm of Sweeney, Dow & Cox, now known as Sweeney, Cox & Sargent. He has been prominent in politics. Served three years as member of Republican State Committee, and has also served as chairman of Republican City Committee. Elected to State Senate in fall of 1905. Appointed Postmaster in July 1906, holding that position until January 1914. Elected District Attorney in the fall of 1015 to fill the unexpired term of Henry C. Attwill, and re-elected in 1916 for three years. He was captain of Battery C, Light Artillery, for three years. In September 1917, he was appointed a colonel in the State Guard. Mr. Cox is married and has two children. Note— Mr. Cox was appointed Justice of the Superior Court March 27. 1918.

BERNARD M- SHERIDAN Superintendent of Schools. –Bernard M. Sheridan was born in Wellesley, Mass., October 26, 1866. He was educated in the public schools of his native town. He was graduated from the Wellesley High School in 1883 and from Boston College in 1887. He received the degree of A. M. from his Alma Mater in 1893. The year after his college graduation, he began teaching in Amsterdam, N.Y. The following year he became principal of a grammar school on Cape Cod, where so many other well-known educators served their apprenticeship. Soon after, he was promoted to the High School principalship in the same town. In 1895, he was elected master of the John K. Tarbox grammar school of this city. In 1897, he succeeded B. F. Dame as principal of the Oliver school. He remained in this position until his unanimous election as Superintendent of Schools in April 1904. Mr. Sheridan is well versed in educational matters. He is a member of the National Education Assn., Massachusetts Superintendents' Assn., New England Superintendents' Assn., National Council of Teachers of English, and the Essex County Teachers' Assn. He is the author of "*Speaking and Writing English,*" a course of study in elementary English which has given him a national reputation. Mr. Sheridan is married and has one child.

JAMES D. HORNE, Master of High School. - James D. Home was born in Biddeford. Me., July 21, 1860, coming to Lawrence in 1862. He was educated in the public schools of this city and Methuen, Phillips-Andover Academy and Dartmouth College, being graduated from the last named institution in 1884 with an A. B. degree and with Phi Beta Kappa rank in scholarship. In 1890, Dartmouth conferred the degree of A M. upon him. For three years prior to this academic training, he worked in the weaving room of the Arlington Mills, and he taught district schools in the last three winters of his college course. Upon graduation from college, he began the study of Law in the office of Hon. J. N. Marshall of Lowell; also attended Boston University Law School. During the law course, he served as principal of the Lowell Evening High School. In June 1886, he was admitted to the Massachusetts Bar, and in July 1887, to the Minnesota Bar, having gone to St. Paul, Minnesota, the spring previous. In the fall of 1887, he returned to Lowell. Giving up the practice of law for school teaching, he was elected Sub-Master of the Haverhill High School in 1888. He became Principal of the Brattleboro, Vt., High School in 1891. He came to Lawrence as Principal of the Lawrence High School in 1894.

DANIEL J. MURPHY, City Solicitor. - Daniel J. Murphy was born in Lawrence November 15, 1875. He attended the public schools, and was graduated from the Lawrence High School. He then went to Harvard College, was elected to the Phi Beta Kappa, and completing his college work, entered the Harvard Law School. In June 1903, he was graduated from the law school, having previously been admitted to the bar, in March, at Boston. While attending law school he taught in the college as an assistant in History. For a short time, he was in the office of Judge J. F. Quinn at Salem. He began the practice of law in Lawrence in October 1903. was later a member of the firms of Knox, Coulson & Murphy, and Coulson & Murphy, and since 1909 has conducted law offices of his own. He has been City Solicitor from 1906 to 1908 and from 1910 to date. Counsel to the Lawrence Bridge Commissions, and Associate or Town Counsel for the Town of .Andover, since 1906. As City Solicitor for the City of Lawrence, he has defended the city in important cases, in which his contentions have been established as precedents in municipal law. In 1905, Mr. Murphy married Mary T. Curran of Andover. He has three children.

DR. PETER L. McKALLAGAT, Assistant City Physician.- Dr. Peter L. McKallagat was born in Lawrence February 13. 1883. He received his preparatory education in the public schools of this city, being graduated from the Lawrence High School in 1902. In the fall of that year, he entered Columbia Medical School of New York City, and upon completing his course of studies there in 1906, he was given his degree. For the two years following, he was house surgeon at St.Vincent's Hospital, New York City, and during the summer of 1909 he had charge of the Seaside Floating Hospital of St. John's Guild, New York. On October 15. 1909, he took up general practice in Lawrence. Dr. McKallagat has established a large practice, having had remarkable success in his cases, particularly in the surgical line. He was appointed Assistant City Physician in 1915. He handles all the surgical cases at the Municipal Hospital, which has been well equipped for such service by the Department of Public Health and Charities. Facilities are provided to meet the requirements for major operations, as well as the minor surgical cases. Dr. McKallagat is married and has two children.

DR. WILLIAM J. SULLIVAN, City Physician. Dr.-William J. Sullivan was born in Lancaster, Mass., June 17, 1860. He was educated in the public schools of Lancaster and the New York University and Bellevue Hospital Medical College, being graduated from the latter institution on March 15, 1886. He came to Lawrence in July of that year. For many years, he has been prominently identified with the medical profession here, and he is one of the city's oldest practitioners. In 1893, he was appointed United States Examining Surgeon for Pensions by President Cleveland, and he still holds that position. He served as President of the Board of Trade in 1909 and 1910 and as Chairman of the Board of Health in 1910. For several years be was a member of the Democratic State Committee, and in 1906 he served on the executive committee of that organization. In 1912, he was appointed Assist. City Physician. He was named City Physician Jan. 5, 1915 and by virtue of that office he is also a member of the Board of Health. As City Physician, he has supervision of the Municipal and Tuberculosis Hospitals. He has been connected with the Massachusetts Medical Society for the past 29 years, and was President of the Essex North District of that society in 1907 and 1908. Dr. Sullivan is married, and has one son.

JOHN J. DONOVAN, Chairman of Central Bridge Commission. –John J. Donovan was born in Lawrence January 1, 1862. He attended the public schools of the city, and was graduated from the Lawrence High School in 1880. Upon leaving school, he entered the office of the City Clerk. In 1883, he was appointed Assistant City Clerk and Clerk of Committees, which position he held until 1892. In the fall of 1891, he was elected Register of Deeds for the Northern District of Essex County. He held that office for three years. On November 20, 1894, he took up the study of law in the Boston University Law School, and in 1896 was given a degree magna cum laude. He was admitted to the bar in July 1896, and began the practice of law in Lawrence. He has gained considerable reputation for his success in handling cases in which municipal law was involved. In 1897 and 1898, he was a member of the Licensing Board for the City of Lawrence. He has served for many years on the local Civil Service Board, and is thoroughly familiar with the Civil Service law. He was appointed a member of the Central Bridge Commission by Mayor Cahill in 1911, being elected chairman of that board upon its organization. Mr. Donovan is married and has one child.

FRANCIS J. MORRIS, Deputy Chief of the Fire Department. –Francis J. Morris is a native of Lawrence, being born October 3. 1867. He attended the public schools. After leaving school. For a while, he was employed in the mills, and later at Blacksmithing. In December 1891, he was appointed chief's driver in the fire department, under Chief Melvin Beal. He served in that capacity until July 1, 1900, when he was appointed Captain of Engine 8's company on Ames Street. In 1912. During the big textile strike, he was given a provisional appointment as Deputy Fire Chief, and in April 1913, he received a regular appointment as such. Mr. Morris has had a wide experience as a fire fighter during his 25 years of service in the fire department of Lawrence. For nearly nine years, he was closely associated with Chief Beal who was regarded as a competent department head, and later, as Captain and Deputy Chief, he participated in and directed the successful handling of difficult fires. In January 1918, Deputy Chief Morris was appointed Acting Chief, succeeding Chief Dennis E. Carey, who was removed by the new Director of Public Safety, Alderman Peter Carr. Mr. Morris is married.

DR. JOHN J. DEACY, Health Physician. -Dr. John J. Deacy was born in Lawrence April 6, 1889. He obtained his preparatory education in the public schools of the city and was graduated with the class of 1907 from the Lawrence High School. He entered Tufts College Medical School in 1909, completing the course of studies there and receiving his degree in 1913. During the summer of that year, he was an interne on the Boston Floating Hospital, and the following fall became an interne and a resident surgeon at St. John's Hospital, Lowell. He served fourteen months at the latter institution, leaving to take up practice in Lawrence. Dr. Deacy has made a special study of surgery, and each year spends several weeks attending the best surgical clinics in the country. He was appointed Health Physician for the City of Lawrence in March 1915. He has supervision of all contagious disease cases, which demand the attention of the Municipal Health Department To him is given the responsibility of guarding- against the outbreak of epidemics. That the city has been remarkably free from serious spreading of contagious diseases is due considerably to the careful and capable attention of its Health Physician. Dr. Deacy is not married.

MAURICE F. McKENNA, City Marshal. -Maurice F. McKenna is a native of Lawrence. He was born October 12, 1873. His education was obtained in the public schools of the city. Upon leaving school, he went to work in the Arlington Mills where he was employed in the dyeing and finishing departments for eight years. Later he became a teamster in the Street Department and in 1900 was elected Superintendent of Streets. For a number of years afterward he was engaged in business. In 1914, he was appointed City Marshal by Alderman James W. Cadogan, Director of Public Safety, and continued in that office during 1915, 1916 and 1917. Just prior to the expiration of Alderman Cadogan's second term in office. City Marshal McKenna resigned to take the position of City Purchasing Agent, to which he was elected by the City Council to fill the vacancy caused by the resignation of Hugh S. McConnor, the first Purchasing Agent under the new city charter. The office of Purchasing Agent is one of the most important offices within the gift of the City Government. With the exception of very minor items, all supplies for the municipal departments are bought through the Purchasing Agent. Mr. McKenna is married and has two children. He was succeeded, as City Marshal, by Timothy J. O'Brien.

HON. MICHAEL F. CRONIN, Postmaster.-Michael F. Cronin was born in Ireland March 1, 187S8. When an infant he came to Lawrence with his parents. He obtained his preparatory education in the public schools of the city, and was graduated from the Lawrence High School in 1818. The fall of that year, he took up the study of law at Boston University Law School. He received his degree in June 1901. In the following September he was admitted to the bar. He has been active in local politics, having been prominently identified with the Democratic Party. He was elected to the Board of Aldermen in 1904. He served as chairman of the Democratic City Committee in 1905 and 1906, and in 1909, he was the Democratic candidate for Mayor. On January 1, 1914, he became Postmaster, having been appointed by President Wilson. Lender his administration the Lawrence post office has maintained a high standard of efficiency. Besides handling the great volume of business in Lawrence, the service extends to the towns of North Andover and Methuen. (In January. 1918, the latter town became the City of Methuen, though still a part of the Lawrence post office district). Sub-postal stations have been established in various sections of the city for the convenience of the public. Mr. Cronin is not married.

NATHANIEL E. RANKIN, Clerk of District Court.- Nathaniel E. Rankin is a native of Taunton, Mass., being born Sept. 12, 1874. He came to Lawrence at the age of six years. He attended the public schools here and was graduated from the Lawrence High School in 1895. Upon leaving school, he engaged in the dyeing business for two years. In 1898, he entered Boston University Law School, and received his degree in 1900. In October of that year, he was admitted to the bar. He has been prominent in local politics. For five years, he was a member of the Republican State Committee. In 1908, he was appointed Public Administrator for the Lawrence District by Governor Guild, and in 1909, he was appointed by Judge Davis as local examiner for the Land Court. In December 1916, Governor McCall appointed him Clerk of the Lawrence District Court. This court handles the civil cases of Methuen, Andover, and North Andover, and has concurrent jurisdiction on all criminal matters of those towns, besides the conduct of lower court cases in Lawrence. Mr. Rankin is a member of Division 3 Exemption Board for the examination of local draft cases. He was selected for this position shortly after the passage of the draft law by Congress, following the declaration of war with Germany in April 1917. He is married and has two children.

WALTER COULSON, President of Bar Association. -Walter Coulson was born in Campo Seco, California, and October 10. 1864. He came to Lawrence when five years of age. He attended the public schools and was graduated from the Lawrence High School in 1884. He received his higher education at Harvard University and the Boston University Law School. In October 1889, he was admitted to the bar. While attending law school he was connected with the office of Charles A. DeCourcy, now Supreme Court Justice, of whom he later became a partner and with whom he was associated until Mr. DeCourcy was appointed to the bench in 1902. He is prominent among the local legal fraternity, and he is a member of the County, State, and National Bar Associations, besides being a member of the Executive Committee of the Massachusetts Bar Association. Mr. Coulson is attorney for many of the large corporations of the city. He has made a specialty of corporation law. In the interpretation of which he has gained considerable reputation. He served on the School Committee from 1890 to 1896. In 1911, he was elected President of the Lawrence Bar Association, which position he has since held. His activity in behalf of the organization has inspired a lively interest in its affairs. He is married.

HON. ARCHIE N. FROST, Clerk of Courts.-Archie N. Frost was born in Lawrence July 26, 1872. Graduating from the Lawrence High School in 1890, he studied for one year at Colby College, after which he entered Brown University. He was graduated from Brown with an A. B. degree in 1894. In the fall of that year, he began the study of law at the Boston University Law School. In 1895, he became associated with the law firm of DeCourcy & Coulson, and in 1898, he was admitted to the bar. He served in the Common Council in 1898 and as a Representative in 1899, 1900 and 1901. He was a member of the State Senate in 1902 and 1903. In 1908, he was appointed Special Assistant to the United States Attorney General in charge of the Government land suits in Oklahoma. He returned to Lawrence in 1914, and became a law partner of Walter Coulson. He was elected a delegate to the Republican National Convention, held at Chicago in 1916. In the spring of 1917, he was chosen a member of the State Constitutional Convention. In May 1917, he was appointed by the Supreme Court as Clerk of Courts for Essex County, to fill the vacancy caused by the death of E. B. George, and at the State election following he was elected to that position by the people. Mr. Frost is married and has two children.

THOMAS M. JORDAN, Vice Chairman of School Board. -Thomas M. Jordan was born in Lawrence December 14, 1871. He attended the public schools. Upon leaving school, he went to work in the mills. Later he learned the barbering business, in which he is now established. Mr. Jordan has been prominently identified with the public life of the community. He served in the Common Council in 1908 and 1909 and in he Board of Aldermen in 1910 and 1911. By virtue of his office as President of the Board of Aldermen, he became Acting Mayor in July 1910. Upon the resignation of Mayor White. He served in that capacity until the election of Mayor Cahill by the City Council. He was elected to the School Board in December 1914, being re-elected for another two-year term in 19x6. He was chosen vice chairman of the board in 1917. Mr. Jordan has been an active and progressive member of the government. Among the notable ideas advocated by him was that of paving a certain number of streets each year. That program has been carried out, with the result that today Lawrence is noted for its fine thoroughfares. Another idea of his is the Educational Council, which has proved a valuable adjunct to the School Board, in an advisory way, in educational matters. Mr. Jordan is married and has two children.

MOSES MARSHALL, Register of Deeds. -Moses Marshall is a native of Lawrence, being born November 20, 1870. He attended the public schools, and later for a number of years he was employed in the mills. In 1892, he took up a college preparatory course of study at the Friends School, Providence, and R.I., from which he was graduated in 1896. He then entered Haverford College where he studied for two years. He began the study of law at the Boston University Law School in 1898. He received his degree in 1901, being admitted to the bar the same year. Mr. Marshall has been active in local politics. In 1904, he served in the Board of Aldermen, and in 1906, he was the Republican nominee for Mayor. In the fall of 1907, he was elected Register of Deeds for the Northern Essex District, for a term of five years. He was re-elected to that office in 1912, and for a third term in 1917. As Register of Deeds, he has charge of all papers, deeds and records relating to real estate in the district, which comprises Lawrence, Methuen. Andover and North Andover. His legal training especially adapts him for this responsible duty. By virtue of his office as Register of Deeds, he is also assistant recorder of the Land Court for this district. Mr. Marshall is married.

JAMES H. BRIDE, Vice Chairman of Public Safety Committee. -James H. Bride was born in Lawrence April 16. 1867. He was educated in the public schools. Upon leaving school, he went to work in the mills. He started his career in the plumbing business as a clerk with W. F. Rutter & Company. In that line of activity, he advanced rapidly. Today he is regarded as one of the most prominent men in the business in this section of the country. He was admitted to the Rutter firm in 1891, the firm then comprising William F. Rutter, Sr., William F. Rutter, Jr., and James H. Bride. Upon the death of Mr. Rutter, Jr., a few years later, E. Eben Grimes became a partner, and in 1906, when Mr. Rutter, Sr., retired, the firm became known as Bride, Grimes & Company. For years, this concern has been the leading heating and plumbing contractors in Lawrence. It has installed the heating and plumbing systems in all of the large mills. Mr. Bride takes a keen and active interest in public affairs. In April 1917, upon the organization of the Public Safety Committee to meet emergencies arising from the war with Germany, he was appointed chairman of the Finance Committee, and later named Vice Chairman of the Executive Committee. Mr. Bride is married and has three children.

HON. JOSEPH J. FLYNN, Member of Central Bridge Commission. -Joseph J. Flynn was born in Ireland May 1, 1862. When a little over one year of age he came to Lawrence with his mother. He attended the public schools. At the age of 11 years, he started to work in the Pemberton Mill. In 1881, when the Lawrence Opera House was opened, he took a position there as advertising agent and stage manager, later becoming treasurer and manager. He has also managed a number of summer park theatres, besides having had several shows on the road. Thirty-three years ago, he established the bill posting business to which, since severing his connection with the Opera House in 1900, he has devoted his time exclusively. This business has grown tremendously, now covering 40 cities and towns in three states. Mr. Flynn has been a prominent figure in local politics. In 1895 and 1896, he served as representative and in 1898 and 1904 as senator in the State Legislature. He was also at one time nominated Democratic candidate for State Treasurer, besides securing a nomination for Congress from this district. He was appointed a member of the Central Bridge Commission by Mayor Cahill in 1911. He is married and has five children.

DANIEL J. MURPHY, Superintendent of Sanitation –Daniel J. Murphy was born in Strafford, Vt. October 12. 1861, at the age of four years he came to Lawrence. He was educated in the parochial and public schools, and Carney's Commercial School of this city. Upon leaving school, he entered the office of the McKay Sewing Machine Association as an office boy. During his 25 years with this concern, he worked his way up to the position of paymaster. The plant was located in the building on Haverhill Street, now occupied by the Walton Shoe Company. When it was absorbed by the United Shoe Machinery Company, Mr. Murphy was transferred, as assistant manager, to the Haverhill branch office of the latter concern, where he remained for three years, until he was transferred to the Boston office. Three years later, he took the position of treasurer and general manager of the MurphyTyler Company, Inc., which manufactures waterproofing for shoe leather. He still has a controlling interest in that company. In 1915, he was appointed Superintendent of Sanitation and Chairman of the Health Board, by Alderman Robert S. Maloney. His executive ability has aided greatly in placing the Municipal Health Department on a well-organized basis. Mr. Murphy is married and has one child.

RICHARD WARD, President Chamber of Commerce –Richard Ward was born in Greenfield, N. H. July 14. 1879. He moved to Lancaster, Mass., in 1881. He was graduated from the Lancaster High School in 1896, and in the fall of that year, he entered Dartmouth College. In 1901, he was given an A. B. degree at Dartmouth, the following year receiving a master's degree in commercial science from that institution. Upon completing his college training, he entered the office of the Western Electric Company at Chicago, with which concern he remained for one year. He then became connected with the Hapgoods, employment experts, of St. Louis. In 1905, Mr. Ward went into the lead manufacturing business in St. Louis, under the firm name of the McDuffee, Ward Lead Manufacturing Company, dealing extensively in plumbers' supplies. He came to Lawrence in 1908, when he became president and treasurer of the Wright Manufacturing Company, which controls the Wright braid mill. In 1917, he was elected President of the Chamber of Commerce. His energetic personality and executive ability have infused new life into that organization. Mr. Ward is prominently identified with the banking and commercial, as well as the industrial interests of the city. He is married and has three children.

MICHAEL F. BROGAN, Chairman of License Commission. –Michael F. Brogan was born in Lawrence October 23, 1868. He attended the parochial and public schools. Upon leaving school, he went to work in the mills. At the age of 17 years, he began his career by learning the machinist trade with the McKay Metallic Fastening Association. When that industry moved to Winchester, he went with it. His advance was rapid. He became thoroughly familiar with the manufacture and setting up of every machine produced by the McKay concern and by the United Shoe Machinery Company, with which he later became connected. For 10 years, he travelled all over the United States as a salesman of shoe machinery and findings. During the past 15 years, he has held a position as inventor with the United Shoe Machinery Company. He has evolved many new devices for the manufacture of shoes. Through the products of his inventive mind, he has become prominent in the shoe machinery industry of the country. Mr. Brogan came into public life of the city in 1914, when he was appointed a member of the License Commission, for a term of six years, by Mayor Scanlon. In 1916, he was named chairman of the board by Mayor Hurley. Mr. Brogan is married and has one child.

CHARLES E. BRADLEY, Chairman of Citizens Assn. (1912) –Charles E. Bradley was born in Lowell, December 8, 1862. He came to Lawrence in 1873. Upon leaving school, he went to work in the old fish line mill in South Lawrence. Later he learned the machinist trade and, for a number of years, he was employed in several of the local machine shops. In 1890, he opened a real estate and fire insurance office, with which business he has since been prominently identified. With his brother, William J. Bradley, he is one of the city's largest individual property owners, having extensive and very valuable holdings on the main street. They pay annually to the city in taxes on real estate over $7,000. Charles E. Bradley served in the Common Council in 1888. He has always manifested a keen interest in public affairs, and has been ever ready to lend his support to movements for the city's welfare. Following the great textile strike of 1912, when the Citizens Association was organized for the purpose of rehabilitating Lawrence's good name by overcoming the ill effects of misrepresentations of unscrupulous writers and agitators, Mr. Bradley was chosen Chairman. His activity aided greatly in bringing about the remarkable success of that organization. Mr. Bradley has three children.

RICHARD J. SHEA, City Auditor. Born in Lawrence May 30, 1855. He attended parochial and public schools. At the age of 12 years, he went to work in the mills. Later, for a number of years, he was employed at the grocery business. In January 1886, he was elected Clerk of the Common Council, and the following April he was elected City Auditor, succeeding Walter R. Rowe. Mr. Shea was the last Clerk of the Common Council, holding that office 26 years. He is married and has two children.

EDWARD J. WADE, City Clerk,. Born in Lawrence April 10, 1878. He was educated in the public schools, Villanova College and Boston University Law School, being admitted to the bar in 1903. He became Assistant City Clerk in April 1910, and was appointed City Clerk Sept. 19, 1910, to fill the vacancy caused by the resignation of Cornelius J. Corcoran. The following December he was elected by the people. Mr. Wade has a wide knowledge of municipal affairs. He is married and has five children.

DANIEL SAUNDERS, Member of School Board. A native of Lawrence, born September 25, 1891. He was educated in the public schools of the city, Bowdoin College, Harvard Law School and Boston University Law School. In 1917, he was admitted to the bar. He was elected to the School Board in 1915 for two years, and he was re-elected in 1917. Mr. Saunders is the great grandson of Daniel Saunders, the founder of Lawrence. He is not married.

JOHN J. MURPHY, Chairman of Assessors. Born in Lawrence January 6, 1858. He attended the public schools. At the age of 10 years, he went to work in the mills. In 1890 and 1891, he served in the Common Council. He was elected Assessor in January 1895, and in 1899, he was made chairman of the board. Mr. Murphy has a keen knowledge of property valuation in Lawrence. He is married and has four children.

214

WILLIAM A. KELLEHER, City Treasurer. Born in Lawrence May 27, 1875. He attended the parochial and public schools. Upon leaving school, he went to work in the mills, and later he engaged in the tobacco business for a number of years. He has been prominent in local politics. In 1903 and 1904, he was a member of the Common Council, and in 1908 of the Board of Aldermen. He served as Representative in 1906, 1907 and 1908. In the fall of 1909, he was elected City Treasurer. Mr. Kelleher is married and has one child.

MICHAEL A. FLANAGAN, Representative. Born in Lawrence February 21, 1890. He was graduated from the Lawrence High School in 1906, and Boston College, receiving an A. B. degree from that institution in 1911. He then entered Boston University Law School, getting his degree in law and being admitted to the bar in 1914. In November, 1916, he was elected Representative from the 8th Essex District. He was re-elected in 1917. Mr. Flanagan is not married.

ARTHUR D. MARBLE - City Engineer. Born in Hingham, Mass., April 10, 1853. He attended the public schools and Derby Academy at Hingham. In April 1874, he came to Lawrence, and became first assistant to City Engineer Baldwin Coolidge. In the summer of 1875, the office of City Engineer was abolished, but the department was retained and the City Government continued to employ Mr. Marble as Acting City Engineer. When the office was re-established in 1898, he was elected City Engineer. Mr. Marble has one daughter.

ARTHUR BOWER, Representative. Born in England September 7, 1877. He came to Lawrence in 1887. Upon leaving school, he went to work in the mills, becoming a weaver and later taking up the loom fixing trade. He served in the Common Council in 1907 and 1908. In the fall of 1913, as a Republican, he was elected Representative from the 5th Essex District. He is now serving his fourth term in the lower branch of the State Legislature.

FRED F. FLYNN - Probation Officer. Born in Lawrence April 25, 1873. Upon leaving school, he learned the machinist trade. He was appointed a patrolman in the Police Department in 1896, serving as inspector in 1904 and 1905. In April 1907, he was appointed a member of the Detective Department of the District Police. In that capacity, he served in many important cases in every county of the state. He was appointed Probation and Court Order of the Lawrence District Court September 1, 1916. Mr. Flynn is married.

MICHAEL S. O'BRIEN - "Father" of Playgrounds. Born in Lawrence February 17, 1883, He was educated in the public schools of the city, Dartmouth College, and Harvard Law School. Admitted to the bar in 1909. In 1912, he served as Alderman and first Director of Public Property and Parks under the new city charter. That year he inaugurated the supervised playground movement, which has since become one of the most important functions of the municipality. Mr. O'Brien is married and has two children.

DENNIS F. DONOVAN - City Pharmacist. Born in Lawrence October 27, 1872. He attended the public schools. Upon leaving school, he learned the drug business, taking a course of study at the Massachusetts College of Pharmacy. On May 1, 1905, he was elected City Pharmacist, succeeding Edward L. Barrett, the first to hold that position. The City Pharmacy supplies the Municipal and Tuberculosis Hospitals, the outside poor, and the medicinal needs of other city departments. Mr. Donovan is married.

DR. JOHN H. BANNON - School Physician. Born in Bolton, England, Sept. 10, 1877. He was educated in the parochial schools and the University of Maryland Medical School, being graduated from the latter institution in 1899. He was elected to the School Board in 1904 for a term of three years. In August 1906, he was elected the first School Physician. In 1910, he was again elected to the School Board, but was legislated out of office in 1912 by the new city charter. Dr. Bannon is not married.

WILLIAM A. WALSH - Public Librarian Born in Boston July 11, 1868. He was educated in the Boston public schools and Boston College. For a number of years he was an officer at the Boston Public Library. In May 1901, he was elected Librarian at the Lawrence Public Library, .succeeding Frederick H. Hedge. During his administration, the main library building has been enlarged and three delivery stations have been established. In 1903, Mr. Walsh was honored with an M. A. degree by Boston College. He is married and has three children.

WILLIAM LORD - Superintendent of Cemetery. For nearly 30 years connected with the Cemetery Department of the City of Lawrence. After attending the public schools, he went to work as clerk of that department in 1889. In 1896, he was made superintendent. He has supervision of Bellevue Cemetery.

DR. JOSEPH A. LEVEK - School Physician. Born in Newmarket, N. H. on February 19, 1890. He came to Lawrence in 1903, and was graduated from the Lawrence High School in 1907. He received his degree from Tufts College Medical School in 1913. He was an interne at the Boston City Hospital, Boston Floating Hospital, Massachusetts General Hospital, and the Lawrence General Hospital. In April 1915, he began practice in Lawrence. He was appointed School Physician February 16, 1916. Dr. Levek is married.

DR. GEORGE W. DOW - Medical Examiner. Born in Methuen, September 23, 1852. He was educated at Colby Academy, Brown University, and the Harvard Medical School. He served on the School Board in 1891-'93, and in the Board of Aldermen in 1894 and 1895. For a number of years he was City Physician. He was appointed Medical Examiner in 1902 by Governor Crane. Dr. Dow is married and has one child.

HUGH S. McCONNOR - Purchasing Agent. Born in Lawrence August 10, 1881. He was educated in the public schools and Boston University Law School, being admitted to the liar in 1906. In 1912, when the new city charter went into effect, the City council elected him the city's first Purchasing Agent. He filled this very responsible position creditably until Nov. 1, 1917, when he resigned to become Secretary of the Federal Land Bank at Springfield. Mr. McConnor is married and has one child.

JOHN P. RYAN - State Armorer. Born in Lawrence September 6. 1863. He served in the Common Council in 1892 and 1893. On February 22, 1893, he received his appointment as State Armorer from Governor Russell. He is the custodian of the property of the State Militia, and has charge of the State Armory on Amesbury Street. During his service, he has seen the local militia units off to war on three occasions, and has been very active in their interests. Mr. Ryan is married, and has three children.

DR. MEYER SCHWARTZ - School Physician. Born in Russia, December 25, 1878. He came to this country at the age of seven years. He attended the public schools at Manchester, N. H., and was graduated from the Manchester High School. He studied medicine at the University of Maryland, receiving his degree in 1902. In the fall of that year, he took up practice in Lawrence. He was appointed School Physician in 1909, which office he has since held. Dr. Schwartz is married and has one child.

DR. CHARLES A. McCARTHY - School Physician. Born in Ireland April 18. 1872. He came to Lawrence in 1876, from Boston. He attended the parochial and public schools, being graduated from Lawrence High School in 1890. Upon leaving school, he learned the drug business, at which he spent several years. He was graduated from the New York University and Bellevue Hospital Medical College in 1899. In 1900, 1901 and 1902 he served on the School Board. He was appointed School Physician in 1916. Dr. McCarthy is not married.

MICHAEL H. JORDAN - Representative .Born in Lawrence, February 7, 1862. He attended the parochial and public schools. For a number of years he played professional baseball, being prominently identified with teams of the New England League, the I and I League of the Middle West, the Texas League, and the Atlantic Association. In 1915, he was elected Representative from the 6th Essex District. He was re-elected in 1916 and 1917. Mr. Jordan has two children.

JOSEPH V. BROGAN - Sealer of Weights and Measures. Born in Lawrence, March 16, 1871. He was educated in the parochial and public schools. For a number of years he was employed as a meat and provision clerk, and later became established in that business. In 1901, he was appointed Sealer of Weights and Measures by Mayor Leonard. Mr. Brogan has the supervision of all weights and measures in Lawrence, and supervision of the enforcement of the law relating to peddlers and itinerant venders. He is not marri

FREDERICK BUTLER - Representative. Born in Lawrence, September 21, 1884. He was educated in the public schools of the city. Highland Military Academy and Bryan & Stratton's Commercial School. Upon completing his education, he entered a banker and broker's office. He later became engaged in the clothing business. He was elected, as a Republican, from the 7th Essex District to the Massachusetts House of Representatives in the fall of 1913. He is now serving his fifth term as a Representative.

DENNIS SHINE - City Messenger. Born in Ireland August' 17, 1855. He came to Lawrence in 1879. For 12 years, he was employed in the shoe shops of Haverhill and Lynn. In 1898, he took the position of Assistant City Messenger under William H. Merrow, his predecessor. He was elected City Messenger in January of 1910. He has the care of the auditorium and offices in the City Hall, besides acting as messenger for the City Government. Mr. Shine is married and has three children.

A. B. SUTHERLAND - A. B. SUTHERLAND COMPANY. In the plant of the A. B. Sutherland Company, 309 Essex St., Lawrence has one of the biggest department stores outside of Boston. The concern has almost an acre of selling space, occupying four floors and basement and having a frontage of 85 feet on the main street. The concern was established in 1900, as Robertson, Sutherland & Co., it comprising Archibald M. Robertson, Andrew B. Sutherland, and John J. Mathison. They took over the business of A. W. Stearns, one of Lawrence's pioneer merchants. The remarkable growth of the concern is noted especially by the fact that in 1900 the store had a floor space of 13,950 square feet, as compared to 43,125 square feet now in use. The first step toward expansion was taken in 1904 when possession of the adjoining four-story building was obtained. In 1912, more space was engaged on the upper floors of the Arlington Trust Company building. In 1909, the company was incorporated. In 1916, Mr. Robertson retired, and the name of the firm was changed, in 1917, to the A. B. Sutherland Company. Mr. Sutherland is president, treasurer and manager; John J. Mathison, vice-president, and Mrs A. B. Sutherland, clerk. The shopping advantages of this store have been influential in attracting shoppers from surrounding cities and towns. It is the city's largest mercantile establishment. It has 35 complete departments, selling practically everything that is carried in a modern department store, including women's, misses' and children's garments, millinery, dry goods, carpets, draperies, china, crockery, kitchen goods, groceries, etc. It is reputed to be the best-lighted store in New England. It is situated in the very heart of the business section, within easy access to the main thoroughfares and the railroad stations. All streetcars pass its doors. Among its advantages is a prompt delivery service, with two deliveries daily in Lawrence and to the surrounding districts. The concern employs 150 people.

MICHAEL T. SULLIVAN - MICHAEL J. SULLIVAN, INC. Lawrence's largest furniture house, and one of the biggest north of Boston, is the establishment of Michael J. Sullivan, Inc., 218-226 Essex Street. This concern was first established in 1887, as a partnership, when Timothy J. Buckley, Michael A. McCormick, and Michael J. Sullivan bought out the Business of Patrick Sweeney at 222 Essex Street. Four years later the firm took the adjoining store, 218-220 Essex Street. The growth of the concern has been steady, and from time to time, it has been necessary to secure additional floor space to meet the demand upon its facilities. In 1901, upon the death of Mr. McCormick, the firm became known as Buckley & Sullivan. In 1914, Mr. Buckley retired from the business, which was then incorporated, Mr. Sullivan taking into the firm some of the employees of long standing. The corporation took the name of Michael J. Sullivan, Inc., with Mr. Sullivan as president and treasurer, and Joseph R. Guilfoyle, secretary. The directors are M. J. Sullivan, A. M. Sullivan, J. R. Guilfoyle and John G. Praetz. In the fall of 1914 the large store west of the original location was added on the ground floor, giving a frontage of 90 feet on the main street. The entire four floors and basement have a floor space of about 35,000 square feet. Besides, two large storehouses are used to carry the extensive stock of the concern. The establishment is equipped with all the modern facilities. Its immense show windows and large ground area provide excellent means for displaying the stock. The concern carries a complete line of house furnishings, pianos, talking machines and office furniture. It is the sole agent in the city for most of the nationally advertised household specialties. It is reputed to be the leading rug and carpet house of Lawrence. An important department is the upholstering and cabinet making, a feature of the business that has existed from the beginning. The store attracts many buyers from surrounding cities and towns, it being widely known for its great variety of stock and its shopping advantages.

LEONARD E. BENNINK - REID & HUGHES COMPANY. The Reid & Hughes Company, 225-235 Essex Street, is one of Lawrence's largest mercantile concerns. As a dry goods department store, it is complete in every respect, and it stands high in the estimation of the purchasing public. The business was founded in 1869 by Thomas Simpson and William Oswald who bought out the dry goods business of A.Sharpe at 213 Essex street, and started under the firm name of Simpson & Oswald. The concern soon outgrew the original quarters, and it moved to the present location, taking in Nos. 229, 231, and 233 of the present store. Additions were later made, east and west, until the entire street floor of the present establishment was occupied. After a successful partnership of several years, Mr. Simpson withdrew from the firm. Mr. Oswald took over the entire business, conducting it until 1893 when, his health failing, he sold it to Reid & Hughes, leasing the building for 10 years with the proviso that he could take the business back at the end of that time should he choose to do so. According to the agreement, after 10 years, Mr. Oswald bought back the business. He formed the corporation of William Oswald Company, and he made extensive improvements in the store. However, at the end of the year his health was such that he was forced to retire, and the present corporation of Reid & Hughes Co., was formed by Adam Reid, James J. Hughes, Eugene T. Adams and Leonard E. Bennink, to which George F. Hughes was admitted later. In 1905 occurred the death of James J. Hughes, followed by that of Mr. Reid in 1907 and that of George F. Hughes in 1914, the interests of the latter two being taken over by Mr. Adams and Mr. Bennink. In 1918 the interests of the James J. Hughes estate were acquired by Mr. Bennink, giving him a majority control of the corporation. He immediately proceeded to make radical improvements, after securing an extension of the lease. The store has a frontage on Essex Street of 105 feet, with a depth of 85 feet. The firm occupies the whole building. There are 35,000 square feet of floor space.

STANLEY GRAIN COMPANY. Lawrence has one of the largest grain warehouses in New England in the plant of the Stanley Grain Company, located at the corner of Broadway and Essex Street. This concern handles the greater part of the flour coming into Lawrence. Its facilities are such that the city's entire supply of grain and flour could be easily received and distributed by the company. The concern occupies the old inward freight house of the Boston & Maine Railroad. It is an ideal location for a business of that character. The warehouse is 450 feet long by 50 feet wide. A railroad siding extends the entire length of the building on the west side, while along Broadway, on the east side, is room for delivery trucks and wagons to back up to the numerous exits. A similar number of entrances are on the opposite side, with a great amount of storage space between, so arranged as to make the receiving, storing and delivering of supplies a very simple matter. Twelve cars at a time can be unloaded. At times there are stored between 6,000 and 7,000 barrels of flour. The offices, sales, and display rooms of the concern are located in a building adjoining the storehouse on the north end, and fronting on Essex Street. The Stanley Grain Company was organized in 1896, with ex-Mayor George S. Junkins as president and George A. Stanley as treasurer. It was first located at the corner of Common and Franklin streets. The growth of the concern has been vigorous from the start, although its greatest development came upon the securing, in 1912, of the lease of the Boston & Maine property, which gave much larger room for expansion. In 1901, death deprived the company of the services of its president, and the business has since been conducted under the guidance of Mr. Stanley as treasurer and manager. The firm carries the Bay State, King Arthur, David Stott, and F. W. Stock & Sons brands of flour, besides grain and poultry supplies. Its trade extends into the adjoining towns of Andover, North Andover, and Methuen. It specializes in Brooks Mash scratch feed for poultry, the demand for which comes from all parts of New England.

HENRY J. KOELLEN - HENRY J. KOELLEN & COMPANY. The business of wholesaling and retailing imported and domestic fancy groceries and liquors of all kinds has a leading representative in Lawrence in the firm of Henry J. Koellen & Co., 166-168 Essex St., and 2 Jackson Street. This concern was established in 1900 with a small retail liquor business at 166 Essex St., by Henry J. Koellen and & Oswald Freytag, under the firm name of Koellen & Freytag. In 1903, Mr. Freytag withdrew from the business. Under Mr. Koellen's management, the establishment developed rapidly. In 1905, he secured the adjoining store, conducting in a small way a family grocery, cigar, and wine store. In 1910, he retired from the retail liquor line, and remodeled the store for the carrying on of a wholesale business. Their facilities for handling the trade have been enlarged from year to year. The place is neat and attractive. The fixtures and equipment are of the very best obtainable, while the stock is unsurpassed in variety and quality by any similar concern in Essex County. In fact, this establishment will compare favorably, for its size, with any of its kind in Boston or New York. Mr. Koellen always keeps on hand an excellent stock of goods from the leading manufacturers of the world. It is seldom that one cannot obtain any particular brand he may desire here, no matter how rarely it is to be found in the general market. The fancy groceries are of the choicest sort. Besides, there is carried a fine assortment of candies, favors, cigars, tobaccos, pipes and smokers' articles of every description. The concern deals in an extensive line of fancy liquors, foreign and domestic, including, sherries, ports, brandies and cordials. The cigar department is patronized by the city's most critical smokers. The business

extends over the states of Massachusetts, New Hampshire, and Maine. Mr. Koellen came to Lawrence in 1896. For four years, he was a travelling salesman for the Cold Spring Brewing Company of this city.

JOSEPH SILVERTHORNE - SILVERTHORNE STUDIO. — Photography, as a business as well as an art, has a leading exponent in Lawrence in the Silverthorne Studio, located in the Bicknell block, 467 Essex Street. Few so well equipped studios are found outside of a metropolis. The concern occupies the greater part of two floors. It is provided with the most modern facilities for turning out high-grade photographic work. One floor of the studio is taken up by the reception and display rooms and office, and on the floor above are the light room where the portraits are made, the finishing, dark, enlarging, and stock rooms, which extend the entire length of the building. This studio was established in August 1914, at 477 Essex Street. The following year the business had outgrown its original location, and it was removed to the present commodious quarters. The proprietor, Joseph Silverthorne, came to Lawrence in 1898. Although but 14 years of age at that time, he was a skilled amateur photographer. He took up the art as a profession in 1901, starting with Scheriver of Worcester. He worked in several of the leading studios of the country, until he became established in Lawrence in 1914. The excellence of Mr. Silverthorne's work is not only known in Lawrence, but it has won for him a reputation outside of the city. His exhibits, which have been shown in New York, Philadelphia, and Boston, have been awarded certificates of merit, besides a number of special prizes. He has photographed many people of note. The Silverthorne Studio makes a specialty of portraits. It has introduced many novelties, including clever ideas in posing, coloring, and enlarging. Its pictures of children are studies of child life. Worthy of special mention are its productions of enlarged portraits, worked over in oil colors. The result is that they are hard to distinguish from genuine oil paintings, and at the same time, the correctness of the drawing is far superior to that which is obtained by free hand.

TOOMEY & DEMARA AMUSEMENT CO. - THOMAS F. TOOMEY & NAPOLEON DEMARA. — The theatrical business in Lawrence is largely represented in the enterprises of the Toomey & Demara Amusement Company. This concern controls four of the leading playhouses of the city, embracing three branches of the theatrical profession, viz., drama, vaudeville, and motion pictures. The Empire, given over to vaudeville, is one of the largest and best-equipped theatres in New England. It has a seating capacity of 2,300. The Broadway, with a seating capacity of 1,500, and The Premier, with a seating capacity of 700, are devoted exclusively to motion pictures. The Colonial, whose seating capacity is 1,650, provides drama. The last named is at the present writing sub-leased to a stock company. Thomas Toomey, to whom much of the success of the concern is due, came to Lawrence in 1906, when he opened the old Nickel theatre as a picture house, in what had been the Castro theatre. The first day's receipts were only $8.20. The venture was extremely gloomy at the start, and the following several months he sank $5,300 in keeping the house open. Mr. Toomey's optimism, however, was unbounded. He was confident that as soon as the public got the picture idea, success would be certain and substantial. Results proved he was right. While still striving for success Mr. Toomey took, as a partner in the business, Napoleon Demara, who was general utility man in the old Nickel. They made an excellent team. The business of the old Nickel soon outgrew the premises. The New Nickel came in 1910, and five years later, this structure was replaced by the present handsome and commodious Empire theatre. In turn, the Premier, Broadway, and Colonial theatres, the policies of whose managements had failed, were taken over by Toomey & Demara and placed on a sound basis. From a small beginning, this concern has grown into one of the largest enterprises of its kind in this section.

CURRAN & JOYCE CO., INC. — The Curran & Joyce Co., Inc., was established in 1877 when Maurice J. Curran and John Joyce formed a partnership and took over the small bottling business of William E. Heald, then located at 34 Hampshire Street. From the beginning, energy and enterprise have marked the development of this concern. The business soon 'Out-grew the accommodations of the original location, and in September, 1885, the partners moved into the building on Common Street, which then had a frontage of 50 feet. The structure has been enlarged from time to time, and it now has a frontage of no feet, with four floors and a basement, extending from 433 to 443 Common Street. In 1897, it became known as the Curran & Joyce Company, Joseph Jackson having been admitted as a partner. In 1914 Mr. Joyce retired, as also did Mr. Curran shortly afterward, both having other business interests so extensive as to demand all their time. That year the concern was made a Massachusetts corporation, becoming known as the Curran & Joyce Co., Inc. The stock is now held by Joseph Jackson, Philip A. McCarthy, John F. Murphy and Patrick F. Finn, the last three mentioned having been for a number of years, employees of the Curran & Joyce Company. The firm is the sole representative in Lawrence of the Harvard Brewing Company, besides having favorable connections with several of the biggest vineyards and distilleries in the country. The manufacture and distribution of ginger ale, soda waters, and tonics has always been an important feature of the business. The concern practically controls the local market for ginger ale. It has well equipped bottling works, with a capacity of 87 bottles a minute. The equipment also includes an artesian well with a depth of 575 feet, which produces 40 gallons a minute. Besides the building at 433-443 Common Street, which it owns, the firm has a lease of the four-story Slayton building at 570 Common Street and two-thirds of the Boston & Maine inward freight shed. Nearby is a cold storage house, which is used and owned by it. The two latter buildings have track facilities for handling of car lots. There are 55 people employed by the company, and the annual pay roll is nearly $50,000. Six auto trucks and 14 delivery wagons are used in connection with the business.

DIAMOND SPRING BREWERY

DIAMOND SPRING BREWERY - HOLIHAN BROS. — Holihan Bros., brewer of the well-known Diamond Spring beers, was first established in 1856 when Peter Holihan and Patrick Holihan formed a partnership for the sale of fine groceries and liquors. The original firm was known as P. & P. Holihan. After the death of Patrick Holihan in 1882, the business was carried on by Davis & Murphy, but in 1890, the present firm again took control. Until 191,7 the partnership consisted of James P. Holihan, Joseph P. Holihan and Charles A. Holihan. That year Charles A. Holihan died, and the business has since been conducted by the first two named partners. The concern is established in a four-story block at the corner of Common and Hampshire streets. It carries a general line of wholesale liquors, including all the leading brands, besides the beers of its own manufacture. Its growth has been steady and substantial, and its goods have a wide distribution throughout eastern New England territory. In 1912 the Diamond Spring brewery was built on the site of the old Knowles farm at the corner of Andover and Beacon streets. The main building is a five-story structure, with two four-story storage buildings adjoining, besides engine and boiler houses adjacent. Here are brewed the Diamond Spring ales, porter, and lager. The capacity of the plant is 75,000 barrels a year. For 40 years the spring water, now used in the manufacture of Diamond Spring beers, was sold to the people of Lawrence as the Knowles Diamond Spring water, and enjoyed an enviable reputation for its purity and excellence. The beverages now produced from it are admitted to be leaders in their line. In 1917, the concern increased the variety of its products, when it began the manufacture of the Diamond Spring ginger ale, the demand for which is growing rapidly. In this connection, a large assortment of tonics is also manufactured and distributed by the firm. A specialty is made of fruit tonics, the flavoring for the strawberry, raspberry, orange, and

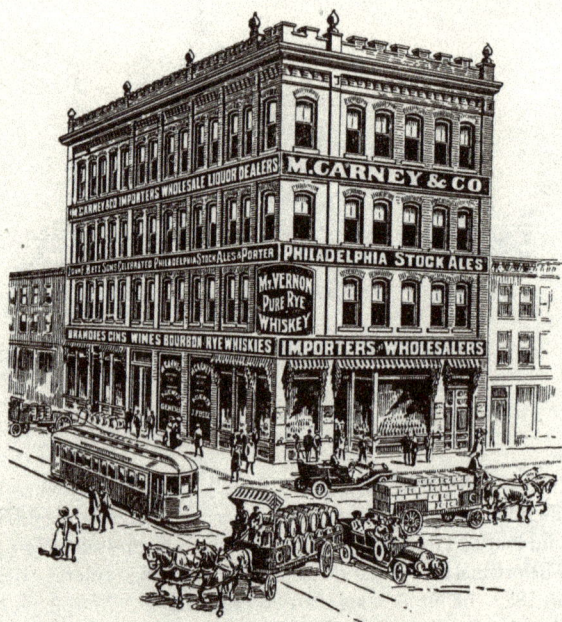

lemon beverages being made from the real fruit. This department is developing into an important feature of the business. The firm employs about 75 people.

M. CARNEY & COMPANY — M. Carney & Company is one of the oldest liquor houses in New England. It was established over 50 years ago by Michael Carney and his brother, Matthew Carney, under the firm name of M. Carney & Brother. It was first located on White Street, and later moved to the corner of Hampshire and Concord streets. Twenty-four years ago, the present location, corner of Hampshire and Common streets, was secured. Some years after the establishment of the business, the Carney brothers dissolved partnership, and later the firm became known as M. Carney & Company. Matthew J. Carney, a nephew of the original partners, becoming a member. Michael Carney died in 1913, his death being preceded by that of Matthew J. Carney, and on May 1,1914, the estate took James C. Corcoran into the firm. The latter was for a number of years an employee of the concern. He has since been the general manager. The firm owns the building in which it is located, and occupies the entire four floors,

with basement. It carries a general line of liquors, wines, cordials and beers, and has the reputation of dealing in the finest grades, both imported and domestic.

COLD SPRING BREWING CO. — Among the minor industries of the city, which have a reputation for the excellence of their products, is the Cold Spring Brewing Company, located on South Union Street. This concern was established in 1895, being incorporated the same year. Its growth has been steady from the beginning. Today the plant covers three acres. Besides the main building of three stories, there are several smaller structures. The equipment embraces every improvement and facility known to the industry, is strictly sanitary, and is scientifically operated. The products consist of ales, porter, and lager, all widely known and largely consumed brands. They are shipped all over Essex County, by case and barrel. The concern has a large bottling trade in Lawrence. The capacity of the plant is 75,000 barrels a year. Under normal conditions, 65 people are employed in the various departments. The president of the company, August Stiegler, served for a number of years as treasurer and general manager, and the successful development of the concern is due in a large measure to his capable management. He has had many years experience in the brewing business. Mr. Stiegler still acts in an advisory capacity in the management of the plant, which is now under the direction of Walter A. Singer, as treasurer and general manager. Louis K. Siegel is clerk of the corporation and secretary of the board of directors. The board of directors is composed of August Stiegler, David Bailey, Herman Yunggebauer, Hugo Moeser, Charles E. Trumbull, Herbert W. Home, Henry C. Schoenland, Henry J. Koellen and Gustav Plisch.

General Statistics

YEAR	POP.	VALUATION	TAX RATE	POLLS	SCHOOL CHILDREN
1892	45,616	$32,527,937	$16.80	12,328	9005
1893	46,204	33,207.372	16.80	12,946	9059
1894	47,804	33,436,593	16.80	12,780	8609
1895	52,654	33,533,588	16.00	14,124	9263
1896	54,635	34,884,223	15.60	14,973	9635
1897	56,616	36,208,166	15.60	15,295	9816
1898	58,597	37.576,798	15.60	15,709	10,085
1899	60,578	38,614,722	15.60	15,817	10,045
1900	62,559	39,841,697	15.60	16,630	10,057
1901	64,035	40,654,758	15.60	17,244	10,889
1902	65,511	41,660,738	15.60	17,935	11,462
1903	66,987	42,882,047	16.40	17,773	11,428
1904	68,463	44,110,964	16.40	17,639	11,782
1905	69,939	46,235,468	16.80	18,230	12,546
1906	73,129	51,044,934	16.00	19,820	12,841
1907	76,319	54,246,294	16.40	20,895	13,200
1908	79,509	56,473,458	16.80	20,482	12,729
1909	82,699	59,434,446	16.40	21,201	13,240
1910	85,892	65,446,007	16.40	22,764	13,500
1911	86,765	70,836,993	17.60	22,639	13,351
1912	**84,638	75,449,814	17.60	21,737	13,840
1913	88,511	78,710,803	18.00	20,963	14,818
1914	89,384	79,813,490	18.00	20,804	14,320
1915	90,258	82,695,620	18.80	20,608	14,703
1916	100,054	82,955,470	18.80	20,634	17,251
1917	102,000	84,077,651	18.80	21,755	18,975

**Estimate shows decrease due to conditions caused by great textile strike.

Note: Since 1895, with the exception of the official census year, that is, every year divisable by five, the population given is nothing more than an estimate based on the computation of the average annual increases. The figure for 1916 is in accordance with a report given out by the Federal Census Bureau for Massachusetts and rating Lawrence as the ninth city in the state.

SELECTMEN OF LAWRENCE

1847   William Swan, Charles F. Abbott, Nathan Wells,
James Stevens, Lorenzo D. Brown.

1848   Daniel J. Clark, Charles F Abbott, Wm. D. Joplin,
Levi Spragne, John M. Smith.

1849   Charles F. Abbott, Levi Sprague, Isaac Fletcher.

1850   Artemus Parker, Jr., William Gile, William R. Page.

1851-'52 William R. Page, Levi Sprague, Joseph Norris.

TOWN AND CITY CLERKS

E. W. Morse	1847-1849
George W. Benson	1850-1852
George W. Benson	1853
Benjamin Boardman	1854
William Morse	1855-1856
George R. Rowe	1857-1874
Walter R. Rowe	1875-1876
James E. Shepard	1877-1883
Timothy Kane	1884
William T. Kimball	1885-1891
Timothy F. O'Hearn	1892
William T. Kimball	1893-1897
*Cornelius J. Corcoran	1898-1910
+Edward J. Wade	1910-to date

+Elected by City Council to fill unexpired term. —Elected by the people at the next city election.

*Resigned September 19th, 1910.

1853	Charles S. Storrow		
1854	Enoch Bartlett	1886	Alexander B. Bruce
1855	Albert Warren	1887	Alexander B. Bruce
1856	Albert Warren	1888	Alvin E. Mack
1857	John R. Rollins	1889	Alvin E. Mack
1858	John R. Rollins	1890	John W. Crawford
1859	Henry K. Oliver	1891	Lewis P. Collins
1860	Daniel Saunders, Jr.	1892	Henry P. Doe
1861	James K. Barker	1893	Alvin E. Mack
1862	William H. P. Wright	1894	Charles G. Rutter
1863	William H. P. Wright	1895	Charles G. Rutter
1864	Alfred J. French	1896	George S. Junkins
1865	Milton Bonney	1897	George S. Junkins
1866	Pardon Armington	1898	James H. Eaton
1867	Nathaniel P. H. Melvin	1899	James H. Eaton
1868	Nathaniel P. H. Melvin	1900	James F. Leonard
1869	Frank Davis	1901	James F. Leonard
1870	Nathaniel P. H. Melvin	1902	James F. Leonard
1871	Smith B. W. Davis	1903	Alexander L. Grant
1872	Smith B. W. Davis	1904	Cornelius F. Lynch
1873	John K. Tarbox	1905	Cornelius F. Lynch
1874	John K. Tarbox	1906	John P. Kane
1875	Robert H. Tewksbury	1907	John P. Kane
1876	Edmund R. Hayden	1908	John P. Kane
1877	Caleb Saunders	1909	William P. White
1878	James R. Simpson	*1910	William P. White
1879	James R. Simpson	††1910	John T. Cahill
1880	James R. Simpson	1911	John T. Cahill
1881	Henry K. Webster	1912-13	Michael A. Scanlon
1882	John Breen	**1914	Michael A. Scanlon
1883	John Breen	††1914-15	John P. Kane
1884	John Breen	1916-17	John J. Hurley
1885	James R. Simpson	1918-	John J. Hurley

*Resigned.

†Elected by City Council August 29th to fill unexpired term.

**Died in office August 16th.

††Elected at city election to fill unexpired term.

TOWN AND CITY AUDITORS

A. C. Radcliffe	1859
Artemus Harmon	1859–'60
Henry N. Butman	1860–'61
L. E. Rice	1861–'63
S. E. Stone	1863–'64
Elbridge B. Osgood	1864–'74
John E. Cushing	1874–'85
Walter R. Rowe	1885–'86
Richard J. Shea	1886 to date

A. C. Radcliffe was apparently the first regular City Auditor. For the years ending in March, 1849, 1850 and 1851, Ivan Stevens audited the town accounts. From that time until 1859 the accounts were audited by a finance committee, except that in 1854 Dana Sargent was paid $25 for auditing all the city accounts but those of the city treasurer.

SUPERINTENDENTS OF SCHOOLS

James D. Herrick

George Packard

Henry F. Harrington

Henry K. Oliver

Joseph L. Partridge

Gilbert E. Hood

Harrison Hume

George A. Littlefield

John L. Brewster

George E. Chickering

William C. Bates

Jeremiah E. Burke

Bernard M. Sheridan

1853 George D. Cabot, Edmund B. Herrick, Alvah Bennett. Albert Warren, Walker Flanders, Samuel S. Valpey.

1854 Albert Blood, Samuel Gould, Monoram F. Cram, David Wentworth, Elkanah F. Bean, Charles F. Abbott.

1855 John B. Atkinson, Wadleigh Goodhue, Joseph W. Kimball, Elbridge Josselyn, Benjamin Osgood, Gorham P. Higgins.

1856 Wyllis G. Eaton, William H. Fernald, Artemus Parker, Jr., Eldridge Josselyn, *Cyrus Hutchinson, †Elkanah F. Bean, Gorham P. Higgins.

1857 Wyllis G. Eaton, Aaron Ordway, William H. Boardman, Amasa Bryant, Cyrus Williams, Nicholas G. Paul.

1858 Samuel S. Crocker, Aaron Ordway, Artemus Harmon. Amasa Bryant, Clark L. Austin, Nicholas G. Paul.

1859 Eben L. Chapman, John S. Statfford, George A. Fuller, Joseph Norris, Oliver Bryant, James D. Herrick.

1860 Nathaniel P. H. Melvin, Reuben W. French, Nathaniel G. White, William H. Bridgeman, John Gale, Joseph N. Gage.

1861 Morris Knowles, Hezekiah Plummer, Artemus W. Stearns. William Thomas, Archibald McFarlin, Alenizies C. Andrews.

1862 John C. Hoadley, William R. Spalding, Samuel M. Stedman, Thomas S. Stratton, Luther Ladd, Menizies C. Andrews.

1863 James Byrom, James A. Treat, Joshua Pillsbury, Jr., Albert Emerson, Samuel B. Kimball, John Q. A. Burridge.

1864 Morris Knowles, Milton Bonney, James Payne, William Thomas, Alfred Lang, John Q. A. Burridge.

1865 William A. Russell, Joseph Norris, James Payne, William Thomas, Alfred Lang, John Q. A. Burridge.

1866 Richard R. Harriman, John Beetle, John D. Glidden, George W. Sargent, Daniel Hardy, William Smith.

1867 Nicholas Chapman, George A. Walton, John D. Glidden, Albert Emerson, Samuel M. Davis. William Smith.

1868 Nicholas Chapman, Hezekiah Plummer, Alfred A. Lamprey, John Kiley, Samuel M. Davis, William Smith.

1869 John R. Rollins. Parker C. Kirk, James H. Eaton, George Littlefield, Samuel M. Davis, Warner Bailey.

1870 Marcus S. Dodge, John R. Perry, James Payne, John Hart, William Bower, Alonzo Winkley.

1871 Aaron A. Currier. Hezekiah Plummer, James Payne, James A. Treat, George Lamb, William F. Cutler.

1872 Aaron A. Currier, Hezekiah Plummer, James Payne. James A. Treat. George Lamb, Edwin Ayer.

1873 Marcus S. Dodge, Charles T. Emerson. Alfred A. Lamprey, Matthew Carney, Nathaniel P. H. Melvin, Caleb Saunders.

1874 Daniel B. Webster, Benjamin F. Chadburn, Moses Perkins, Matthew Carney, John France, Fred W. Taylor.

1875 Thomas Clegg, Hezekiah Plummer, Abel G. Pearson, Dyer S. Hall, Charles Smith, Edwin Ayer.

1876 Thomas Clegg, Lurandus Beach, Jr., Albert R. Field, Edwin Lyford, William P. Clark, Jesse Moulton.

1877 Pardon H. Armington, David T. Porter, Hector P. Linn, Peter Holihan, John H. Prescott, **John B. Howard, †Silas H. Loring.

1878 Thomas Clegg, James G. Abbott, Joseph Shattuck, George Sanborn, Luther Ladd, Silas H. Loring.

1879 Henry P. Danforth, James G. Abbott. John F. Cogswell, George Sanborn, John Abercrombie, William T. McAlpine.

1880 Marcus W. Copps. Phineas B. Robinson, Henry B. Dyer, J. Clinton White, Samuel Smith, William T. McAlpine.

1881 Henry P. Danforth, Henry Dolbier, Henry B. Dyer, Henry P. Doe, Samuel Smith, Caleb Saunders.

1882 Henry B. Thompson, Henry Dolbier, Abiel Morrison, James W. Joyce, Samuel Barrett, Caleb Saunders.

1883 Henry B. Thompson, C. Henry Schoenland, Abiel Morrison. James W. Joyce, George A. Lindsey, William T. McAlpine.

1884 Henry B. Thompson, C. Henry Schoenland, Patrick Ford, James W. Joyce, Alexander B. Bruce, Patrick A. Lenane.

1885 George L. Gage, William E. Gowing, Henry B. Dyer, Henry A. Buell, James C. Brown, Nathan A. Holt.

1886 Samuel Knowles, Samuel W. Fellows, David Cahill, James J. Stanley, Edward McCabe, William Luscomb.

1887 Samuel Knowles, William E. Gowing, D. Frank Robinson, John Russell, James W. Joyce, Nathan A. Holt.

1888 Thomas Clegg, Charles T. Main, Charles H. Davis, George I. Haeberle, Franklin Butler, John Hartley.

1889 Thomas Clegg. Charles T. Main, Charles H. Davis. George I. Haeberle, Franklin Butler, John Hartley.

1890   Frederick M. Libbey. Charles T. Main, George B. Elliott, Arthur A. Bailey, Otis Freeman, Jr.. Lewis P. Collins.

1891   George W. Hall, August Stiegler, Andrew F. Shea, George S. Junkins, Otis Freeman, Jr., Jeremiah F. Driscoll.

1892   James H. Martin, Richard W. Doyle, Josiah S. Whitehouse, William J. Butler, Daniel Gallagher, John W. Bolton.

1893   Herman Bruckmann. Fred N. Abbott, Gilbert H. Kittredge, George S. Junkins, Ezra W. Hodgkins, Richard W. Ellis.

1894   Herman Bruckmann, Fred N. Abbott, Gilbert H. Kittredge, George W. Dow, John A. Abercrombie, Richard W. Ellis.

1895   Edward H. Humphrey, George H. Goldsmith, George W. Dow, Albert E. Butler, John A. Abercrombie, Adelbert C. Varnam.

1896   Edward H. Humphrey, George H. Goldsmith, A. Herbert Robinson, Ira D. Blandin, William H. Howarth, John Haigh.

1897   Charles G. Kidder, George P. Low, Charles W. Currier, Omar E. Couch, William H. Howarth, John H. Bedell.

1898   William F. King, Cornelius F. Lynch, Louis Matthes, Narcisse E. Miville, Thomas Bevington, Patrick O'Brien.

1899   Hugo E. Dick, Cornelius F. Lynch, Louis Matthes. Narcisse E. Miville. Andrew A. Caffrey, Henry B. Lane.

1900   Frederick F. Sherman, Daniel H. Logue, Andrew Griffin, Jr., Narcisse E. Miville, Andrew A. Caffrey, Edmund B. Belknap.

1901   Frederick F. Sherman, James P. Flynn, William P. White, William H. Forbes, Robert F. Pickels, Edmund B. Belknap.

1902   H. Richard Parthum, Fred H. Eaton, William P. White, Eli Lacaillade, Charles H. Choate, Henry B. Lane.

1903   H. Richard Parthum, William C. Cusack, Henry P. Hart, Eli Lacaillade, Simeon Viger, Edmund B. Belknap.

1904   Julius J. McCormick, Michael F. Scanlon, Henry P. Hart, Joseph Dooley, Moses Marshall, Michael F. Cronin.

1905   George T. Stanstield, Charles A. Salisbury, William A. Kelleher, David Daigle, Benjamin L. Weeks, John McGillis.

1906   Patrick Lyons, James J. Ahearn, John C. Needham, J. Frank James, Benjamin L. Weeks, John J. O'Brien.

1907   Patrick Lyons, James J. Ahearn, John C. Needham, Michael M. Garvey, Timothy F. Donovan, Joseph A. Woodhall.

1908   John F. Young, Edward A. Dolan, John J. Breen, Michael M. Garvey, John Tobin, Joseph A. Woodhall.

1909 Carl A. Woekel, Jr. Rudolph Miller, Matthew Burns, Robert S. Maloney, Xavier Legendre, William Moss. Jr.

1910 William H. Callahan, Thomas M. Jordan, John Jos. Ford, Michael A. Scanlon, John Tobin. William Moss, Jr.

1911 William H. Callahan, Thomas M. Jordan, Joseph Hayes, Michael A. Scanlon, James R. Walker, John Hennessey.

Note:-The Aldermen are named in the order of the ward represented, one being elected for each of the six wards.

*Resigned.   †To fill vacancy.   **Died.

COMMON COUNCILMEN OF LAWRENCE

1853 John T. Loring, William B. Gallison, James H. Harding, Jackson Gordon, William R. Spalding, Abner N. Whittaker, Josiah Osgood (President), Nathaniel G. White, Elisha Winch, Dana Sargent, Edwin L. Gowen, Isaac K. Gage, Elkanah F. Bean, Eldridge Weston, Daniel Hardy, William M. Tyler, James Stevens, John Lear.

1854 Elisha C. Hopkins, Charles Stark Newell, Enoch Hewins, Thomas A. Parsons, Andrew D. Blanchard, Benjamin McAllister, John Beith, Thomas W. Floyd, Oliver Pearl, William Clark, Henry Withington, Leonard Hoyt (President), Isaac K. Gage (President), Asa M. Bodwell, Elijah B. Dolloff, Daniel Hardy, George H. Parker, John Caldwell, John Q. A. Burridge, George Richardson, Gorham P. Higgins.

1855 David P. Foster, Rufus Reed, Sylvester A. Furbush, Reuben W. French, William A. Carleton, Adolphus Durant, William H. Fernald, Thomas W. Floyd, Thomas S. Stratton, Amos Carter, Sullivan Simonds, John C. Wadleigh (President), George Littlefield, Jefford M. Decker, Charles Hutchinson, Harvey White, William Hardy, Hezekiah Plummer, Samuel M. Davis, Edwin Ayer.

1856 Elijah M. Mooers, Thomas G. Peckham, William J. Merrill, Julius H. Morse, John Q. A. Batchelder, Stillman Towne. Abner N. Whittaker, Sewell Sylvester, Phineas M. Gage, Lyman Daniels, Jefford M. Decker, David Wentworth, William H. Cook, William Hardy (President), Cyrus Williams, John P. Gale, Hezekiah Plummer, George A. Fuller, Henry F. Pasho, Jr., Paschal Abbott.

1857   Abel Webster, Thomas G. Peckham (President), Thatcher Merriam, John S. Stafford, George W. Sargent, John Q. A. Batchelder, Sewell Sylvester, William H. Whitmarsh, Elihu W. Colcord, William Murray, Joseph Norris, Heaton Bailey, William H. Cook, William Thomas, Alfred Lang, Eli Wentworth, Albert Drew, David C. Richardson, John Bailey, Oliver C. Demeritt, Emulus W. Burbank.

1858   John M. Currier, Thomas S. Winn, Richard R. Harriman, John Q. A. Batchelder, John S. Stafford, John Beetle, Terence Brady, Algernon S. Wright, Abiel Morrison, Joseph Norris, Heaton Bailey, William P. Frost (President), Carlos C. Closson, Rollins A. Kempton, Luther E. Stevens, Horace J. Durgin, David M. Pasho, William Smith.

1859   Lafayette Branch, Thomas Scott, Isaac B. Cobb, Leonard Wheeler, Hezekiah Plummer, Eben T. Colby, William D. Lamb (President), Abel G. Pearson, Caleb T. Briggs, Leonard F. Cressey, William Thomas, Lawson Rice, Allen Wilson, Carlos C. Closson, Rufus Fuller, George S. Merrill, John Q. A. Burridge, James Clark, Alonzo Winkley.

1860   Samuel W. Jackson, Alfred Hall, Abner Hosmer, Eben T. Colby, George Wilkins, Jr., Augustus M. Fay, William Barbour, Albert R. Brewster, Terence Brady, Joseph Stowell, James Corcoran, Michael P. Merrill (President), Archibald McFarlin, Rufus Fuller, George S. Merrill, Paschal Abbott, Alonzo Winkley, Philemon C. Parsons.

1861   Samuel W. Jackson, Alfred Hall, Oliver Collins, Lemuel A. Bishop, Eben T. Colby (President), Joseph W. George, Joshua Pillsbury, Jr., James E. Morris, Nathaniel R. French, Albert Emerson, Stevens Dockham, Philip Yeaton, Samuel M. Davis, George S. Merrill, Orange Wheeler, Ezekiel W. Matthews, Joel Barnes, George Poor.

1862   Charles A. Brown, Reuben Maynard, Edwin F. Bailey, John F. Cogswell, Lemuel A. Bishop (President), Daniel S. Jordan, Joshua Pillsbury, Jr., Perley Ayer, James E. Morris, Albert Emerson, Jonathan D. Boothman, Frank L. Runals, Rufus Fuller, William P. Frost, Joseph M. Freese, Joel Barnes, Ezekiel W. Matthews, George Poor.

1863   Charles A. Brown, Reuben Maynard, George Ordway, John F. Cogswell, Franklin Edwards, William H. Jaquith, Baruch C. Whitcomb, David Beatty, James R. Simpson, Jonathan D.

Boothman, Asa M. Wade, Jeremiah J. Desmond, Frederick Butler. Milton Bonney (President), George W. Chandler, Alonzo Winkley, William Smith, Paschal Abbott.

1864 Abel Webster, Ebenezer L. Chapman, Seth D. Paul, W. Fiske Gile (President), Franklin Edwards, Isaac Fletcher, John Stow, Terence Brady, Baruch C. Whitcomb, Moses Perkins, David S. Swan, Henry J. Couch, Humphrey Desmond, George W. Chandler, George W. Dame, William W. Colby, Alonzo Winkley, William Smith, Nathan T. Plummer.

1865 Augustus M. Fay, Melvin Beal, Aaron A. Currier, Byron Truell, John E. Dustin, Lurandus Beach, Jr., George S. Merrill (President), Merrill N. Howe, Samuel W. Knights, Thomas H. Fernald, James H. Stannard, Woodbridge S. Lyford. William W. Colby. George W. Dame, James A. Storer, Joel Barnes, David C. Richardson, Nathan T. Plummer.

1866 Alonzo S. Winn, Lewis Stratton, Rufus M. Howard, Alanson Briggs, Edward Devlin, James H. Eaton, George S. Merrill (President), George A. Smith, Jeremiah D. Drew, Thomas H. Fernald, Charles T. Young, John Bamford, James A. Storer. Albert Blood, John France, James R. Balloch, Moses A. Bailey, Henry K. Flint.

1867 Lewis Stratton, F. C. Drew, Albert F, Coburn, Perley Ayer, James H. Eaton (President), Alanson Briggs, William L. Thompson, Jeremiah D. Drew, Jonathan C. Bowker, John Stone, George K. Wiggin, John Kiley, William Clark, Tempest Birtwell, John France, Levi Emery, George W. Horn, Alonzo Winkley, Caleb Saunders, James Clark.

1868 Alanson Dixon, Horatio Dennett, Ebenezer L. Chapman, Samuel Langmaid, Edward Devlin, Moses B, Kenney, John J. Doland (President), Daniel C. O'Sullivan, Herbert P. Damon, John Hart, William Clark, Henry J. Couch, Levi Emery, Asa M. Bodwell, George Lamb, Alonzo Winkley, Caleb Saunders, James Clark.

1869 Aaron A. Currier. Thomas J. Cate, Winslow Eager, Moses B. Kenney, Samuel Langmaid, Smith B. W. Davis, John J. Doland (President), Daniel C. O'Sullivan, Samuel Gould, Waldo L. Abbott, James Kiley, Henry J. Couch, George Lamb, James W. Bailey, William Bower, Edward Burke, Warren Stevens, Mark Manahan, Caleb Saunders.

1870 Thomas J. Cate, Winslow Eager, William F. Farnham, Smith B. W. Davis (President). Andrew C. Stone, Edward McCoy.

Augustus S. Bunker, Martin O'Sullivan, William F. Gearin, Henry J. Couch, Patrick Murphy, James Kiley, James W. Bailey, Cyrus Williams, Richard Wheelwright, Mark Manahan, Frank E. Wheeler, George A. Nelson.

1871 Winslow Eager, George B. Smart, James F. Megin. J. Frank Gilbert, Edward McCoy, Andrew C. Stone (President), James G. Abbott, Augustus S. Bunker, Martin O'Sullivan, Timothy Deacey, Henry J. Couch, Patrick Murphy, Patrick Foster, Cyrus Williams, Richard Wheelwright, James Miles, Frank E. Wheeler, Edwin Ayer, Warren Stevens.

1872 George B. Smart, Abel Webster, George W. Russell. James G. Abbott, Charles H. Littlefield. Charles T. Emerson, Timothy Deacey, Henry P. Doe, James W. Joyce, Henry J. Couch, James Murphy, William Hanrahan, James Miles, Levi Emery. Lorenzo D. Sargent (President), Elisha B. Cutler, John L. Webster, John Dane.

1873 George W. Russell, Baldwin Coolidge, Louis Hefner, Charles H. Littlefield, Granville M. Stoddard, Charles C. Whitney, James W. Joyce, William W. Emery, James Noonan, Duncan Wood, William Hanrahan, John Gilmartin. Everett P. Richardson, Lorenzo D. Sargent (President), Cyrus T. Moore, John L. Webster, John Dane, E. B. Cutler.

1874 William Cannon, Henry P. Chandler, Henry E. Burckel, Patrick J. Kelley, Charles H. Schoenland, Edward Devlin, James O'Dea, James Noonan, James Watts. James Murphy, Daniel F. Dolan (President), George O. Clifford, Everett P. Richardson, Thomas Scott, Cornelius J. Tighe, Samuel White, John L. Webster, George Littlefield.

1875 Charles W. Stevens, James S. Hutchinson, John Brown, John L. Brewster (President), C. H. Ernest Keilhau, Thomas Kenney, Prescott G. Pillsbury, James Watts, D. Frank Robinson, Robert Haughton, Edwin Lyford, George Sanborn, Levi Emery, Lewis G. Holt, Samuel Hardacre, William T. McAlpine, Jesse Moulton, Thomas Dean.

1876 Charles W. Stevens, Albin Yeaw, William F. Wiesner, John L. Brewster (President), Thomas Kenney, C. H. Ernest Keilhau, John Breen, John F. Hogan, Prescott G. Pillsbury, George Sanborn, Robert Haughton, Josiah N. Pratt, Samuel Hardacre, Lewis G. Holt, Levi Emery, William C. Luscomb, John Daley, James Moffett.

1877 Albin Yeaw, James S. Barrie (President), Joseph Cleveland,
      Patrick Sweeney, Michael Rinn, Edward H. Dickie, Edgar H.
      Drew, William H. Keefe, John Breen, Michael Mann, Nathaniel
      Ambrose, J. Clinton White, George N. Austin, George H.
      McFarlin, George W. Horn, Joseph Barnes, Samuel Barrett,
      James McLaughlin, James B. Wiggin, George E. Follansbee, John
      Foley.

1878 Seth F. Dawson, Marcus W. Copps, Henry P. Danforth, Edward
      H. Dickie, Andrew Sharpe, Henry Behrmann, William H. Keefe,
      Michael Mann, Daniel F. McCarthy, Francis Gorman, George N.
      Austin, J. Clinton White, Henry K. Webster (President), George
      W. Horn, Joseph Barnes, John Phillips, Joseph H. Stafford,
      Charles E. Knowles, William T. McAlpine.

1879 James Moorehouse, Marcus W. Copps, George W. Stafford,
      Andrew Sharpe, Charles Morrison, Charles McCarthy, Daniel F.
      McCarthy, Francis Gorman, James Murphy, Henry K. Webster
      (President), Merrill N. Howe, Charles H. Davis, John Phillips,
      John Paisley, Jr., Charles H. Bean, Michael A. McCormick, John
      O'Sullivan, George S. Williams, Timothy J. Buckley.

1880 James Moorehouse, Oscar A. Frye, F. W. Theodor Erler, John
      P. Kennedy, Charles Morrison, Portal M. Black, Thomas Griffin,
      Cornelius Sullivan, James A. Coughlin, Merrill N. Howe
      (President), Charles H. Davis, Thomas Ayrey, Charles H. Bean,
      John Paisley, Jr., George W. Chandler, Michael A. McCormick,
      Michael F. Collins, John Hartley.

1881 Oscar A. Frye, Gustave Graichen, James C. Fisher, William A.
      Kelleher, Herbert S. Rice, Charles U. Bell (President), Patrick
      O'Connor, James A. Coughlin, Thomas Griffin, Thomas Ayrey,
      Alfred L. Mellen, Charles L. Place, George Collins, Charles A.
      Trumbull, Cornelius Whitehead, Michael F. Collins, John J.
      Kilbride, Wendell W. Beal.

1882 James C. Fisher, Harry E. Smith. Ernest E. Dick, Charles U. Bell,
      Edward Costello, William A. Kelleher, Patrick O'Connor,
      Maurice Lyons, Anthony Corwan, Eugene A. McCarthy, Henry A.
      Buell, Moses F. Hutchinson (President), Cornelius Whitehead,
      John N. Ellingwood, John H. Stafford, Patrick A. Lenane, John J.
      Kilbride, Franklin B. Davis.

1883 Rufus Andrews, George L. Gage, John L. Cross, Richard Doyle,
      John F. McQueeney, Thomas F. Condon, Patrick Ford, John
      Morrissey, Patrick F. Halley, Thomas J. Morrissey, Charles H.

Littlefield, Eugene A. McCarthy (President), Charles Lacaillade, John N. Ellingwood, Joseph E. Watts, William Sharrock, Patrick A. Lenane, Franklin B. Davis, John J. Nugent.

1884 Rufus Andrews, Henry E. Burckel, Andrew S. Arthur, Richard Doyle, John F. McQueeney, Thomas Murray, Thomas J. Morrissey, Patrick F. Halley (President), Anthony Corwan, William H. Burnham, Charles Lacaillade, Archelaus Bolduc, Milton B. Townsend, Joseph E. Watts, James G. Abbott, John J. Nugent, John Campbell, Dennis W. Murphy.

1885 Harry E. Smith, Joseph H. Wheeler, James Lane, William G. Hill, William H. Abbott, Geeorge L Haeberle, James O'Neill, Timothy F. O'Hearn, Michael F. Sullivan, John O'Brien, Phineas W. Haseltine, John A. Brackett, Peter W. Lyall, James G. Abbott, Jr., (President), Thomas H. Soemerville, William J. Hinchcliffe, William Cooney, Jonathan Auty, Dennis W. Murphy.

1886 William Hooper, William H. Dawson, John M. Graham, Frederick M. Libbey, William J. Barry, Owen F. Malley, Thomas Goodwin, William J. McCarthy, Michael F. Sullivan (President), John O'Brien, Moses E. Woodbury. Benjamin P. Cheney, Martin Golden, Richard H. Fox, Thomas H. Somerville, William J. Hinchcliffe, John F. McCarthy, Patrick C. Ward, Patrick J. Graham.

1887 Frederick M. Libbey, William Henderson, Walter H. Langshaw, Owen F. Malley, William F. Sheedy, Timothy J. Kelleher, David Doyle, James H. Weldon. James McConville, Moses E. Woodbury, Henry A. Musk, Thomas Gilmartin, Richard H. Fox (President). William Chadwick, William W. Dean, Patrick J. Graham, John F. McCarthy, Harry Whittemore.

1888 Frederick M. Libbey (President), William Henderson, William E. Bradbury, Timothy J. Kelleher, William F. Sheedy. Michael J. Clark, David Doyle, James McConville, James H. Weldon, Henry A. Musk, Charles W. Howard, James M. Learned, William Chadwick, George Hartley, William L. Seaver, Charles E. Bradley, Robert E. Burke, John J. O'Brien.

1889 William E. Bradbury (President), Emil C. Stiegler, George W. Hall, Michael J. Clark, Henry E. Sugatt, John F. Doyle. Dennis E. Halley, John M. Lynch, William Nicholson, Charles W. Howard, James M. Learned, Arthur A. Bailey, George Hartley, William L. Seaver, James H. Derbyshire, William Barrage, Lewis P. Collins, Ellsworth W. Hastings.

1890 George W. Hall (President), Emil C. Stiegler, A. Herbert Robinson, John F. Doyle, Henry E. Sugatt, Fred N. Abbott, Dennis E. Halley, John M. Lynch, John D. Mahoney, Robert Barker, George S. Junkins, Isaac N. Wilson, Benjamin C. Ames, Charles F. Sargent, James H. Derbyshire, John W. Bolton, John J. Murphy, Ellsworth W. Hastings.

1891 A. Herbert Robinson, Henry W. Gesing, George C. Bosson, Jr., Fred N. Abbott, George H. Goldsmith, H. Dennie Morse, John D. Mahoney, Maurice Ryan, Cornelius Sullivan, Robert Barker, Isaac N. Wilson, Harry R. Dow, Benjamin C. Ames, Charles F. Sargent (President), Ezra W. Hodgkins, John J. Murphy, William R. Sawyer, Michael J. Sullivan.

1892 John T. Beanland, Edwin J. Cate, Charles E. Wingate, Thomas A. Brooks, John P. Kane (President), Frank J. Whelan (President), William G. Kennedy, John A. McGowan, John P. Ryan, Harry R. Dow, Arnie D. V. Bourget, Patrick J. Finn, Ezra W. Hodgkins, James H. Barnes, Fred R. Warren, Edward Braithwaite, Michael J. Dempsey, Robert Thompson,

1893 John T. Beanland, Edwin J. Cate, Benjamin H. Forbes, James O'Neill, Fred A. Sylvester, Frank S. Turner, William G. Kennedy, John P. Ryan, Thomas J. Burns, Harry R. Dow (President), J. Frank James, William A. Schenk, James H. Barnes, Fred R. Warren, John R. H. Ward, Andrew A. Chalmers, Dennis F. Durgin, John W. Godin.

1894 John T. Beanland (President). Benjamin H. Forbes, Charles H. Guenther, James O'Neill, John Davey, Peter M. Sweeney, Thomas J. Burns, John E. Ganley, John I. Hart, Ira D. Blandin. Albert S. Lang, Nathan O. Magoon, John R. H. Ward. William H. Rankin, Frank A. Rowell, Andrew A. Chalmers, Dennis F. Durgin, John W. Godin.

1895 Benjamin H. Forbes, Charles H. Guenther, Willoughby W. Lathrop, John P. S. Mahoney (President), Andrew J. McCarthy, Bernard T. O'Connell, John E. Ganley, John J. Hart, Edward F. Joyce, John J. Hartley, Jeremiah J. Desmond, William H. Forbes, Fred A. Gray, Frederick Patch, Frank A. Rowell, Edward L. Arundel, John P. Black, Jeremiah O'Leary.

1896 Willoughby W. Lathrop, George Campbell, Jr., Charles E. Pearce, George P. Low, George W. Smith, Andrew J. McCarthy. Edward F. Joyce, Jeremiah J. Carey, Edward P. Morton, John E. Barr, Omar E. Couch, John F. Shea, Frederick Patch (President),

Alexander H. Rogers, Walter E. Rushforth, Edward L. Arundel, John H. Bedell, Andrew Craig.

1897   George Campbell, Charles A. Knox, Louis K. Siegel, Andrew J. McCarthy (President), Michael H. Bradley, Michael F. Sullivan, Thomas F. Hadley, Frank J. O'Brien, John F. Sullivan, John F. Shea, William Daley, John A. Patterson, Alexander H. Rogers, Joseph S. Chambers, John E. H. Latham, James Forbes, Walter A. Savage, Joseph A. Woodhall.

1898   Charles A. Knox (President), George Mowat, Louis K. Siegel, Archie N. Frost, Daniel H. Logue, John F. Quinn, Edward C. Callahan, Dennis H. Finn, John F. Hannon, William Collins, William Daley, George Theberge, Ezra G. Hinckley, Orrin J. Randlett, Walter E. Rushforth, Frederick A. Carr, Henry B. Lane, Walter A. Savage.

1899   George Mowat, Emil J. Muehlig, John H. Spinlow, John Casey, James P. Flynn, Daniel H. Logue (President), Edward C. Callahan, Andrew Griffin, Jr., Bartholomew A. Young, William Collins, John F. Connor, George Theberge, Albert H. Evans, Robert F. Pickels, Frank Smith, Thomas A. Arundel, Harmon T. Drew, William H. Knowles.

1900   John H. Spinlow, Emil J. Muehlig, William Hoffarth, James P. Flynn (President), Michael F. Scanlon, James E. Gurry, Henry P. Hart, William Farrell, Joseph F. Kennedy, William B. Bartley, John F. Connor, Fred S. McCarthy, Frank Smith, Albert H. Evans, Charles H. Choate, Timothy Lynch, John Donohue, Thomas Maxwell.

1901   Gustav Plisch, Richard Koerner, Walter W. Hager, Richard A. Linehan, John Casey, Michael F. Scanlon, Henry P. Hart, Joseph F. Kennedy, James E. Ryan, William B. Bartley (President), Fred S. McCarthy, John W. Tatham, Charles H. Choate (President), Charles H. Morgan, John A. Evans, George Beedles, Andrew W. Campbell, John Halsted.

1902   Richard Koerner (President), Walter W. Hager, Emil H. Wilde, Timothy F. O'Neill, William C. Cusack, Jeremiah F. Gearin, Michael P. Finnegan, Joseph P. Garvey, James A. Mulcahey, Joseph Doyle, Arthur A. White, Joseph L. Dooley, Priestly Fitzgerald, John A. Evans, Charles H. Morgan, Andrew W. Campbell, George Beedles, John Halstead.

1903   Alfred J. Burckel, Charles A. Salisbury, James Forlies, Timothy O'Neill (President), Fred W. Gay, Alexander W. Sheriff, Michael

P. Finnegan, William A. Kelleher, Jeremiah Mahoney, Arthur A. White, John J. Collins, Joseph L. Dooley, Orrell Ashton, Priestly Fitzgerald, James R. Tetler, William H. Knowles, John McCrillis, John J. O'Brien.

1904   Alfred J. Burckel, Anton L. Weidner, George T. Stansfield, James J. Ahearn, Frederick Gehring, Edward J. Ward, James A. Connors, William A. Kelleher (President), Jeremiah J. Mahoney, Daniel W. Mahony, John P. O'Brien, John J. Collins, James R. Tetler, Benjamin L. Weeks, Albert Wilkinson, John J. O'Brien, John McCrillis, Fenn W. Boody.

1905   Anton L. Weidner, Lewis H. Schwartz, Alvin L. Hofmann, James J. Ahearn, Edward J. Ward, John P. Lahey, James A. Connors, John T. Kilcoyne, Frank A. Sullivan, Daniel W. Mahoney, John P. O'Brien, Michael Welch, Jr., Joseph A. Edmond, Harry Simpson, Albert Wilkinson, Andrew E. Cantwell, Charles Cate, John J. O'Brien (President).

1906   Alvin L. Hofmann, Fred Knight, Lewis H, Schwartz, Edward A. Dolan, Eugene B. Griffin, Thomas F. Scanlon, James J. Finegan, Stephen J. Scully, Joseph A. Tosney, John T. Manion, Michael A. Scanlon, Michael Welch Jr. (President), Joseph A. Edmond, Harry Simpson, Henry H. Wildes, Patrick J. Casey, Charles Cate, Patrick W. Connors.

1907   Arthur Bower, Henry C. Gebelein, John F. Young, Edward A. Dolan, Eugene B. Griffin, Thomas F. Scanlon, Daniel Fitzpatrick, Joseph Hayes, Joseph A.Tosney. John T. Manion (President). Daniel McCabe, Michael Welch. Jr., Timothy Bee, Joseph A. Mosher, Henry H. Wildes, Patrick J. Casey, Florence D. McCarthy, John J. McCarthy.

1908   Arthur Bower, Herman Grunwald, Carl A. Woekel, Jr., James A. Coyne, Thomas M. Jordan, Henry J. Nichols, Michael Brown, Joseph Hayes, Joseph A. Kennedy, Bernard J. Bresnahan, David D. O'Connell, Fred J. Watson. Timothy Bee, Thomas Hughes, Joseph A. Mosher, George F. Hoar, Florence D. McCarthy, John J. McCarthy (President).

1909   Jacob Doerr, Herman Grunwald, Albert E. Knuepfer, Seth Cooper, John J. McCarthy, Thomas M. Jordan, John Joseph Ford, John J. Holley, John T. Busby, Michael J. Dooley, Joseph H. Maxwell, Eugene A. McCarthy, Jr., Frederick W. Briggs, Thomas Hughes (President), Charles P. Rushforth, Frank E. Ferguson, Ambrose J. Godin, John Hennessey.

1910   Joseph F. Adams, Jacob Doerr, Albin Ulrich, Bernard J. Keaveny,
        Henry J. Nichols, David Noonan, Thaddeus J. Begley, Frank D.
        Foley, John F. Morrissey, Michael J. Dooley, Joseph H. Maxwell,
        Eugene A. McCarthy, Jr. (President), Charles P. Rushforth,
        Joseph Spencer, L. Morton Taylor, Thomas A. Welch, Edgar W.
        Shea, John J. Nugent, Jr.

1911   Adam Boehm, Robert Leupold, Albin Ulrich, Michael H.
        Collopy, Bernard J. Keaveny (President), David Noonan,
        Thaddeus J. Begley, Frank D. Foley, Jolin F. Morrissey, Michael
        Joseph Fay. John McMahon, John A. O'Donnell, Frederick W.
        Briggs, James J. Carney, Joseph A. Hurley, Joseph M. O'Dowd,
        James H. Quinn, Thomas A. Welch.

Note: The Councilmen are named in the order of the wards they represented, three being elected from each of the six wards. Common Council
abolished under new charter in 1912.

COMMISSION GOVERNMENTS

1912   Mayor Michael A. Scanlon
                Aldermen
        Paul Hannagan Director of Engineering
        Michael S. O'Brien Director of Public Property and Parks
        Cornelius F. Lynch Director of Public Safety
        Robert S. Maloney Director of Public Health and Charities

1913   Mayor Michael A. Scanlon
                Aldermen
        Cornelius F. Lynch Director of Public Safety
        John S. Todd Director of Public Health and Charities
        Paul Hannagan Director of Engineering
        Alfred Bradbury Director of Public Property and Parks

1914   Mayors
        Michael A. Scanlon (Died August 16 1914)
        John P. Kane (Elected to fill vacancy)
                Aldermen
        Paul Hannagan Director of Engineering

244

Alfred Bradbury Director of Public Property and Parks

James W. Cadogan Director of Public Safety

John S. Todd Director of Public Health and Charities

1915 Mayor John P. Kane

    Aldermen

James W. Cadogan Director of Public Safety

Robert S. Maloney Director of Public Health and Charities

John F. Finnegan Director of Engineering

1916 Mayor John J. Hurley

    Aldermen

James W. Cadogan Director of Public Safety

John A. Flanagan Director of Public Property Parks

John F. Finnegan Director of Engineering

Robert S. Maloney Director of Public Health and Charities

1917 Mayor John J. Hurley

    Aldermen

James W. Cadogan Director of Public Safety

John A. Flanagan Director of Public Property Parks

John F. Finnegan Director of Engineering

Robert S. Maloney Director of Public Health and Charities

1918 Mayor John J. Hurley

    Aldermen

John A. Flanagan Director of Public Property Parks

John F. Finnegan Director of Engineering

Peter Carr Director of Public Safety

Robert S. Maloney Director of Public Health and Charities

1853	C. S. Storrow, Whig, 577	1870	N. P. H. Melvin, dem., 1518
	Dana Sargent, dem., 484		John B. Atkinson, rep., 1363
	Scattering, 21	1871	S. B. W. Davis, rep., 1665
1854	Enoch Bartlett, dem., 651		John J. Doland, dem., 1522
	Geo. W. Benson, Whig, 529	1872	S. B. W. Davis, rep., 1726
	James D, Herrick, ind., 67		John J. Doland, dem., 1604
	Scattering, 12		Daniel Hardy, pro., 55
1855	Albert Warren, k. not'g, 1037	1873	John K. Tarbox, dem.,A 1959
	Elkanah F. Bean, dem., 81		S. B. W. Davis, rep., 1685
	Nathan W. Harmon, Whig, 82	1874	John K. Tarbox, cit., 2211
	Scattering, 7		Scattering, 124
1856	Albert Warren, k. not'g, 758	1875	R. H. Tewksbury, rep., 2396
	John R. Rollins, ind., 386		N. P. H, Melvin, dem., 1555
1857	John R. Rollins, ind., 801	1876	E. R. Hayden, dem., 2162
	Thomas Wright, whig, 570		William S. Knox, rep., 1843
	Scattering, 6	1877	Caleb Saunders, dem., 2283
1858	John R. Rollins, ind., 720		A. A. Currier, rep., 2010
	Nathaniel G. White, dem., 76	1878	James R. Simpson, rep., 2365
	Scattering, 4		Caleb Saunders, dem., 1795
1859	Henry K. Oliver, rep., 886	1879	James R, Simpson, rep., 2087
	Daniel Saunders, Jr., dem., 589		Thomas F. Tucker, dem., 1519
	Scattering, 5		H. W. K. Eastman, gr., 443
1860	Daniel Saunders, Jr., dem., 820	1880	James R. Simpson, rep., 2341
	John R. Rollins, rep., 646		John K. Tarbox, dem., 2006
1861	James K. Barker, rep., 967	1881	Henry K. Webster, rep., 2556
	Benj. F. Watson, dem., 567		John Breen, dem., 2363
	Scattering, 3	1882	John Breen, dem., 2932
1862	Wm. H. P. Wright, rep., 805		Wm. T. McAlpine, rep., 2363
	Nathaniel G. White, dem., 506	1883	John Breen, dem., 2934
	James K. Barker, rep., 87		Charles U. Bell, rep., 2656
1863	Wm. H. P. Wright, rep., 759	1884	John Breen, dem., 3062
	N. P. H. Melvin, dem., 632		Charles U. Bell, rep., 2582
1864	Alfred J. French, rep., 720	1885	James R. Simpson, rep., 3052
	John Beetle, dem., 615		A. B. Bruce, dem. 2425
1865	Milton Bonney, rep., 762	1886	A. B. Bruce, dem., 2961
	Nicholas Chapman, dem., 270		Byron Truell, rep., 2302
1866	Pardon Armington, rep., 894	1887	A. B. Bruce, dem., 2559
	Nathaniel G. White, cit., 828		P. B. Robinson, rep., 1972
1867	N. P. H, Melvin, dem., 959		Daniel Hardy, pro., 94
	Lemuel A. Bishop, rep., 831	1888	Alvin E. Mack, rep., 3177
1868	N. P. H. Melvin, dem., 1406		D. F. McCarthy, dem., 2521
	Frederick Butler, rep., 668	1889	Alvin E. Mack, rep., 3530
1869	Frank Davis, rep., 1551		A. B. Bruce, dem., 2332
	N. P. H. Melvin, dem., 1396	1890	J. W. Crawford, dem., 2914

Alvin E. Mack, rep., 2815

1891   Lewis P. Collins, rep., 3418

D. F. McCarthy, dem., 2766

C. R. Lawrence, pro., 57

1892   Henry P. Doe, dem., 3448

Lewis P. Collins, rep., 3025

1893   Alvin E. Mack, rep., 3627

Charles G. Rutter, dem., 3457

1894   Charles G. Rutter, dem., 3874

John L. Brewster, rep., 3624

1895   Charles G, Rutter, dem., 3723

George S. Junkins, rep., 3641

1896   George S. Junkins, rep., 4302

James F. Leonard, dem., 3437

1897   George S. Junkins, rep., 4241

James F. Leonard, dem., 4225

1898   James H, Eaton, rep., 4968

James E. Donoghue, dem., 4083

1899   James H. Eaton, rep., 4431

John P. S. Mahoney, dem., 4243

1900   James F. Leonard, dem., 4515

James H. Eaton, rep., 4188

1901   James F. Leonard, dem., 5058

Richard W. Ellis, rep.. 3967

1902   James F. Leonard, dem., 4604

Alexander L. Grant, rep., 4417

1903   Alexander L. Grant, rep., 5220

James F. Leonard, dem., 4101

1904   Cornelius F. Lynch, dem., 5722

Henry B. Lane, rep., 4019

1905   Cornelius F. Lynch, dem., 4990

Moses Marshall, rep., 4353

1906   John P. Kane, dem.,; 5142

Moses Marshall, rep., 4623

1907   John P. Kane, dem., 5178

Robert F. Pickels, rep., 3897

1908   John P. Kane, dem., 4524

Wm. P. White, ind. cit., 3540

Alvin E. Mack, rep., 1950

1909   W. P. White. rep., ind. 1., 6233

Michael F. Cronin, dem., 3690

1910   Wm. P. White, rep., 5157

John T. Cahill, dem., 4671

Joseph Donovan, ind., 146

1911   John T. Cahill, dem., 5216

Rudolph Miller, rep., 3045

COMMISSION GOVERNMENT

1912-13   Michael A. Scanlon, 5975

Michael J. Sullivan, 3977

*1914   Michael A. Scanlon, 4968

William P. White, 4801

**1914-'15   John P. Kane, 5474

William P. White, 5177

1916-17   John J. Hurley, 5786

John P. Kane, 5258

1918–19   John J. Hurley, 6506

John P. Kane, 4253

* Died August 16, 1914

* * Elected at City Election to fill unexpired term.

TOWN AND CITY TREASURERS

1847	Daniel Saunders
1848	Nathaniel White
1849	Daniel Saunders
1850-'52	George W. Sanborn
1853	Brackett H. Clark
1854	Daniel Hardy
1855-'64	Nathaniel Wilson
1865-'73	Robert H. Tewksbury
1874	Elihu W. Colcord
1875-'82	Albert V. Bugbee
1883-'86	Patrick Murphy
1887-'91	Edward P. Poor
1892	Daniel C. O'Sullivan
1893-'94	Walter R. Rowe
1895	Franklin B. Davis
1896-'97	Walter R. Rowe
1898-'01	Arthur A. Bailey
1902-'03	William H. Russell
1904	Daniel F. Murray
1905-'08	Barry T. O'Connell
1909	William N. Hamel
1910 –	William A. Kelleher

VOTE ON LICENSE

*1881 Yes, 3158 – No, 1858

1882 Yes, 3427 – No, 1319

1883 Yes, 3158 – No, 968

1884 Yes, 2441 – No, 878

1885 Yes, 2380 – No, 1232

1886 Yes, 2529 – No, 1346

1887 Yes, 2460 – No, 2688

1888 Yes, 3708 – No, 1937

1889 Yes, 2792 – No, 2393

1890 Yes, 3326 – No, 2655

1891 Yes, 3182 – No, 3085

1892 Yes, 2965 – No, 4004

1893 Yes, 3932 – No, 3390

1894 Yes, 3857 – No, 3423

1895 Yes, 4182 – No, 3331

1896 Yes, 4539 – No, 3775

1897 Yes, 4863 – No, 3897

1898 Yes, 5105 – No, 3269

1899 Yes, 5283 – No, 2673

1900 Yes, 5623 – No, 2892

1901 Yes, 5812 – No, 2868

1902 Yes, 5595 – No, 3153

1903 Yes, 5965 – No, 3376

1904 Yes, 5188 – No, 3749

1905 Yes, 5692 – No, 3602

1906 Yes, 5515 – No, 2944

1907 Yes, 5931 – No, 3177

1908 Yes, 5931 – No, 3743

1909 Yes, 6145 – No, 3292

1910 Yes, 5280 – No, 2493

1911 Yes, 6389 – No, 3117

1912 Y.es, 6224 – No, 2813

1913 Yes, 5969 – No, 3367

1914 Yes, 5520 – No, 4918

1915 Yes, 6989 – No, 4844

1916 Yes, 6617 – No, 4527

1917 Yes, 6854 — No, 3736

*Beginning of Local Option on the License Question.

Note :–From 1852 to 1875 prohibition was in effect, except from.1870 to 1875 the sale of beers and light wines was permitted. From 1875 to 1881 the question was left to the discretion of the Board of Aldermen. From 1881 to date, local option in vogue–Question determined by the people and, until 1895, licenses were granted by the Board of Aldermen. In 1895 the first grant was made by the newly appointed License Commission. On July 1st, 1888, the so–called High License statute went into effect, affecting the licenses granted the following May. The first License Commission comprised :–John P. Sweeney, chairman; Walter E. Parker and James E. Donoghue.

JUDGES OF POLICE COURT

Joseph Couch (Trial justice) 1846-48

William Stevens 1848-76

Wm. H. P. Wright (served) 1877

Nathan W. Harmon 1878-1887

Andrew C. Stone 1887-1905

Jeremiah J. Mahoney 1905 to date

CHIEFS OF POLICE

Gilman F. Sanborn, 1847 to 1848

Nathaniel Ambrose, 1848 to 1849

James D. Herrick, 1849 to 1850

Nathaniel Ambrose, 1850 to 1853

Harvey L. Fuller, 1853 to 1854

Leonard Stoddard, 1854 to 1855

Chandler Bailey, 1855 to 1856

Joseph H. Keyes, 1856 to 1857

John S. Perkins, 1857 to 1859

George W. Porter, 1859 to 1860

Edmund R. Hayden, 1860 to 1861

Noah Parkman, 1861 to 1862

John W. Porter, 1862 to 1864

Chandler Bailey, Jan. to Aug. 1864

Chase Philbrick, Aug. 1864 to 1870

James E. Shepard, 1870 to 1871

Chase Philbrick, 1871 to 1873

Lyman Prescott, 1873 to 1875

James M. Currier, Jan. to Aug., 1875

M. Batchelder, Aug., 1875 to 1877

Jas. T. O'Sullivan, 1877 to 1878

Moulton Batchelder, 1878 to 1881

Hiram R. Neal, 1881 to 1882

Jas. T. O'Sullivan, 1882 to 1885

Hiram R. Neal, 1885 to 1886

Jas. T. O'Sullivan, 1886 to 1888

Clinton P. Vose, 1888 to July, 1891

John Sheehan, July, 1891 to 1896

David Bailey, 1896 to 1898

Michael J. Murphy, 1898 to 1900

Jas. T. O'Sullivan, 1900 to 1906

John Sheehan, 1906 to 1909

Richard Fox, 1909 to 1911

Jas. T. O'Sullivan, 1911 to Mar. 1912

*John J. Sullivan, Mar. 1912 to 1914

Maurice F. McKenna, 1914 to 1918

*Timothy J. O'Brien, 1918–

* acting Chief of Police

CHIEFS OF FIRE DEPARTMENT

James D. Herrick, 1849 to 1851

Samuel I. Thompson, 1851 to 1852

William M. Kimball, 1852 to 1854

Luther Ladd, 1854 to 1857

Lorenzo D. Sargent, 1857 to 1859

Luther Ladd, 1859 to 1862

Benjamin Booth, 1862 to 1868

George K. Wiggin, 1868 to 1871

Luther Ladd, 1871 to 1873

Albert R. Brewster, 1873 to 1875

Melvin Beal, 1875 to 1877

Dennis Wholley, 1877 to 1878

William E. Heald, 1878 to 1884

Michael F. Collins, 1884 to 1885

Zachary T. Merrill, 1885 to 1891

F. L. Calderwood, Jan. to †June, 1891

Melvin Beal, June 1891 to 1900

Charles G. Rutter, May, 1900 to 1909

J. A. Hamilton, May '09 to Oct. '10

*Wm. McCreadie, Oct.'10 to Feb.'11

Dennis E. Carey, Feb., 1911 to 1918

*Francis J. Morris, 1918 to —

*Acting Chief.

† Department reorganized, when the system of electing chief engineers was changed.

CLERKS OF POLICE COURT

William H. Parsons

William H. P. Wright

Edgar J. Sherman

Charles E. Briggs

Henry L. Sherman

Jesse G. Gould

Henry F. Hopkins

William F. Moyes

Daniel W. Mahony

Nathaniel E. Rankin

CITY SOLICITORS

1854 Daniel Saunders, Jr.

1855 *Benjamin Boardman

   †George W. Benson

1856 George W. Benson

1857-'58 Daniel Saunders, Jr.

1859 N. W. Harmon

1860 B. F. Watson

1861 Gilbert E. Hood

1862-'65 N, W. Harmon

1866-'67 Thomas Wright V.

1868-'69 Thomas A. Parsons

1870 Caleb Saunders

1871-'73 Thomas A. Parsons

1874 John C. Sanborn

**1875-'77

1878-'81 E. T. Burley

1882-'83 John K. Tarbox

1884 William F. Moyes

1885 Andrew C. Stone

1886-'87 William F. Moyes

1888-'91 William S. Knox

1892 Charles A. DeCourcy

1893-'98 Charles U. Bell

1899-'05 John P. Kane

1896-'08 Daniel J. Murphy

1909 Frederic N. Chandler

1910- Daniel J. Murphy

*Resigned March 13th.

†Elected March 20th to fill vacancy. ·

**Original ordinance, establishing office of City Solicitor was repealed February 10, 1875. This ordinance had been adopted February 28, 1854. Office reestablished by ordinance February 18, 1878. During interval, 1875-'77, it appears that attorneys were engaged as the occasion demanded.

POSTMASTERS OF LAWRENCE

*Geo. A. Waldo, Sept., 1846 to 1848

William Peirce, 1848 to 1849

Nathaniel Wilson, 1849 to 1853

Benjamin F. Watson, 1853 to 1861

George S. Merrill, 1861 to 1886

Patrick Murphy, 1886 to 1890

Lewis G. Holt, 1890 to 81894

John P. Sweeney, 1894 to 1898

Sidney H. Brigham, 1898 to 1902

Byron Truell, 1902 to 1906

Louis S. Cox, 1906 to Jan., 1914

Michael F. Cronin, Jan., 1914 to —

*When George A. Waldo was first appointed the Post-office, now designated as Lawrence, was known as Merrimack, the latter name being retained until the incorporation of the town in 1847.

STATE SENATORS AND REPRESENTATIVES
SENATORS FROM LAWRENCE

1851	Daniel Saunders, Jr.	1895	George L. Gage
1853	Thomas Wright	1896	James H. Derbyshire
1854	Thomas Wright	1897	James H. Derbyshire
1856	Benjamin Osgood	1898	Joseph J. Flynn
1863	Thomas Wright	1899	Charles F. Sargent
1864	Thomas Wright	1902	Archie N. Frost, R.
1872	John K. Tarbox	1903	Archie N. Frost, R.
1873	Nathan W. Harmon	1904	Joseph J. Flynn, D.
1874	Horace C. Bacon	1906	Louis S. Cox, R.
1877	Byron Truell	1907	Joseph Donovan, R.
1878	Byron Truell	1908	Dennis E. Halley, D.
1880	Andrew C. Stone	1911	Dennis E. Halley, D,
1882	Andrew C. Stone	1912	Dennis E. Halley, D.
1887	Edward F. O'Sullivan	1913	Dennis E. Halley, D.
1888	William T. McAlpine	1914	James R. Tetler, R.
1889	Edward F. O'Sullivan	1915	James R. Tetler, P. P., R.
1892	Richard A. Carter	1916	James R. Tetler, P. P., R.
1893	Richard A. Carter	1917	James R. Tetler, R., D.
1894	George L. Gage	1918	James R. Tetler, R.

Note :-In the years not mentioned in the above list, the Senator serving came from elsewhere in the district. In the earlier years the Senatorial district, including Lawrence, comprised practically the whole of Essex County. Party designation is given where there has been a record of such.

REPRESENTATIVES FROM LAWRENCE

1851   James K. Barber, Morris Knowles, George D. Luna.

1852   E. B. Currier, Charles S. Merrill, Josiah Osgood.

1853   Enoch Bartlett, Enoch Pratt, David Wentworth.

1854   Amassa Bryant, Timothy V. Coburn, John A. Goodwin.

1855   John Gale, Benjamin Harding, James R. Johnson.

1856   John Gale, Benjamin Harding, Thomas W. Floyd.

1857   Walker Flanders, William Hardy, Nathan W. Harmon.

1858   William Hardy, John C. Hoadley.

1859 A. J. French, George W. Benson.

1860 Thomas A. Parsons, Henry K. Oliver.

1861 Thomas A. Parsons, Harrison D. Clement, Cyrus Williams.

1862 John J. Doland, Harrison D. Clement, Cyrus Williams.

1863 John J. Doland, Lemuel A. Bishop.

1864 Thomas A. Parsons, Lemuel A. Bishop.

1865 Henry Barton, Edgar J. Sherman.

1866 Henry Barton, Edgar J. Sherman.

1867 William H. P. Wright, Henry M. McIntire, Albert Blood.

1868 William H. P. Wright, Albert Blood, John K. Tarbox.

1869 William A. Russell, Frederick Butler.

1870 John K. Tarbox, Patrick Sweeney, Robert Bower.

1871 John K. Tarbox, Robert Bower, George E. Davis.

1872 Horace C. Bacon, Patrick Murphy.

1873 George E. Davis, Horace C. Bacon.

1874 William S. Knox, Henry J. Couch.

1875 William S. Knox, Byron Truell.

1876 yron Truell, Edwin Ayer.

1877 Timothy Dacey, John C. Sanborn, Levi Emery, Edwin Ayer.

1878 Michael Rinn, Abel Webster, Levi Emery, Melvin Beal.

1879 Abel Webster, Joseph J. Nichols, Levi Emery, Jesse Moulton.

1880 Henry P. Danforth, Joseph J. Nichols, Edward P. Poor, Daniel F. Dolan.

1881 Daniel Donovan, Joseph J. Nichols, Edward P. Poor, Thomas Scott.

1882 Dennis Gilmartin. Dennis A. Sullivan, Jonathan D. Boothman, John B. Campbell.

1883 Dennis Gilmartin, Dennis A. Sullivan, Samuel M. Davis, Daniel F. Dolan.

1884 Edward F. O'Sullivan, Henry P. Danforth, John H. Stafford, Richard T. Butler.

1885 Edward F. O'Sullivan, John F. McQueeney, Charles Murphy, Milton B. Townsend.

1886 Timothy F. O'Hearn. John F. McQueeney, James Murphy, Milton B. Townsend.

1887 Timothy F. O'Hearn, Michael Carney, William J. Hinchcliffe, Harry M. Fames.

1888 Michael F. Sullivan, Michael Carney, William J. Hinchcliffe, Harry M. Fames.

1889 Michael F. Sullivan, John F. Howard, Phineas W. Haseltine, John H. Stafford.

1890 John O'Brien. John F. Howard, Richard A. Carter, John H. Hulford.

1891 John O'Brien, William Cannon, Richard A. Carter, Frank McAnnally.

1892 Dennis E. Halley, William Cannon, William H. Hart, Frank McAnnally.

1893 Dennis E. Halley, Thomas A. Brooks, James H. Derbyshire, John Haigh.

1894 John M. Lynch, Thomas A. Brooks, James H. Derbyshire, John Haigh.

1895 John M. Lynch, Joseph J. Flynn, Harry R. Dow, Charles F. Sargent.

1896 Cornelius F. Sullivan, Joseph J. Flynn, Harry R. Dow, Charles F. Sargent.

1897 George B. Smart, Benjamin C. Ames, Richard Cullinane, Cornelius F. Sullivan.

1898 George B. Smart, Richard Cullinane, Joseph H. Joubert, Cornelius F. Sullivan.

1899 Archie N. Frost. R., Richard Cullinane. D., William Daly, D., Mortimer D. A. Murphy, D.

1900 Archie N. Frost, R., Amedee Cloutier, D., William Daly, D., Mortimer D. A. Murphy, D.

1901 Archie N. Frost, R., Amedee Cloutier, D., Jeremiah J. Desmond, D., John T. Maloney, R.

1902 Karl M. Ebert, R., Jeremiah J. Desmond, D., Simon B. Ryan, D., John T. Maloney, R.

1903 John H. Spinlow, R., Dennis H. Finn, D., Simon B. Ryan, D., Frank J. Stanley, D.

1904 Otto Mueller, D., Edward C. Callahan, D., Dennis H. Finn, D., William J. Graham, D.

1905 John H. Spinlow, R., Dennis C. Callahan. D., William J. Graham, D., John P. Whelan, D.

1906 Emil J. Muehlig, R.. Edward C. Callahan. D., William J. Graham, D., William A. Kelleher, D.

1907 Emil J. Muehlig. R., William A. Kelleher, D., George S. J. Hyde, R., William J. Graham, D.

1908 George McLane, Jr., R., William A. Kelleher. D., George S. J. Hyde, R., William J. Graham, D.

1909 Alfred J. Burckel, R., William A. Hester, D., James R. Tetler, R., William J. Graham, D.

1910 Alfred J. Burckel, R., William A. Hester, D., James R. Tetler, R., William J. Graham, D.

1911 John C. Sanborn, D., Frederick W. Schlapp, D., Eugene A. McCarthy, Jr., D., Charles H. Morgan, R., William J. Graham, D.

1912 John C. Sanborn, D. P., D., Frederick W. Schlapp, D. P., Daniel Fitzpatrick, D.. Charles H. Morgan, R., William J. Graham. D.

1913 John C. Sanborn, D., Frederick W. Schlapp, D., Daniel Fitzpatrick, D., Charles H. Morgan, R., William J. Graham, D.

1914 Arthur Bower, R., John E. Cuddy, Jr., D., Peter Carr, D., Frederick Butler, R., James T. O'Dowd, D.

1915 Arthur Bower, P. P., R., Peter Carr, D., Frederick Butler, R., P. P., James T. O'Dowd, D.

1916 Frederick Butler. R., Michael H. Jordan, D., James T. O'Dowd, D., Frederick W. Schlapp, D.

1917 Frederick Butler, R., Michael H. Jordan, D., Michael A. Flanagan, D., Arthur Bower, R.

Note:–Party designation is given where there has been a record of such.

DESTRUCTIVE FIRES
(WHERE THE LOSSES WERE $10,000 AND UPWARDS)

1849 November 28. The Merrimack House on Turnpike, near Tremont Street, - $25,000

1850 February 28. The Bangor block and five other houses on Common Street, near Newbury, Street 12,000

August 16. Car shops of the Boston & Maine railroad, in South Lawrence, 25,000

1851 Februar y 11. The armory of the Lawrence Light Infantry, with its contents, and B. H. Clark's store on Merchants' row, consumed, 12,000

1859 August 12. The United States hotel, Church block, courthouse burned, also spire of Unitarian church destroyed, 52,000

1860 May 2. Wilson & Allyn's factory on Lowell street, 20,000

August 26. W. W. Briggs' cashmere mill at mouth of Spicket, 18,000

1865 January 27. Everett mills dye house, 50,000

September 26. Russell's paper mill. 20,000

1866 May 14. Ashworth's brewery, and Flanders & Severance's shop in the Essex yard, 15,000

June 28. Pemberton mill storehouse, containing $40,000 worth of yarn.

August 12. Boston & Maine car shops in South Lawrence, 100,000

October 9. The Arlington mills totally consumed 200,000

1867 April 8. Desmond's hat factory on Broadway, 40,000

September 1. Gale & Ames' carriage shop on Lowell Street, 12,000

1868 November 17. H. K. Webster's grist mill, Pillsbury's machine shop and Davis' foundry. loss about, 30,000

1869 July 8. Thomas S. Stratton's hat factory in Essex yard 17,000

September 3. O'Sullivan Bros.' hat factory on Daisy Street, 35,000

1870 October 19. Lawrence Lumber Co.'s planing mill on Lowell St., 125,000

1871 June 23. The building at northeast corner of Common and Amesbury streets and Stowell's shop burned, 30,000

July 18. Clement & Cressey's shops in Essex yard, 17,000

1875 October 4. West wing of Washington mills, 50,000

1877 October 11. Everett mills dye house, 18,000

1878   January 13. Pacific mills' print works, 130,000

September 1. Gale's carriage shop on Lowell Street, 20,000

1881   July 17. The Broadway Bridge over the Merrimack, 60,000

1882   June 23. Pacific Mills' storehouse, 400,000

1883   August 6. Wright Mfg. Co.'s braid mill, 150,000 '

1885   January 1. Lawrence Lumber Co.'s building, Essex yard, also Briggs & Allyn's shops, 17,000

February 18. Russell paper mill, 30,000

March 18. Packard school-house in South Lawrence, 25,000

September 12. Lee, Blackburn & Co.'s chemical works at which Fireman James Keegan lost his life by falling into a vat of vitriol.

1886   April 10. The river building of the Pemberton mills, when George McKenzie and John Miller were fatally burned, 100,000

1887   May 4. The Union street (Duck) bridge over the Merrimack

May 17. No. 1 mill of the Washington Corporation, 150,000

1889   March 28, Essex Savings Bank building, 10,000

1890   January 13. Merrimack Spinning Co.'s mill on Island street, 20,000

1892   April 15. Boston & Maine freight depot on Broadway, 30,000

1896   October 25. Washington mill, 200,000

1897   March 22. Gleason building, on Essex street, 62,000

1899   March 25. D. W. Pingree Co.'s box shop 13,500

November 13. Hartley Bros.' wool scouring mill on Island st., 13,500

1902   October 17. Hamblett Machine Co.'s shop on Island street, 14,000

Dec. 30. F. P. Berry & Co.'s furniture store, and W. H. Godfrey's storehouse on Essex Street, 15,800

1907   July 23. City Flour Mills on South Broadway totally destroyed, 90,000

September 11. Robertson & Sutherland Co.'s store on Essex st., 10,000

1908   December 14. G. W. Dodson Co.'s stove store and plumbing shop (Adams' Block) on Essex street. 25,000

1909   April 29. Lawrence Market Co.'s store on Essex Street, 10.000

1910   March 15. National Fibre Board Co.'s plant (known as the Clegg mill) on the South canal, 21,500

December 7. Old High Schol Building on Haverhill Street totally destroyed, 60,000

1911 January 25. Plymouth fibre mills on Marston Street, 41,000

August 3. Robertson & Sutherland Co.'s store on Essex Street, 12,000

August 28. Bradley block of ten-footers on Essex Street, 25,000

October 19. Archibald Wheel Co.'s plant, 50,000

November 13. H. K. Webster's grain elevator and storehouse, 25,000

November 28. Regan Bros.' foundry on Merrimack Street, 11,000

1912 July 26. Lawrence Ice Co.'s ice houses on Water Street, 10,000

December 17. Lawrence Boiler Works plant on Water Street, 20,000

1913 February 2. State Armory on Amesbury Street, 10,000

February 7. Lawrence Street Congregational church totally destroyed, 23,000

May 4. M. J. Cahill's dry goods store on Essex Street, 15.000

June 14. U. S. Bobbin Co.'s shop on Lowell Street, 10,000

1914 December 26. Smith machine shop building on Essex Street, 21,000

1915 February 9. Cold Spring brewery on South Union Street, 10,000

1916 March 31. Jak Katz and Joseph E. Walworth residences on Campo Seco Street, former totally destroyed and Mrs, Aaron A.Currier and daughter, Ella Currier, burned to death, 20.000

1917 July 31. Franklin House stable and adjoining property, 561-7 Common Street, 16,000

November 14. R. J. Macartney Company's clothing store, 431-5 Essex Street, 47,000

December 5. Morehouse's bakery, 7 Mill Street, 12,000

December 22. Boston & Maine round house, 22,000

INDEX

6th Essex Representative District 201
6th Mass. Regiment 121, 167
8th Mass. Regiment 121
9th Mass. Regiment 122

A

A. B. Sutherland Company 220
A.G. Walton & Co. Inc. 164
Abbott, a young man 15
Abbott, Charles F. 229, 232
Abbott, Fred N. 234, 241
Abbott, James G. 233, 238, 240
Abbott, James G. Jr. 240
Abbott, Mrs. Nellie E. 184
Abbott, Paschal 235, 236, 237
Abbott, Samuel 22
Abbott, Waldo L. 130, 237
Abbott, William H. 240
Abercrombie, John A. 233, 234
Acadia Corporation 158
Acadia Mills 156, 158
Adams, Eugene T. 221
Adams, George G. 138
Adams, Joseph F. 244
Adolph, William 61
Adolph, William, Pemberton victim 61
Advent Christian church 115
Agawam tribe 13
Ahearn, James J. 234, 243
Ahern, Ellen, Pemberton victim 61
Alder street 104

Alexander B. Bruce grammar school 104
Alexander Bruce School 51, 104
Alexander, John W. 160
Alfred Kimball Shoe Company 165
Allegbro, Secundo 66
the Alleghaney 122
Allen, Dr. Granville S. 126
Almshouse Hospital 139
Ambrose, Nathaniel 94, 102, 179, 239, 250
the American 180
American Federation of Labor 200
American Red Cross 125
American Red Cross War Fund 125
American Woolen Co. 46, 47, 48, 70, 149
Ames, Benjamin C. 189, 241, 255
Ames farm 19, 185
Ames, Samuel 18, 19
Ames street 22, 92, 104, 185
Amesbury, Mass. 20
Amesbury street 18, 20, 22, 31, 71, 84, 91, 103, 113, 136, 139, 147, 191, 218, 257, 259
Amesbury Street Armory 71
Amesbury Street Baptist Church 113
Amoskeag Company 43
Amoskeag Manufacturing Company 92
the Amphitheatre 133
Andover Bridge 19, 22, 23, 24, 25, 27, 31, 32, 41, 185, 187, 188, 189, 190, 258
Andover, Mass. 13, 14, 15, 17, 21, 22, 35, 38, 98, 143, 174, 187, 204, 208, 222
Andover street 19, 24, 27, 45, 63, 184, 185, 225

Andrew, F. M. 170
Andrew, Thomas E. 77
Andrews, Alenizies C. 232
Andrews, Clinton O. 126, 169, 170
Andrews, Menizies C. 232
Andrews, Rufus 239, 240
Anzeiger und Post 181
Apitz, Oswald 124
Appleton, Nathan 26
Appleton street
    82, 83, 87, 99, 114, 135,
    138, 191
Appleton street, 42
Archibald Wheel Co. 259
Archibald Wheel Company 164
Arlington Day Nursery 142
Arlington district 174, 183
Arlington, Mass. 193
Arlington Mills
    19, 45, 46, 47, 48, 49, 70,
    154, 155, 156, 158, 183, 204,
    207, 257
Arlington National Bank 170
Arlington Trust Company 170, 220
Arlington Union Church 116
Arlington Woolen Mills 155
Armenian Congregational church
    115
Armenian National Apostolic
    Church 118
Armington, Pardon H.
    60, 231, 233, 246
Armory 257
Arthur, Andrew S. 240
Arundel, Daniel A. 120
Arundel, Edward L. 241, 242
Arundel, Thomas A. 242
Ashkexazy, Joseph D. 124
Ashton, Orrell 243
Ashworth, Augusta, Pemberton
    victim 61
Ashworth's brewery 257
Asrath Noshim 142

Assumption of Mary church 115
Assumption school for boys and
    girls 109
Atkinson, John B. 232, 246
Atkinson, Moses L. 31
Atkinson road 183
Atlantic Mill boarding house 32
Atlantic Mills
    27, 34, 36, 46, 49, 58,
    71, 86, 93, 98, 161, 194
Augustinian Fathers 114
Austin, Clark L. 232
Austin, George N. 239
Auty, Jonathan 240
Avon Street 116, 117
awke, a place 13
Ayer, D. M. 169
Ayer, Edwin 233, 235, 238, 254
Ayer, Frederick 47, 149
Ayer Mills 47, 48, 52, 71
Ayer, Perley 236, 237
Ayrey, Thomas 239

B

Bacon, Horace C. 169, 253, 254
Bailey, Arthur A. 64, 234, 240, 248
Bailey, Chandler 250
Bailey, David 227, 250
Bailey, Edwin F. 236
Bailey, Heaton 236
Bailey, James W. 237, 238
Bailey, John 236
Bailey, Joseph, Pemberton victim 61
Bailey, Moses A. 237
Bailey, Robert M. 155
Bailey street 92
Bailey, Warner 232
Ballard, Walter C. 160
Balloch, James R. 237
Baltimore, Md. 41
Bamford, John 237
Bangor Block 257

Bannan, Mary Ann, Pemberton
    victim 61
Bannon, John H, 216
Baptists 112
Barber, James K. 253
Barbour, William 236
Barker family 18
Barker, James K. 138, 231, 246
Barker, Robert 241
Barnard family 18
Barnard road 183
Barnes, Charles 112
Barnes, James H. 241
Barnes, Joel 236, 237
Barnes, Joseph 239
Barr, John E. 241
Barrage, William 240
Barrett, Mary, Pemberton victim 61
Barrett, Samuel 233, 239
Barrie, James S. 239
Barry, William J. 240
Bartlett, Enoch 231, 246, 253
Bartlett, Mayor 40
Bartley, Dr. J. J. 77
Bartley, William B. 242
Barton, Henry 89, 254
Batchelder, John Q. A.
    60, 235, 236
Batchelder, Moulton 250
Batchelder, Samuel 157
Bates, General James 122
Bates, Gov. John L. 197
Bates, William C. 231
bathhouse, No. 1 66
bathhouses 53, 67
Battershill, John O. 147
Battery building 113
Battery C, 102nd Field Artillery
    64, 71, 122, 124, 125, 203
Bay State Bank 36, 165, 166, 191
Bay State Bank building 165
Bay State block 51

Bay State building 147, 173, 175
Bay State Mills
    27, 32, 34, 35, 36, 38,
    46, 47, 58, 84, 88, 98
Bay State road 143
Bay State Street Railway 143
Beach, Lurandus Jr. 233, 237
Beacon street 183, 225
Beal, Chief 206
Beal, Melvin 237, 251, 254
Beal, Wendell W. 239
Bean, Charles H. 82, 239
Bean, Elkanah F. 232, 235, 246
Bean, N. S. 43
Beanland, John T. 241
Beatty, David 236
Beatty, Hannah 64
Bedell, John H. 234, 242
Bee, Timothy 243
Beedles, George 242
Beetle, John 232, 236, 246
Beevers, Frank 124
Begley, Thaddeus J. 244
Behrmann, Henry 239
Beith, John 235
Belanger, Joseph 66
Belden, David A. of Haverhill 145
Belknap, Edmund B. 234
Bell, Charles U.
    120, 137, 239, 246, 253
Bellevue Cemetery 38, 61, 217
Bellevue Hospital Medical College
    218
Belt line 144
Bennett, Alvah 232
Bennink, Leonard E. 77, 125, 221
Benson, George W.
    229, 246, 253, 254
Benton, Senator Thomas H. 196
Berkeley street 144
Bernard, Rudolph 77
Berwick, Thomas 124
Bethel Armenian Congregational
    church 118

Bevington, Thomas 234
Bicknell block 223
Bigelow, Charles H.
    27, 29, 57, 58, 82, 134
Birtwell, Tempest 237
Bishop, Lemuel A. 236, 246, 254
black house 192
Black, John P. 241
Black, Portal M. 239
Blackburn, George 61
Blanchard, Andrew D. 235
Blandin, Ira D. 234, 241
Blood, Albert 232, 237, 254
Blythe, William 66
Board of Aldermen 249
Board of Trade 64, 174
Boarding houses 32, 34, 50
Boardman, Benjamin 229, 253
Boardman, William H. 232
Bodkin, John 124
Bodwell, Alpheus 19
Bodwell, Asa M. 235, 237
Bodwell family 18, 184
Bodwell farm 19
Bodwell, Mr. 15, 16
Bodwell, Mrs. 184
Bodwell Park 27, 133
Bodwell street 133, 194
Bodwell Street Methodist Episcopal
    church 116
Bodwell's Falls
    13, 20, 22, 25, 33, 45, 185
Bodwell's Ferry 15, 22
Boehm, Adam 244
Bolduc, Archelaus 240
Bolster, William 66
Bolton, John W. 234, 241
Bonney Light Battery 92
Bonney, Milton
    92, 168, 231, 232, 237, 246
Boody, Fenn W. 172, 243
Booth, Benjamin 251
Booth, John 124

Booth, Joseph W. 163
Boothman, Jonathan D. 236, 254
Bordman, Benjamin 179
Bosson, George C. 155, 241
Boston & Maine Railroad
    38, 54, 63, 146, 183, 221, 222,
    224, 257, 258
Boston & Maine round house 259
Boston & Northern Street Railway
    143
Boston City Hospital 217
Boston College 215, 217
Boston Floating Hospital 217
Boston, Mass. 54
Boston Public Library 217
Boston University Law School
    204, 206, 208, 209, 214,
    215, 218
Bourget, Arnie D. V. 241
Bowditch, Alfred 99
Bowdoin College 214
Bower, Arthur 243, 256
Bower, Robert 180, 254
Bower, William 232, 237
Bowker, Jonathan C. 237
Boxford Street 117
Boynton, E. M. 176
Brackett, John A. 148, 171, 240
Bradbury, Alfred
    131, 132, 244, 245
Bradbury, William E. 240
Bradford street 18, 115, 117, 136
Bradford Street, No. 32 & No. 34
    185
Bradley block 259
Bradley, Charles E. 77, 240
Bradley, Michael H. 242
Bradley, William J. 120, 213
Brady, Terence 236, 237
Braithwaite, Edward 241
Branch, Lafayette, Pemberton victim
    61, 236
Brechin block 91, 170

Breen, John
    171, 231, 234, 238, 239, 246
Brennan, Owen, Pemberton victim
    61
Bresnahan, Bernard J. 243
Brewster, Albert R. 236, 251
Brewster, Frank 99
Brewster, John L. 231, 238, 247
Bride, Grimes & Company 211
Bride, James H. 77, 125, 170, 211
Bride, T. H. 169
Bridgeman, William H. 232
Bridgman hall 113
Briggs & Allyn 258
Briggs, Alanson 237
Briggs, Caleb T. 236
Briggs, Charles E. 251
Briggs, Frederick W. 243, 244
Briggs, W. W. 257
Brigham, Sidney H. 253
Broadway
    17, 18, 19, 31, 32, 38, 45,
    63, 72, 84, 90, 95, 137, 170,
    174, 179, 184, 191, 221, 257,
    258
The Broadway theater 223
Broadway Savings Bank 168
Broadway, South 24
Broder, Bridget, Pemberton victim
    61
Brogan, James A. 171, 172
Brogan, Joseph V. 219
Brooks Mash 222
Brooks, Thomas A. 241, 255
Brown & Becket 179
Brown, Charles A. 236
Brown, David 171
Brown, James C. 233
Brown, John 238
Brown, Lorenzo D. 229
Brown, Michael 243
Brown, Miss, a teacher 102
Brown University 217

Bruce, Alexander B. 233, 246
Bruckmann, Herman 234
Bryan & Stratton's Commercial
    School 219
Bryan, William J. 196
Bryant, Aldermen 195
Bryant, Amassa 232, 253
Bryant, Oliver 232
Buckley & Sullivan 220
Buckley, Timothy J. 172, 220, 239
Buell & Co., Henry A. 32
Buell, Henry A. 233, 239
Bugbee, Albert V. 248
Bull Dog Field 184
Bunker, Augustus S. 179, 238
Burbank, Emulus W. 236
Burckel, Alfred J. 242, 243, 256
Burckel, Henry E. 238, 240
Burke, Edward 237
Burke, Jeremiah E. 231
Burke, Mary, Pemberton victim 61
Burke, Robert E. 240
Burley, Elbridge T. 120, 253
Burnham, William H. 240
Burns, Matthew 235
Burns, Thomas J. 241
Burridge, John Q. A. 232, 235, 236
Busby, John T. 243
Butler, Albert E. 170, 234
Butler, Franklin 64, 99, 233
Butler, Frederick
    219, 237, 246, 254, 256
Butler, Gen. Benjamin 176
Butler, Richard T. 254
Butler, William J. 234
Butman, Henry N. 231
Byrom, James 232

C

Cabot, George D.
    29, 98, 137, 165, 232

Cadogan, James W. 207, 245
Caffrey, Andrew A. 234
Cahill, David 233
Cahill, John T.
    148, 206, 210, 211, 231, 247, 259
Cahill's dry goods store 259
Cain, William, Pemberton victim 61
Caldwell, John 235
Callahan, Edward C. 242, 255
Callahan, Hannah, Pemberton
    victim 61
Callahan, Mary, Pemberton victim
    61
Callahan, Peter, Pemberton victim
    61
Callahan, William H. 235
Camp Alger, Dunn Loring, Va. 122
Campbell, Andrew W. 242
Campbell, George 242
Campbell, George Jr. 241
Campbell, John B. 132, 240, 254
Campo Seco Street 259
Canadian Army 124
Canal Street 71
Cannon, William 238, 255
Cantwell, Andrew E. 243
Cape Hatteras 122
Carden, Richard 77
Carey, Dennis E. 94, 206, 251
Carey, Jeremiah J. 241
Carleton, William A. 235
Carletonville 63
Carnegie Hero Fund 67
Carney, James J. 244
Carney, Matthew J. 226, 233
Carney, Michael 226, 254, 255
Carney's Commercial School 212
Carpenter, John A. 29
Carr, Frederick A. 242
Carr, Peter 77, 201, 206, 256
Carter, Amos 235
Carter, Rev. Clark 64, 65, 142
Carter, Richard A. 253, 255

Casey, John 242
Casey, Patrick J. 243
the Castro theatre 224
Cate, Charles 243
Cate, Edwin J. 241
Cate, Thomas J. 124, 237
Catholic Democrats 41
Catholic Young Men's Association
    109
caves 185
Cemetery Department 217
Center street 145
Central Bridge 53, 146, 147
Central Bridge Commission
    148, 206, 211
Central Congregational Church 114
Central fire station 52, 91, 92, 93
Central Grammar School 40, 200
Central Methodist church 112
Chadbourne, Capt. Benjamin F.
    87, 233
Chadwick, William 240
Chalmers, Andrew A. 241
Chamber of Commerce
    55, 174, 212
Chamberlain, Albert H. 156, 170
Chambers, Joseph S. 242
Champion-International Paper
    Company 48, 162
Chandler, Frederic N. 77, 253
Chandler, George W. 237, 239
Chandler, Henry P. 238
Chapin, William C. 60
Chapman, Ebenezer L. 232, 237
Chapman, Nicholas 232, 246
Charities Department of the city 139
Charles Storrow school 104
Charlestown, Mass. 187
Chase, John E. 61
chemical fire engine 93
Cheney, Benjamin P. 240
Chestnut street 112
Chicamauga, Ga. 122

Chickering, George E. 231
Chickering pianos 45
Chickering Street 140
Children's Home 141
Children's Nursery and Home 141
Chinese residents 130
Choate, Charles H. 234, 242
Christmas Club 173
Christmas Savings Club 173
Chubb, H. Christopher 126
Church Block 42
Church of Assumption of Mary
    (German Catholic) chu 116
Church of Holy Rosary (Italian
    Catholic) street 117
Citizens Association 77, 213
City Block 191
city charter 52
City Council 106, 148, 194, 195
City Farm 19
City Flour Mills 258
City Hall
    15, 38, 40, 59, 71, 78, 81,
    83, 87, 114, 137, 191
City Hall pump 194
city hill 37
City Hose carriage 92
City Hose company 91
city water works. 38
Civil War 38, 41, 42, 47, 50, 58,
    92, 129, 163, 193
Clark, Brackett H. 248, 257
Clark, Daniel J. 229
Clark, James 236, 237
Clark, Michael J. 240
Clark, William P. 233, 235, 237
Clarke, Catherine, Pemberton victim
    61
Clarke, Frederick E. 61, 130, 168
Clegg mill 258
Clegg, Thomas 233
Clement & Cressey 257
Clement, Harrison D. 254

Cleveland, Joseph 239
Clifford, George O. 238
clock and bell in the City Hall tower
    85
Closson, Carlos C. 236
Cloutier, Amedee 255
Clover Hill 20, 111, 142
Cobb, Isaac B. 236
Coburn, Albert F. 237
Coburn House, 32
Coburn, Timothy V. 253
Cocheco Manufacturing Company
    152
Cocheco Mills 49
Cochichewick Brook 13
Cochichewick, Lake 20
coffer dam 57
Cogswell, John F. 233, 236
Cogswell, Thomas M. 170
Colbert, Ellen, Pemberton victim 61
Colby Academy 217
Colby, Eben T. 236
Colby, John 31
Colby, Kimball G. 77, 169, 181
Colby, William W. 237
Colcord, Elihu W. 236, 248
Cold Spring Brewery 222, 227, 259
Coleman, Margaret, Pemberton
    victim 61
Collins, Annie 63
Collins, Elizabeth 64
Collins, George 239
Collins, John J. 243
Collins, Lewis P.
    64, 231, 234, 240, 247
Collins, Michael F. 65, 239, 251
Collins, Oliver 236
Collins, William 242
Collopy, Michael H. 244
The Colonial theater 224
Columbia mills 153
Columbia, S. C. 152
Combination No. 6 92

Combination No. 7 92
Combination No. 8 92, 94
Combination No. 9 92
commission form of government 79
Common Council
209, 210, 213, 214, 215, 218,
235, 244
Common Pond 89
Common street
31, 32, 36, 38, 52, 82, 84,
87, 90, 95, 98, 106, 112, 113,
114, 115, 119, 138, 192, 222,
224, 225, 226, 257
Common street, No. 570 224
Common street, Nos. 433-443 224
Common street, Nos. 561-7 259
Company F, 101st Infantry 124
Company F, 9th Mass. Infantry
64, 71, 121, 122, 125
Company L, 103rd Infantry 124
Company L, 8th Mass. Infantry
71, 121, 122, 125
Concert Hall 112
Concord, Mass. 19
Concord, N.H. 13, 24, 187
Concord street
91, 93, 115, 117, 118, 135, 136
Condon, Thomas F. 239
Congregation of Anshea Sfard
(Jewish) 117
Congregation of Sons of Israel
(Jewish) 116
Congregational Church 116
Congregationalists 112
Conner, Ellen, Pemberton victim 61
Conners, Catherine, Pemberton
victim 61
Connor, John F. 242
Connors, James A. 243
Connors, Patrick W. 243
Constance, Sister Superior 108
Cook, Eli 82
Cook, William H. 235, 236

Cooke, Homer A. 179
Coolidge, Baldwin 215, 238
Coolidge, Benjamin 29
Coolidge street 117
Cooney, Catherine, Pemberton
victim 61
Cooney, William 240
Cooper, Maurice 77
Cooper, Seth 243
Cooper-Corliss 159
Copps, Marcus W. 233, 239
Corcoran, Cornelius J.
77, 172, 214, 229
Corcoran, James 236
Corcoran, James C. 226
Corcoran, Margaret, Pemberton
victim 61
Cornelie, Thomas 130
Corporation Reserve 191
Cortwright, Charles W. 157
Corwan, Anthony 239, 240
Costello, D. Y. 170
Costello, Edward 239
Cote, John 66
Cottage Hospital 139
Couch, Joseph 95
Couch, Albert I. 125, 166, 168
Couch, Henry J. 237, 238, 254
Couch, Joseph 250
Couch, Omar E. 234, 241
Coughlin, James A. 239
Coulson & Murphy 204
Coulson, Walter 99, 120, 209
Count Rumford 184
County Court House 137
the Courier 179, 181
Court of Common Pleas 83, 84
Cox, Louis S. 77, 120, 203, 253
Coyne, James A. 243
Craig, Andrew 242
Cram, Monoram F. 232
Crane, Governor 217
Cranston, John 124

Crawford, John W. 64, 231, 246
Cregg, Matthew A. 120, 126
Cressey, Leonard F. 236
the Critic 181
Crocker, Samuel S. 232
Cronan, Joanna, Pemberton victim 61
Cronin, Michael F. 208, 234, 247, 253
Crosby, Arthur J. 170
Crosby, Bridget, Pemberton victim 61
Crosby, Irene, Pemberton victim 62
Crosby, Josiah 32
Crosby street 91, 92
Cross, a pioneer 16
Cross, J. W. 169
Cross, John L. 239
Cross street 103
Cross, Y. W. 170
Cross-roads settlement 185
Cuba 122
Cuddy, John E. Jr. 256
Cullen, Alice, Pemberton victim 62
Cullinane, Richard 255
Culloten, Mary, Pemberton victim 62
Curran & Joyce Co., Inc. 224
Curran & Joyce Company 224
Curran, Mary T. 204
Curran, Maurice J. 170, 224
Currant Hill 38
Currier, Aaron A. 65, 233, 237, 246
Currier, Charles W. 234
Currier, E. B. 253
Currier, Ella 259
Currier, James M. 250
Currier, John M. 236
Currier, Mrs. Aaron A. 259
Currier, W. D. 169, 170
Cusack, William C. 234, 242
Cushing, John E. 231

Cutler, Elisha B. 238
Cutler, Helen H. 63, 64
Cutler, Henry 18
Cutler house 63
Cutler, William F. 233

D

D. W. Pingree Co. 258
Dacey, Timothy 254
Daigle, David 234
the Daily American 180
the Daily Journal 180
the Daily News 180, 181
Daisy street 257
Daley, John 77, 238
Daley, William 242
Daly, William 255
Dame, Arthur C. 170
Dame, B. F. 203
Dame, George W. 237
Damon, Herbert P. 237
Damphouse, Joseph 124
Dana, James 157
Dane, John 238
Danforth, Henry P. 233, 239, 254
Daniels, Lyman 235
Danvers, Mass. 144
Dartmouth College 212, 216
Davey, John 241
Davis & Murphy 225
Davis, Benjamin H. 148
Davis, Charles H. 233, 239
Davis' foundry 15, 257
Davis, Franklin B. 231, 239, 240, 246, 248
Davis, George E. 254
Davis, Samuel M. 232, 235, 236, 254
Davis, Smith B. W. 231, 237, 246
Dawson, Seth F. 239
Dawson, William H. 240
Deacey, Timothy 238

Dean, Thomas 238
Dean, William W. 240
Dearborne, John C., Pemberton
    victim 62
Decker, Jefford M. 235
DeCourcy & Coulson 209
DeCourcy, Charles A.
    64, 120, 174, 203, 209, 253
deep waterway 53
Deer Jump 20
Demara, Napoleon 223
Demeritt, Oliver C. 236
Democratic party 40
Democrats 39
Dempsey, Michael J. 241
Den Rock Cemetery 14, 185
Den Rock Park 185
Dennett, Horatio 237
Dental Clinic 140
Depot Square 51
Derbyshire, James H.
    240, 241, 253, 255
Desmond, Humphrey 237
Desmond, Jeremiah J.
    237, 241, 255
Desmond's hat factory 257
Devil's Slide 185
Devlin, Edward 237, 238
Diamond Match Company 48
Diamond Spring Brewery 225
Dick, Ernest E. 239
Dick, Hugo E. 234
Dickie, Edward H. 239
Dineen, Ellen, Pemberton victim 62
Dineen, James A. 77
District Board of Appeals 126
district court 55
Dixon, Alanson 237
Dockham & Place 180
Dockham, Stephen 144, 236
Dodge, Marcus S. 167, 232, 233
Doe, Henry P. 231, 233, 238, 247
Doerr, Jacob 243, 244

Dolan, Daniel F. 238, 254
Dolan, Edward A. 234, 243
Doland, John J. 237, 246, 254
Dolbier, Henry 233
Dolloff, Elijah B. 235
Donnelly, Margaret, Pemberton
    victim 62
Donoghue, James E. 181, 247, 249
Donohue, John 242
Donovan, Daniel 254
Donovan, Frank L. 77
Donovan, Gen. W. H. 77
Donovan, John J. 120, 147, 206
Donovan, Joseph 247, 253
Donovan, Major Frank L. 77
Donovan, Timothy F. 234
Dooley, A. X. 77
Dooley, Joseph L. 234, 242, 243
Dooley, Michael J. 243, 244
Dorgan, Maurice B. 172
Douglas, Gov. William. L. 95
Douglass, Harrison 179
Douglass, Stephen A. 196
Dover, N.H. 152
Dow, George W.
    126, 217, 234, 255
Dow, Harry R. 120, 241
Dow, Henry R. 241
Dow, John C. 31
Doyle, David 240
Doyle, John F. 240, 241
Doyle, Joseph 242
Doyle, Richard W. 234, 239, 240
Doyle street 22
Draft Exemption Boards 126
Drew, Albert 236
Drew, Edgar H. 239
Drew, F. C. 237
Drew, Harmon T. 242
Drew, Jeremiah D. 237
Driscoll, Jeremiah F. 234
Duchesney, Captain L. N. 64
Duck and Machine Shop 27

Duck Bridge 71
Duck Mills 48, 70, 71
Dunn, Harvey A. 122
Dunn, Elizabeth, Pemberton victim
    62
Durant, Adolphus
    18, 19, 183, 188, 235
Durant district 102
Durant paper mill 45
Durgin, Dennis F. 241
Durgin, Horace J. 236
Durham street 63
Dustin, John E. 237
Dyer, Arthur W. 174
Dyer, Henry B. 233

E

Eager, Winslow 237, 238
the Eagle 180
Eagle Hose Company 92
East Haverhill street
    16, 18, 19, 90, 116, 144, 183, 184
East Haverhill Street Bridge 19
East Pepperell, Mass. 162
Eastman, H. W. K. 246
Easton, James H. 231
Eaton, Fred H. 131, 234
Eaton, James H.
    137, 144, 166, 232, 237, 247
Eaton, Wyllis G. 232
Ebert, Karl M. 255
Edge, Father 109, 114
Edge, Rev. Louis M. 114
Edison Electric Illuminating Com-
    pany 98
Edmond, Joseph A. 243
Edwards, Franklin 236, 237
electric street lights 97
Eliot Congregational church 114
Ellicott, Henry 130
Ellingwood, John N. 239, 240
Elliott, George B. 64, 234
Ellis, Richard W. 234, 247

Elm street 16, 91, 95, 117, 184
Emerson, Albert 232, 236
Emerson, Charles T. 233, 238
Emerson, Jacob Jr. 169
Emerson, Ralph Waldo 136
Emery Hill 90
Emery, Levi 19, 237, 238, 254
Emery, William W. 238
Emmet street 63
Emmon Loom Harness, Co. 165
Emmons, A. B. 170
Emmons, Nathaniel H. 99
Emmons, R. W. 99
the Empire theater 223
Empire House 191
the Engine 180
Erler, F. W. Theodor 239
Essex Company
    23, 25, 26, 29, 31, 32, 33,
    34, 35, 36, 37, 38, 39, 58,
    63, 82, 88, 97, 98, 102, 103,
    113, 129, 133, 135, 136, 137,
    148, 152, 157
Essex County
    55, 166, 173, 222, 227
Essex County Teachers' Assn. 203
Essex County Training School
    20, 138, 190
the Essex Eagle 180
Essex House 189, 193
Essex Mission 112
Essex Savings Bank
    36, 131, 165, 166, 258
Essex street
    21, 31, 32, 35, 39, 40, 42, 52, 72,
    90, 91, 119, 137, 144, 147, 166,
    167, 170, 173, 191, 193, 221,
    222, 258, 259
Essex street, No. 213 221
Essex street, No. 222 220
Essex street, No. 229 221
Essex street, No. 231 221
Essex street, No. 233 221

Essex street, No. 263 171, 172
Essex street, No. 264 170, 172
Essex street, No. 309 220
Essex street, No. 467 223
Essex street, No. 477 223
Essex street, No.166 222
Essex street, Nos. 166-168 222
Essex street, Nos. 218-226 220
Essex street, Nos. 225-235 221
Essex street, Nos. 431-5 259
Essex yard 34, 257, 258
Ettor, Joseph J. 71, 72, 74, 76
Evans, Albert H. 242
Evans, John A. 242
the Evening Tribune 180
Everett Classics 156
Everett Mills
     27, 34, 39, 46, 48, 58, 70, 144, 156,
     157, 257
Exeter, N.H. 180

F

F. P. Berry & Co. 258
F. W. Stock & Sons 222
Fallon, Margaret, Pemberton victim
     62
Fallon, Thomas J. 124
Fames, Harry M. 254, 255
Farnham, William F. 237
Farrell, William 242
Farwell Bleachery 97, 165
Fay, Augustus M. 236, 237
Fay, Michael Joseph 244
Federal Land Bank 218
Felician Sisters 110
Fellows, Samuel W. 233
Ferguson, Frank E. 243
Fernald, Thomas H. 237
Fernald, William H. 232, 235
ferry house 185
Ferry road 38
Ferry street 22
Field, Albert R. 233

Field, H. W. 170
Field, Jeremiah S. 31
Finegan, James J. 243
Finn, Dennis H. 242, 255
Finn, Patrick F. 224
Finn, Patrick J. 241
Finnegan, John F. 201, 245
Finnegan, Michael P. 242
Fire Department 18
Fire engine
     chemical 93
     chemical, No. 3 92
fire engine
     Essex 36
     Niagara 2 91
     No. 2 92
     No. 3 92
     No. 4 52, 92
     No. 5 93
     No. 6 51
     No. 7 51
     No. 8 51, 206
     No. 9 52
     steam, Atlantic No. 2 92
     steam, Essex No. 4 93
     steam, Essex No.4 93
     steam, Washington No. 5 93, 94
     Syphon 3 91
     the Lawrence 43
fire engines 36, 43
fire truck, ladder 92, 93
Firemen's Relief Association 93
first
     attorney 31
     bank 36
     Baptist organization 113
     boarding house 32
     bookstore 31
     brass band 32
     brick store buildings 32
     Catholic burying-ground 38
     Christmas service celebrated 111
     clothing dealer 31

druggist 31
dry goods dealer 31
dwelling house 32
fire alarm telegraph system 43
fraternal organization 32
grammar school 32, 103
grocery store 32
high school 32
hook and ladder truck 92
hotel 32
house of worship 32
lockup 95
lumber dealer 31
mechanic 31
mill 32
physician 31
police court 38
police force 94
post office 32
private school 32
Superior court 38
trial justice 31
First Baptist church 22, 91, 113
First Church of Christ (Scientist) 117
First Free Baptist church 113
First Methodist Episcopal church 112
First Protestant Episcopal Church of Methuen 111
First Spiritual Church 118
First Universalist Society 113
Fisher, James C. 239
Fitzgerald, Priestly 242, 243
Fitzpatrick, Daniel 243, 256
Flanagan, John F. 245
Flanagan, John A. 200
Flanagan, Michael A. 215, 256
Flanders & Severance 257
Flanders, Henry 31
Flanders, Walker 232, 253
Fleming, Michael P. 77
Fletcher, Isaac 229, 237
Flint, Henry K. 237
Flint, Lizzie D., Pemberton victim 62

Floyd, Daniel 32
Floyd, Thomas W. 235, 253
Flynn, Fred F. 77
Flynn, James P. 234, 242
Flynn, Joseph J. 147, 211, 253, 255
Foley, Frank D. 244
Foley, John 239
Foley, Margaret 62
Foley, Martin 77
Follansbee, George E. 239
Forbes, Benjamin H. 241
Forbes, James 242
Forbes, William H. 234, 241
Forbes, Y. C. 170
Ford, John Joseph 235, 243
Ford, Miss, a teacher 102
Ford, Patrick 233, 239
Ford's Hall 70
Forlies, James 242
Fort Slocum, N.Y 125
Fort Sumpter, Ga. 84, 121
Foss, Gov. Eugene 71
Foster, Charles W. 93
Foster, David P. 235
Foster house 19
Foster, Patrick 238
Fox, G. V. Ass. Sec. of the Navy 84
Fox, Richard H. 240, 250
Foye, Lewis A. 168, 170
France, John 233, 237
Franco-American Methodist Episcopal street 117
Franklin House 32
Franklin House stable 259
Franklin Library 18, 36, 51, 55, 80, 134, 191
Franklin street 18, 20, 91, 135, 222
Freeman, Otis, Jr. 64, 234
Freese, Joseph M. 236
French, Alfred J. 161, 169, 231, 246, 254
French, Father 112

273

French, Nathaniel R. 236
French, Reuben W. 232, 235
French, Rev. Charles 112
French System 159
French War 184
Freytag, Oswald 222
Frost, Archie N. 209, 242, 253
Frost, William P. 236
Frost. Archie N. 255
Frye, a pioneer 16
Frye, Newton P. 120
Frye, Oscar A. 239
Fuller, George A. 144, 232, 235
Fuller, Harvey L. 250
Fuller, Rufus 236
Fulton Mills, Fulton, N. Y. 149
Furbush, Sylvester A. 60, 235
Fyfe, Charles G. 124

G

G. W. Dodson Co. 258
Gage farm 129
Gage, George L. 233, 239, 253
Gage, Isaac K. 235
Gage, Joseph N. 32, 232
Gage, Phineas M. 17, 18, 235
Gale & Ames' carriage shop
    257, 258
Gale, John P.
    42, 183, 232, 235, 253
Gale's Hill 51, 183
Gallagher, Daniel 234
Gallan, Bridget 62
Gallison house 184
Gallison, William B. 184, 235
Game well system 94
Ganley, John E. 241
Garden street
    18, 86, 91, 92, 93, 112
Garden Street Methodist Episcopal
    church 112
Garfield, Frederick H. 85
Garvey, Joseph P. 242

Garvey, Michael M. 234
Gaudette, Gerry 124
Gaudette, Ronaldo 66
Gay, Fred W. 242
the Gazette 181
Gearin, Jeremiah F. 242
Gearin, William F. 238
Gebelein, Henry C. 243
Gehring, Frederick 243
Gelineau, George 172
General Hospital 51
General Lawton Post, 146, G. A. R.
    132
George, E B. 209
George E. Kunhardt Corporation
    163
George, Joseph W. 236
German Methodist Episcopal
    church 116
German Old Folks Home 141
German Presbyterian church 116
German Ruth Society 142
Germany 123
Gesing, Henry W. 241
Gilbert E. Hood grammar school
    104
Gilbert, J. Frank 238
Gile, W. Fiske 237
Gile, W. H. 169, 170, 229
Gilman, John 132
Gilmartin, Dennis 254
Gilmartin, John 238
Gilmartin, Thomas 240
Gilmore & Carpenter 29
Gilmore, Father 109
Gilson, Lorinda, Pemberton victim
    62
Giovannitti, Arturo 72, 74, 76
Gleason building 258
Glidden, John D. 232
Glover, Jesse 169
Godfrey, W.H. 258
Godin, Ambrose J. 243

Godin, John W. 241
Goffs Falls, N.H. 145
Golden, Martin 240
Goldsmith, George H.
    180, 234, 241
Gomorrah 17
gondola, in the Merrimack 31
Goodell, Henry 31
Goodhue, Wadleigh 232
Goodwin, John A. 179, 253
Goodwin, Thomas 240
Gordon, George A. 179
Gordon, Jackson 235
Gorman, Francis 239
Gorman-Wilson tariff 149
Goss, Charles E. 144
Gould, Jesse G. 251
Gould, Samuel 232, 237
Gowen, Edwin L. 235
Gowing, William E. 233
Grace Episcopal Church
    32, 104, 110, 112, 114, 188, 194
Graham, John M. 240
Graham, Patrick J. 240
Graham, William J. 255, 256
Graichen, Gustave 239
Grand Army of the Republic
    85, 129, 130
Grant, Alexander L. 231, 247
Grant, Gen. U. S. 81, 196
Graves family 18
Graves Hill 20
Graves, John 18
Gray, Fred A. 241
Gray Nuns 141
Great Stone Dam 29
Grecian Lodge of Masons. 119
Greeley, Horace 31
Green street 117
Greene, Edwin Farnhani 153
Greenwood, William 77
Griffin, Andrew Jr. 234, 242
Griffin, Eugene B. 243

Griffin, Mary, Pemberton victim 62
Griffin, Thomas 239
Grimes, E. Eben 211
Grosvenor's Corner 111
Groton street 117
Grunwald, Herman 243
Guenther, Charles H. 241
Guild, Gov. 208
Guilfoyle, J. R. 220
Gurley-Flynn, Elizabeth 72
Gurry, James E. 242
Gutherie, William J. 124
Gutterson & Gould 183

H

H. K. Webster's grist mill 257
Hadley, Thomas F. 242
Haeberle, George I. 233
Haeberle, George L 240
Hager, Walter W. 242
Haggett's Pond 20, 38, 88
Haigh, John 234, 255
Hale, Richard A. 29
Halifax disaster 126
Hall, Alfred 236
Hall, Dyer S. 233
Hall, George W. 234, 240, 241
Hall, Henry H. 29
Hall, Maria, Pemberton victim 62
Halley, Dennis E.
    240, 241, 253, 255
Halley, Patrick F. 239
Halstead, John 242
Hamblett, G. W. 169, 170
Hamblett Machine Co. 258
Hamel, William N. 248
Hamilton, J. A. 251
Hamilton, Margaret, Pemberton
    victim 62
Hamilton Print Works 153
Hammond, P. A. 163

Hampshire street
    32, 39, 103, 106, 109, 112,
    113, 115, 119, 133, 134,
    135, 145, 225, 226
Hampshire street, No. 34 224
Hannagan, Paul 77, 244
Hannon, Catharine 62
Hannon, John F. 242
Hanrahan, William 238
Hardacre, Samuel 238
Harding, Benjamin 253
Harding, James H. 235
Hardy, Daniel
    169, 232, 235, 246, 248
Hardy, William 235, 253
Harmon, Artemus 95, 231, 232
Harmon, F. C. 172
Harmon, Nathan W.
    95, 246, 250, 253
Harold, Dora, Pemberton victim 62
Harrigan, Catharine, Pemberton
    victim 62
Harriman, Richard R. 232, 236
Harrington, Henry F. 104, 179, 231
Harrington School 104
Harrison, William H 196
Hart, John I. 241
Hart, E. A. 172
Hart, Henry P. 234, 242
Hart, John 77, 130, 232, 237, 241
Hartley Bros. 258
Hartley, George 240
Hartley, John J. 233, 239, 241
Hartshorne, W. D. 169, 170
Harty, James, Pemberton victim 62
Harvard Brewing Company 224
Harvard Law School 120, 214, 216
Harvard Medical School 217
Haseltine, Phineas W. 240, 255
Hastings, Ellsworth W. 240, 241
Hastings, Walter M. 159
Haughton, Robert 238
Haverhill High School 204

Haverhill, Mass.
    16, 17, 18, 20, 144, 174, 219
Haverhill road 22
Haverhill street
    18, 19, 20, 22, 48, 82, 90, 102, 108,
    104, 109, 112, 113, 114, 115,
    134, 136, 258
Hayden, Edmund R.
    130, 231, 246, 250
Hayes, Joseph F. C.
    11, 35, 179, 235, 243
Haywood, William O. 72
Heald, William E. 224, 251
Health and Charities Department
    200
Health Department 139, 140
Hedge, Frederick H. 217
Hefner, Louis 238
Henderson, William 240
Hendry, John 126
Hennessey, John 235, 243
Hennessey, Joseph 66
Henry J. Koellen & Co. 222
the Herald 180
Herrick, Edmund B. 232
Herrick family 18
Herrick, Horatio G. 130
Herrick, James D.
    94, 102, 108, 231, 232, 246, 250, 251
Herrick, Nehemiah 18
Herrick, Robert F. 154
Hester, William A. 256
Hewett, Alfred 124
Hewins, Enoch 235
Hey, George 77
Hickey, Catharine , Pemberton
    victim 62
Hickey, Ellen, Pemberton victim 62
Higgins, Gorham P. 232, 235
Higgins, Michael 63
High Schol Building 258
High school 102, 105
high speed steam engine 47

High street 90
Highland Military Academy 219
Hildreth & Rogers 180
Hildreth, F. H. 180
Hill, Charles F. 11
Hill, William G. 240
Hinchcliffe, Henry 67
Hinchcliffe, William J.
   240, 254, 255
Hinckley, Ezra G. 242
Hoadley, John C. 60, 232, 253
Hoar, George F. 243
Hobbs, Franklin W. 49, 155, 156
Hodgkins, Ezra W. 234, 241
Hoffarth, William 242
Hofmann, Alvin L. 77, 243
Hogan, John F. 65, 77, 238
Holihan Bros. 225
Holihan, Charles A. 225
Holihan, James P. 225
Holihan, Joseph P. 225
Holihan, Patrick 225
Holihan, Peter 169, 225, 233
Holley, John J. 243
Hollifield, Bernard, Pemberton
   victim 62
Holmes, Oliver Wendell 136, 191
Holt, Lewis G. 238, 253
Holt, Nathan A. 233
Holy Rosary (Italian) church 117
Holy Rosary for Italian boys and
   girls 110
Holy Trinity (Polish Catholic)
   church 117
Holy Trinity school for Polish boys
   and girls 110
Home, Herbert W. 170, 227
Home, James D. 131, 204
Home, James E. 170
Home, L E. 169
the Home Review 179
Hood, Ernest N. 158, 159
Hood, Gilbert E.

   104, 169, 196, 231, 253
Hood school 51, 104
Hooper & Co. of Boston 86
Hooper, H. N. 86
Hooper, William 240
Hopkins, Elisha C. 235
Hopkins, Henry F. 251
Horn, George W. 237, 239
horse drawn patrol and ambulance
   96
Horse Railroad 39
Hosmer, Abner 236
House of Correction 40, 138
Houston, James 170
Hovey, Lewis R. 176
Howard, Charles W. 240
Howard, John B. 233
Howard, John F. 255
Howard, Mary, Pemberton victim
   62
Howard, Rufus M. 237
Howard street 92, 104
Howarth, William H. 234
Howe, George 58
Howe, Merrill N. 237, 239
Howe, Thorndike D. 77
Hoyt, Leonard 235
Hudson avenue 185
Hudson, N.H. 145
Hughes, George F. 221
Hughes, James J. 221
Hughes, John, Pemberton victim 62
Hughes, Martin, Pemberton victim
   62
Hughes, Thomas 243
Hulford, John H. 255
Hume, Harrison 231
Humphrey, Edward H. 234
Humphreys, C. J. R. 98, 99, 170
Hurley, Joanna, Pemberton victim
   62
Hurley, John J. 247
Hurley, John J.

171, 172, 213, 231, 245, 247
Hurley, Joseph A. 244
Huse family 18
Huse, Stephen 18
Huse, Susan 19
Hutcheson, Elwood C. 124
Hutchinson, Charles 235
Hutchinson, Cyrus 232
Hutchinson, James S. 130, 238
Hutchinson, Moses F. 239
Hyde, George S. J. 256

I

I.W.W. 70, 71, 72, 74, 75
Immaculate Conception church
    109, 112, 115
Industria seal 130
International Paper Company 162
International Typographical Union
    200
Island street 161, 258
Isolation Hospital 139

J

J. N. Peterson & Co. of Salem 138
J. W. Horne & Sons, Co. 165
Jackson, Joseph 171, 224
Jackson, Patrick T. 26
Jackson, Samuel W. 236
Jackson street
    17, 20, 32, 35, 36, 38, 42,
    72, 95, 103, 112, 113, 114,
    129, 142, 192
Jackson street, No. 2 222
Jackson terrace 16
Jail Common 133
James, J. Frank 234, 241
Jaquith, William H. 236
Jewett, Mary, Pemberton victim 62
Jewett, William S. 77, 180
Jim Syphon, a dog 190
Jitneys 144
John Breen grammar school

52, 104
John K. Tarbox grammar school
    100, 104
John R. Rollins grammar school 104
Johnson, James R. 253
Jones, Roland 66
Joplin, William D. 60
Joplin, Wm. D. 229
Jordan, Thomas M. 243
Jordan, Daniel S. 236
Jordan, Michael H. 219, 256
Jordan, Thomas M. 210, 235, 243
Jordan, William, Pemberton victim
    62
Josselyn, Elbridge 232
Josselyn, Eldridge 232
Joubert, Joseph H. 64, 255
the Journal 181
Jovce, James W. 233
Joyce, John 224
Joyce, Edward F. 241
Joyce, James W. 233, 238
Junketing 189
Junkins, George S.
    222, 231, 234, 241, 247

K

Kane, John P.
    77, 120, 231, 241, 244, 245, 247, 253
Kane, Timothy 229
Kaplan, Samuel 124
Katama Mill 48, 160
Katz, Jak 259
Keaveny, Bernard J. 244
Keefe, John 67
Keefe, William H. 239
Keegan, James fireman 258
Keilhau, C. H. Ernest 238
Kelleher, Catharine, Pemberton
    victim 62
Kelleher, Timothy J. 240
Kelleher, William A.
    215, 234, 239, 243, 255, 256

Kellett, John 124
Kelley, Patrick J. 238
Kelly, Bridget, Pemberton victim 62
Kempton, Rollins A. 236
Kendall, Frank O. 130
Kennedy, John P. 239
Kennedy, Joseph A. 243
Kennedy, Joseph F. 242
Kennedy, William G. 241
Kenney, Everett R. 124
Kenney, Moses B. 237
Kenney, Thomas 238
Kent, General 122
Keyes, Joseph H. 250
Kidder, Charles G. 234
Kilbride, John J. 239
Kilcoyne, John T. 243
Kiley, James 237, 238
Kiley, John 232, 237
Kimball, Elizabeth R., Pemberton
    victim 62
Kimball, Joseph W. 232
Kimball, Samuel B. 232
Kimball, William M. 251
Kimball, William T.
    11, 64, 77, 131, 229
King Arthur flour 222
King, William F. 234
Kirk, Parker C. 169, 232
Kittredge, Alfred 88
Kittredge, Gilbert H. 234
Knapp, James Hoyt 163
Knight, Fred 243
Knight, S. W. 169
Knights of Columbus 125
Knights of Columbus War Fund
    125
Knights, Samuel W. 237
Know Nothing party 179
Know-Nothing party 40, 192
Knowles, Charles E. 239
Knowles Diamond Spring water 225

Knowles farm 225
Knowles, Morris 23, 168, 232, 253
Knowles, Samuel 233
Knowles, William H. 242, 243
Knox, Charles A. 242
Knox, Coulson & Murphy 204
Knox, William S.
    120, 170, 246, 253, 254
Knuepfer, Albert E. 243
Koellen & Co. 222
Koellen & Freytag 222
Koellen, Henry J. 222, 227
Koerner, Richard 242
Koffman, Edward I. 171
Kunhardt, George E. 163, 170
Kunhardt Mills 46, 48, 70, 71

L

Lacaillade, Charles 240
Lacaillade, Eli 234
Ladd, Luther 232, 233, 251
Ladies' Choral Union 130
Lafayette, General 24, 187
Lahey, John P. 243
Lake Street chapel 116
Lamb, George 233, 237
Lamb, William D. 60, 102, 236
Lamprey, Alfred A. 232, 233
Lancaster High School 212
Lane, Henry B. 234, 242
Lane, James 240
Lang, Albert S. 169, 241
Lang, Alfred 232, 236
Langmaid, Samuel 237
Langshaw, Walter H. 240
Lanigan, James F. 171
Latham, John E. H. 242
Lathrop, Willoughby W. 241
Laurel grove 14, 15, 193
Lawrence & Methuen Street Railway
    Company 145

Lawrence, Abbott 6, 26, 35, 134
Lawrence, Alison 84
Lawrence Almshouse 139
the Lawrence American 179
Lawrence Aqueduct Company 88
Lawrence armory 139
Lawrence Athenaeum 134
Lawrence Bank 169
Lawrence Bar Association
    120, 138, 209
Lawrence Board of Trade 174
Lawrence Boiler Works 183, 259
Lawrence Boys' Club 142
Lawrence Brass Band 32
Lawrence Bridge 24
Lawrence Bridge Commissions 204
Lawrence, C. R. 247
Lawrence Canoe Club 67
Lawrence Chamber of Commerce
    174
Lawrence City Mission 142
Lawrence Commercial School. 201
Lawrence Common
    27, 39, 65, 128, 133
the Lawrence Courier 85
Lawrence dam
    13, 20, 24, 28, 29, 30, 34, 35, 36, 45, 57, 88
Lawrence Duck Co. 46, 48, 164
Lawrence Electric Light Company
    97, 98
Lawrence Encampment, I. O. O. F.
    119
Lawrence Fire department
    42, 45, 52, 55, 64, 91, 93, 94,
    190, 201
Lawrence Gas Company
    32, 36, 98, 114
Lawrence General Hospital
    141, 217
Lawrence Hall 190
Lawrence High School
    204, 206, 208, 209, 215, 217, 218
Lawrence Home for Aged 142

Lawrence Ice Co. 259
Lawrence Jail 40
The Lawrence Journal 180
Lawrence Law Library 138
Lawrence Light Infantry 257
Lawrence Lumber Co. 257, 258
Lawrence Lyceum 134
Lawrence Machine Shop
    27, 34, 43, 46, 144, 157
Lawrence Market Co. 258
Lawrence Music Hall 113, 137
Lawrence National Bank 169, 170
Lawrence Opera House 211
Lawrence Park Commissioners 185
Lawrence Park Department 129
Lawrence Police Department
    74, 94, 96, 201
Lawrence Police Precinct 8 92
Lawrence Police Station 55, 95
Lawrence Post Office
    32, 51, 55, 137
Lawrence Protective company 91
Lawrence Public Library
    51, 134, 137, 217
Lawrence Pumping Station 89
Lawrence Reform School 138
Lawrence Reservoir 27, 89
Lawrence, Samuel 25, 35, 84
Lawrence Savings Bank 167
Lawrence schools 101
Lawrence street
    18, 21, 38, 82, 90, 91, 95,
    103, 111, 112, 113, 114,
    116, 118, 119, 166, 167, 170,
    173, 259
the Lawrence Telegram 180
Lawrence Trust Company 172, 173
Lawrence Woolen Company
    46, 163
the Leader 181
Lear, John 235
Learned, James M. 240
Lee, Ashton 170

Lee, Blackburn & Co. 258
Legendre, Xavier 235
Lemay, Samuel 77
Lenane, Patrick A. 233, 239, 240
Leonard, Dennis, Pemberton victim
    62
Leonard, James F. 219, 231, 247
Leupold, Robert 244
Levek, Joseph A. 172, 217
Lewis Scouring Mill 165
Lexington, Mass. 19
Libbey, Fred A. 64
Libbey, Frederick M. 234, 240
Liberty bonds 173
Liberty Loans 125, 173
License Commission 249
Lighthouse Mission 118
Lincoln, Abraham 81
Lindsey, George A. 233
Linehan, Richard A. 242
Linn, Hector P. 233
Lithuanian Catholic church
    115, 118
Little River 13
Littlefield, Charles H. 11, 238, 239
Littlefield, George
    231, 232, 235, 238
Locke, Langdon E. 169, 170
Logan, Samuel C. 71
Logue, Daniel H. 234, 242
Lombard, Charles A. 155
Londonderry Turnpike
    17, 18, 31, 95, 102, 184, 188
LoPezzi, Anna 71, 72, 74, 76
Lord, William 217
Loring, John T. 235
Loring, Silas H. 233
Lot, the inkeeper 17
Loughrey, Bridget, Pemberton victim
    62
Lovejoy, Rev. George E. 131
Low, George P. 234, 241
Lowell, John A. 26

Lowell, Mass.
    13, 18, 20, 25, 38, 39,
    143, 153, 174, 177, 184,
    193, 204, 213
Lowell road 102, 139, 184
Lowell street
    90, 91, 92, 93, 115, 184,
    257, 258, 259
lumber dock 183
Luna, George D. 253
Lunney, Richard, Pemberton victim
    62
Luscomb, William C. 233, 238
Lyall, Peter W. 240
Lyford, Edwin 233, 238
Lyford, Woodbridge S. 237
Lynch, Aldermen Cornelius F. 77
Lynch, Cornelius F.
    73, 94, 171, 231, 234, 244
Lynch, Felix 124
Lynch, John M. 240, 241, 255
Lynch, Timothy 242
Lynn, Mass. 219
Lyons, Mary 64
Lyons, Maurice 239
Lyons, Patrick 234

M

M. Carney & Brother 226
M. Carney & Company 226
M.V. Horse Railroad 39
Macartney Company's clothing store
    259
Macdonald, Peter M. 172
Mack, Alvin E. 168, 231, 246, 247
Magoon, Nathan O. 241
Mahoney, Charles A. 65
Mahoney, Daniel W. 243
Mahoney, Ellen, Pemberton victim
    62
Mahoney, Jeremiah J.
    68, 95, 243, 250
Mahoney, John D. 241

Mahoney, John P. S. 120, 241, 247
Mahony, D. D. 170
Mahony, Daniel W. 243, 251
Main, Charles T. 64, 233, 234
Mair, Alexander of Boston 82
Malley, Owen F. 240
Malone, Robert S. 245
Maloney, John T. 255
Maloney, Robert S. 77, 200, 235
Manahan, Mark 237, 238
Manchester and Lawrence Railway
    39
Manchester High School 218
Manchester, N.H. 145, 218
Manion, John T. 243
Mann, Horace 103
Mann, Michael 239
Maple street 141
Marbel, Arthur D. 215
Marble, Arthur D. 11, 14
Marist Brothers 110
Market street 27
Marsh, William S. 65
Marshall, J. N. 204
Marshall, Moses 234
Marston family 18
Marston street 98, 138, 139, 259
Marston's ferry 22
Martin, Asenath P., Pemberton
    victim 62
Martin, Charles A. 124
Martin, James H. 77, 234
Martinelli, Monsignor 196
Masons 119
Massachusetts Bar Association 209
Massachusetts General Hospital
    217
Massachusetts Hospital Life
    Insurance Company 60
Massachusetts Normal school 106
Massachusetts Northeastern Street
    Railway 145
Massachusetts State Guard 126

Mathew, Father Theobald 196
Mathison, John J. 220
Matthes, Louis 234
Matthews, Ezekiel W. 236
Maxwell, Joseph H. 243, 244
Maxwell, Thomas 242
May Procession 110
May street 19
Maynard, Reuben 236
McAleer, Margaret, Pemberton
    victim 62
McAllister, Benjamin 235
McAlpine, William T.
    233, 238, 239, 246, 253
McAnnally, Frank 255
McCabe, Daniel 243
McCabe, Edward 233
McCall, Gov. Samuel 177, 202, 208
McCann, Alary 62
McCann, Joseph 66, 67
McCarthy, Andrew J. 241, 242
McCarthy, Charles 218, 239
McCarthy, Charles A. 172, 218
McCarthy, Cornehlius A. 171
McCarthy, Cornelius A. 171
McCarthy, Daniel F. 239, 246, 247
McCarthy, Eugene A. 239, 240, 256
McCarthy, Eugene A. Jr. 243, 244
McCarthy, Florence D. 243
McCarthy, Fred S. 242
McCarthy, John F. 240
McCarthy, John J. 243
McCarthy, Joseph 77, 131
McCarthy, Philip A. 224
McCarthy, William J. 240
McClellan, Gen. George B. 196
McConnor, Hugh S. 207, 218
McConville, James 240
McCormick, Julius J. 234
McCormick, Michael A. 220, 239
McCoy, Edward 237, 238
McCreadie, Wm. 251
McCrillis, John 243

McDermott, Father 111
McDonald, J. H. 172
McDonald, Warren 124
McDowell, James 172
McDuffee, Ward Lead Manufacturing Company 212
McDuffie, Fred C. 157, 170
McFarlin, Archibald 232, 236
McFarlin, George H. 239
McGillen, Daniel 124
McGillis, John 234
McGowan, John A. 241
McIntire, Henry M. 254
McKallagat, Dr. Peter L. 205
McKay Metallic Fastening Association 213
McKenna, Maurice F. 207, 250
McKenzie, George 258
McLane, George Jr. 256
McLaughlin, James 239
McMahon, John 244
McManus, Rev. Michael T. 65
McNabb, John, Pemberton victim 62
McQueeney, John F. 239, 254
Meagher, Thomas Francis 196
Medford, Mass. 187
Medical Examiner 217
meetinghouse 42
Megin, James F. 238
Mellen, Alfred L. 239
Mellen, George A. 171
Melvin & Young of Boston 82
Melvin, Nathaniel P. H. 231, 232, 233, 246
Mena, an island 13
Menomack 13
Menzie, James R. 77, 131
Mercer, John T. 156
Merchants Association 175
Merchants National Bank 169, 170, 172
Merchants Row 32, 191, 257

Merchants Trust Company 169, 170
Merriam, Thatcher 236
Merrill & Wadsworth 180
Merrill, Charles G. 180
Merrill, Charles S. 253
Merrill, Daniel 17
Merrill, George S. 180, 236, 237, 253
Merrill, Michael P. 236
Merrill, Reuben 130
Merrill, William H. 171
Merrill, William J. 235
Merrill, Winfield G. 180
Merrill, Zachary T. 251
Merrimack, (Lawrence) 35, 253
Merrimack Co-operative Bank 171
Merrimack Congregational Society 113
the Merrimack Courier 32, 35, 179
Merrimack Hall 36, 114
Merrimack House 32, 257
Merrimack Mills 153
Merrimack Paper Company 165
Merrimack river 13, 16, 17, 20, 21, 22, 24, 25, 30, 39, 45, 53, 54, 57, 63, 66, 88, 89, 115, 133, 135, 147, 175, 190, 197, 201, 258
Merrimack Spinning Co. 258
Merrimack street 259
Merrimack Valley Horse Railroad 143
Merrimack Valley Waterway Board 176
Merrimack Water Power Association 25
Merrow, William H. 219
the Messenger 179
Messer, a pioneer 16
Metcalf, William, Pemberton victim 62

Methodist Episcopal Church
115, 116
Methodists 112, 116
Methuen, Mass.
13, 17, 21, 22, 35, 39, 49,
98, 102, 111, 139, 143, 144,
156, 158, 168, 174, 187,
188, 204, 208, 217, 222
Methuen Orthodox church 111
Methuen street 32, 114
Metropolitan Park police 70, 74
Mexico 123
Michael F. Brogan 213
Michael J. Sullivan, Inc. 220
Middleton, Mass. 144, 174
Midgeley, Richard, Pemberton victim
62
Miles, James 238
militia 24, 72
Mill street, No. 7 259
Miller, John 258
Miller, Rudolph 235
Milliken, James I. 157
Mills, Hiram F. 29, 88
Mitchell's Falls 176
Miville, Narcisse E. 77, 234
Moeser, Hugo 227
Moffett, James
Molineux, Hannah, Pemberton
victim 62
Monomac Spinning Company
48, 159
Montezuma House 31, 32
Monument Association 130
Mooers, Elijah M. 235
Moore, Cyrus T. 238
Moorehouse, James 239
Moose Country 17
Morehouse's bakery 259
Morgan, Charles H. 242, 256
Morgan, Fred 124
Morrill, Governor 187
Morris, Francis J. 94, 206, 251

Morris, James E. 236
Morrison, Abiel 180, 233, 236
Morrison, Charles 239
Morrissey, John F. 239, 244
Morrissey, Thomas J. 239
Morro Castle 122
Morse, E. W. 82, 229
Morse, H. Dennie 241
Morse, Julius H. 235
Morse, William 229
Morton, Edward P. 241
Morton Street 91, 93
Mosher, Joseph A. 243
Moss, William Jr. 235
Moulton, Jesse 233, 238, 254
Moulton, Rev. Arthur Wheelock
112
Mount Zion Church 111
Mowat, George 242
Moyes, William F. 251, 253
Mt. Vernon street 183
Muehlig, Emil J. 242, 255, 256
Mueller, Otto 77, 255
Mulcahey, James A. 242
Mulholland, J. P. 172
Municipal Council 145
municipal filtration plant 51, 54
Municipal Health Department
140, 212
Municipal Hospital 139, 205
municipal sewer 53
municipal swimming pool 53
Murphy, Alice, Pemberton victim 62
Murphy, Charles 254
Murphy, Daniel J.
68, 148, 171, 204, 212, 253
Murphy, Dennis W. 240
Murphy, James 238, 239, 254
Murphy, John F. 224
Murphy, John J. 214, 241
Murphy, Mary, Pemberton victim 62
Murphy, Michael 111
Murphy, Michael J. 250

Murphy, Mortimer D. A. 255
Murphy, Patrick
169, 238, 248, 253, 254
Murphy Tyler Co. 212
Murray, Daniel F. 248
Murray, G. E. 170
Murray, Thomas 240
Murray, William 236
Music hall 84
Musk, Harry B. 77
Musk, Henry A. 240
Mystic pond 20

N

Namoskeag tribe 13
Nash, Orin C. 62
Nashua, N.H. 145
Nashua, tribe 13
National Fibre Board Co. 258
National Guard 125, 126
Neal, Hiram R. 250
Needham, John C. 234-235
Needham, Sumner H. 41, 121
Nelson, George A. 238
Nevins, David 58, 61
New England Baseball League 219
the New Nickel theater 224
New York Universit 218
Newbury street
17, 21, 32, 45, 91, 108, 144, 192, 257
Newburyport, Mass.
20, 31, 39, 137
Newell, Charles Stark 235
newspapers 55
Newton street 63, 104, 111
Nice, Harry 180
Nice, Mary, Pemberton victim 62
Nichols, Henry J. 243, 244
Nichols, Joseph J. 254
Nicholson, William 240
Nickel theatre 224
Nickerson, Albert W. 49
Nickerson, Joseph 49, 155

night school 101
Noonan, David 244
Noonan, James 238
Norcross pond 183
Norris, Alderman 195
Norris, Joseph 229, 232, 236
North Andover, Mass.
19, 21, 24, 33, 34, 38,
98, 144, 168, 174, 208, 222
North canal 20, 30, 37, 50, 148
Norwood, John K. 65
Nova Scotia 126
Noyes, Henry 190
Nugent, John J. 240
Nugent, John J. Jr. 244

O

Oak street
32, 65, 91, 92, 103, 104,
109, 113, 117, 191, 192
Oak street, No. 346 108
O'Brien, Frank J. 242
O'Brien, John 240, 255
O'Brien, John J. 234, 240, 243
O'Brien, John P. 243
O'Brien, Michael S.
77, 131, 133, 216
O'Brien, Patrick 234
O'Brien, Timothy J. 67, 207, 250
O'Brien. Michael, Pemberton victim
62
O'Commor, Frank 124
O'Connell, Barry T. 248
O'Connell, Bernard T. 241
O'Connell, David D. 243
O'Connell, Elizabeth 63
O'Connell, Mary Ann 64
O'Connor, Patrick 239
O'Connor, Patrick, Pemberton
victim 62
Odd Fellows hall 32, 106, 113, 119
O'Dea, James 238

O'Donnell, Rev. James
   38, 108, 114, 244
O'Donovan, William R. 130
O'Dowd, James T. 256
O'Dowd, Joseph M. 244
O'Hearn, Timothy F. 229, 240, 254
O'Hearne, Jeremiah, Pemberton
   victim 62
Old Battery building 92
Old Blue Ledge 63
Old Red Bridge 184
O'Leary, Jeremiah 241
Oliver, Henry K.
   39, 40, 41, 60, 103, 104, 136,
   191, 194, 231, 246, 254
Oliver school
   37, 40, 102, 103, 106, 107, 200
O'Mahoney, Arthur 77
O'Neill, James 240, 241
O'Neill, Timothy 242
O'Neill, Timothy F. 242
Orangemen of Lawrence 193
Orchard street 18
Ordway, a patriot 19
Ordway, Aaron 232
Ordway, George 236
O'Reilly, Rev. James T.
   77, 109, 115, 117
Orphan Asylum and Home for
   Invalids 141
Orr, Eliza, Pemberton victim 62
Osgood, Benjamin 232, 253
Osgood, Elbridge B. 231
Osgood, Josiah 235, 253
Osgood, Timothy 32, 33, 113
O'Sullivan Bros.' hat factory 257
O'Sullivan, Daniel C. 237, 248
O'Sullivan, Dr. John J. 126
O'Sullivan, Edward F.
   179, 253, 254
O'Sullivan, James T. 73, 250
O'Sullivan, John 239
O'Sullivan, Martin 238

Oswald, William 221
Oxford street 92, 93

P

P. & P. Holihan 225
Pacific Mills
   46, 47, 48, 49, 50, 58,
   71, 92, 134, 151, 152,
   153, 258
Pacific National Bank 169, 170
Pacific National Banks 169
Packard, Rev. Dr. George
   104, 106, 112, 188, 194, 231
Packard school 104, 107, 258
Page, William R. 194, 229
Paine, Charles C. 176
Paisley, John Jr. 239
Palmer, Morris E., Pemberton victim
   62
Panama-Pacific International
   Exposition 175
Paper Mill schoolhouse 183
Parent, Alfred 66
Park street 92, 104
park system 52
Parker, Artemus Jr. 229, 232
Parker family 18
Parker, George H. 235
Parker, Lyman 67
Parker, Michael 18, 19
Parker, Nancy 15
Parker street 115
Parker, Walter E.
   137, 153, 166, 170, 249
Parkman, Noah 250
Parnell, Charles Stewart 196
Parnell, Stewart 196
parochial schools 108
Parsons, Philemon C. 236
Parsons, Thomas A. 235, 253, 254
Parsons, William H. 251
Parthum, H. Richard 234
Parthum, Otto 148

Partridge, Joseph L. 231
Pasho, David M. 236
Pasho, Henry F. Jr. 235
Passaconnaway 14
passenger railway 26
the Patch 183, 191
Patch, Frederick 241
Paterson, N. J. 72
Patriots' Tea 141
Patterson, Charles 67
Patterson, John A. 242
Paul, Nicholas G. 232
Paul, Seth D. 237
Paul's self-acting mules 47
Pawtucket Falls 13
Payne, James 168, 169, 232, 233
Pearce, Charles E. 241
Pearl, Oliver 235
Pearl spindle for cotton spinning 47
Pearson, Abel G. 233, 236
Peckham, Thomas G. 235, 236
Pedler, William A. 158
Pedrick, William R. 65
Peel, Robert 124
Peirce, William 253
Pelham, N.H. 145
Pemberton Mill
    27, 46, 47, 56, 57,
    58, 59, 61, 81, 92, 164, 211
Pemberton National Bank 170
Pemberton street
    82, 87, 113, 119, 173, 194
Pennacook tribe 13
Pentucket tribe 13
Perkins, John S. 250
Perkins, Moses 233, 237
Perry, John R. 232
Perry Mill 163
Perry, O. H. 163
Perry, Theodore M. 130
Peters falls 20
Peters family 185
Petroske, J. J. 172

Peverly, H. R. 99
Phelan, Michael F. 202
Philbrick, Chase 250
Philips & Kunhardt 163
Phillips Hill 188, 201
Phillips, John 239
Phillips-Andover Academy 204
Pickels, Robert F.
    77, 234, 242, 247
Pillsbury, Amos D. 31, 173
Pillsbury, C. K. 169
Pillsbury, Joshua Jr. 232, 236
Pillsbury, Joshua Jr. 236
Pillsbury, Prescott G. 169, 238
Pillsbury's machine shop 257
Pine Island 14, 15
Pinta, Flower 66
Pioneer Race Track 188
Place, Charles L. 239
Plain of Sodom 17
the Plains 183
playground system 52
Plisch, Gustav 227, 242
Plummer, Hezekiah
    31, 130, 168, 232, 233, 235, 236
Plummer, Nathan T. 237
Plymouth Mills 163, 259
Police Court 83
police signal system 96
Poor, Ebenezer 18, 22
Poor, Edward P. 60, 248, 254
Poor Family 18, 139
poor farm, Lawrence 22
poor farm, Methuen 17, 18
Poor, George 236
Poor, Henry 189
Poor, John 19, 189
Poor, Theodore 19
Poor, Thomas 18, 19
Porter, David T. 233
Porter, F. L. 169, 170
Porter, George W. 250
Porter, John W. 250

Portland street 63
Portsmouth, N.H. 145
Potter's pond 183
Power, Maurice J. 130
the Plains 191
Praetz, John G. 220
Pratt, Enoch 103, 253
Pratt, Josiah N. 238
The Premier theater 223
Presbyterian church 116
Prescott, John H. 233
Prescott, Lyman 250
Prescott, Roland A. 29
Prospect Hill
        20, 21, 22, 27, 37, 38, 88, 104,
        111, 133, 141, 150, 192
Prospect Hill, schoolhouse 111
Prospect street 19, 103, 193
Prospect street school 183
Protectorate of Mary Immaculate
        141
Public Health and Charities
        200, 205
Public Property and Parks 200, 216
Public Safety Committee 123
Public Service Commission 145
Putnam, John Pickering 58

Q

Quinn, Frank 172
Quinn, James H. 244
Quinn, John F. 242

R

racetrack 24
Radcliffe, A. C. 231
railroad
        24, 26, 34, 35, 38, 39, 145
Randlett, Orrin J. 242
Rankin, Nathaniel E. 126, 208, 251
Rankin, William H. 241
Reading, Mass. 187
Red Cross 125

Reed, Rufus 235
Regan Bros. 259
Reid & Hughes Company 221
Reid, Adam 221
Religious Society of Friends 116
Remi, John 73, 74
Republican National Convention
        209
Republican party 40
Republican State Committee 208
Reservoir street 22
Revere House 19
Revolutionary War 19
Rice, Herbert S. 239
Rice, L. E. 231
Rice, Lawson 236
Richards, David 130
Richardson, Benjamin 18
Richardson, Caleb 18
Richardson, David C. 169, 236, 237
Richardson, Everett P. 238
Richardson family 18
Richardson, George 235
Rinn, Michael 239, 254
river dredging 175
Riverside Congregational church
        116
Riverside Park 134
Roach, Ellen, Pemberton victim 62
Roberts, Julia, Pemberton victim 62
Robertson & Sutherland Co.
        258, 259
Robertson, Archibald M. 220
Robertson, Sutherland & Co. 220
Robinson, A. Herbert 234, 241
Robinson, D. Frank 233, 238
Robinson, Miss, a teacher 102
Robinson, Phineas B. 233, 246
Rogers, Alexander H.
        77, 172, 180, 242
Rogers house 19
Rogers, Thomas 124
Rolfe, Samuel J., Pemberton victim

288

62
Rolley, James L. 77
Rollins, John R.
29, 40, 104, 130, 231, 246
Rollins School 51, 104
Roosevet, Theodore 197
Rowe, George R. 229
Rowe street 133
Rowe, Walter R.
214, 229, 231, 248
Rowell, Frank A. 241
Rowell, Wilbur E.
126, 137, 169, 170
Rumford street 184
Runals, Frank L. 169, 236
Rushforth, Charles P. 243, 244
Rushforth, Walter E. 242
Russell, George W. 238
Russell, George F.
125, 163, 169, 170, 238
Russell, Gov. William R. 218
Russell, John 233
Russell Paper Mill 46, 162, 258
Russell, William 162
Russell, William A.
144, 162, 232, 254
Russell, William H. 171, 248
Russell's paper mill 257
Russll, Ernest 124
Rutter, Charles G. 231, 247, 251
Rutter, William F. 169, 170
Rutter, William F. Jr. 211
Rutter, William F. Sr. 211
Ryan, Bridget, Pemberton victim 62
Ryan, James E. 242
Ryan, John P. 179, 218, 241
Ryan, Mary, Pemberton victim 62
Ryan, Matthew C., Pemberton victim 62
Ryan, Maurice 241
Ryan, Simon B. 255
Ryan, Stephen J. 122

S

Sacred Heart (French Catholic) church 117
Sacred Heart school 110
Sager, Alfred 171
Salem, Mass. 137, 144
Salem, N.H. 145, 174
Salem street 63, 118
Salem Street Primitive Methodist church 118
Salem Turnpike 184
Salisbury Beach 201, 202
Salisbury, Charles A. 234, 242
Salvation Army 118
Sampson, Amos H. 180
Sampson, Augusta L., Pemberton victim 62
San Francisco, Ca. 175
Sanborn, George A. 29
Sanborn, George W. 233, 238, 248
Sanborn, Gilman F. 94, 250
Sanborn, John C. 253, 254, 256
Sanborn, John C. Jr. 120
Santiago de Cuba 122
Sargent, Charles F. 241, 253, 255
Sargent, Dana 231, 235, 246
Sargent, Edwin 18
Sargent family 18
Sargent, George W. 179, 232, 236
Sargent house 18, 20
Sargent, Ignatius 26
Sargent, James 18
Sargent, Lorenzo D. 238, 251
Sargent, Major Charles F. 77
Sargent, Nathaniel 18
Saunders, Caleb
231, 233, 237, 246, 253
Saunders, Charles G. 137
Saunders, Daniel
18, 24, 25, 26, 45, 60, 88, 120, 168, 182, 185, 214, 248
Saunders, Daniel Jr.
40, 59, 60, 231, 246, 253
Saunders family 18

Savage, Walter A. 242
Sawyer, William R. 241
Scanlon, Michael A.
    71, 77, 132, 231, 235, 243, 244, 247
Scanlon, Michael F. 234, 242
Scanlon, Thomas F. 243
Schenk, William A. 241
Scheriver of Worcester 223
Schlapp, Frederick W. 256
Schoenland, Charles H. 233, 238
Schoenland, Henry C. 227
School Board 214
School Physician 218
Schwartz, Dr. Meyer 218
Schwartz, Lewis H. 243
Scott, Thomas
    43, 169, 236, 238, 254
Scully, Stephen J. 243
Sealer of Weights and Measures
    219
Searles, Edward F. 142
Sears, Herbert W. 157
Seaver, William L. 240
Second Baptist church 115
Second Congregational church 42
Selden, G. L. 169
semi-centennial 197
Seminary Hill 187
the Sentinel 180
Shafter, General 122
Shanty pond 183
shanty villages 34
Sharpe, Andrew 221, 239
Sharrock, William 240
Shattuck, Charles 32
Shattuck, Dorothy 131
Shattuck family 18
Shattuck flag pole 65
Shattuck, Joseph
    18, 32, 130, 131, 132, 165, 233
Shattuck, Joseph Jr. 166
Shattuck, Nathan 18
Shattuck street 188

Shattuck's farm 15
Shawsheen corner 24
Shawsheen Fields 14, 24, 187
Shawsheen House 32
Shawsheen Inn 189
Shawsheen river 21, 63
Shawsheen Tavern 19, 189
Shea, Andrew F. 234
Shea, Edgar W. 244
Shea, Hannah 62
Shea, John F. 241, 242
Shea, Richard J. 214, 231
Sheedy, William F. 240
Sheehan, John 250
Shepard, James E. 229, 250
Sheridan, Bernard M. 203, 231
Sheriff, Alexander W. 242
Sherman, Edgar J. 120, 251, 254
Sherman, Frederick F. 234
Sherman, Henry L.
    64, 169, 170, 251
Sherman, J. R. 65
Shields, Gen. James 196
Shine, Dennis 219
Shuttleworth, M. L. 169
Shuttleworth, Moses 171
Siegel, Louis K. 227, 242
Silverthorne, Joseph 223
Silverthorne Studio 223
Simonds, G. H. 170
Simonds, Sullivan 235
Simpson, James R. 65
Simpson & Oswald 221
Simpson, Harry 243
Simpson, James R.
    130, 231, 236, 246
Simpson, Thomas 221
Siskind, A. L. 171
Sisters of Charity 110, 141
Sisters of Good Shepherd 110
Sisters of Holy Union of Sacred
    Heart 110

Sisters of Notre Dame
    108, 109, 110, 114
Sisters of St. Domenic 109
Slayton building 224
Smart, George B. 238, 255
Smith, Albert 32
Smith, Capt. Daniel C. 77
Smith, Capt. John 19
Smith, Charles 233
Smith, Frank 242
Smith, George A. 237
Smith, George W. 241
Smith, Harry E. 239, 240
Smith, J. W. 169
Smith, John 169
Smith, John M. 83, 229
Smith, Joseph 32
Smith machine shop 259
Smith, Maggie J., Pemberton victim
    62
Smith, Peter 169
Smith, Samuel 233
Smith, William 232, 236, 237
Soldiers' and Sailors' Monument
    127, 130, 132, 193
Somerville, Thomas H. 240
Souhegan tribe 13
South Broadway
    24, 45, 92, 93, 102, 115, 185
South Broadway Branch library 134
South Broadway Fire House 93
South canal 30, 148, 258
South Congregational church 115
South Congregational Sunday
    School 115
South Lawrence
    14, 18, 19, 31, 54, 63, 91, 111,
    134, 183, 191, 213
South Union Park 63
South Union street
    14, 117, 133, 159, 160, 227, 259
Spalding, William R.
    31, 144, 168, 232, 235

Spalding, William W. 168
Spanish War Veterans 122
Spencer, Joseph 244
Spicket Falls 16
Spicket river
    13, 16, 17, 18, 19, 21, 27,
    33, 34, 42, 45, 135, 183,
    184, 191, 257
Spinlow, John H. 242, 255
Spiritualist Temple 118
Sprague, Levi 229
Springfield Street 63
St. Anne's (French Catholic) church
    116
St. Anne's school for boys 110
St. Anthony's Syrian Maronite
    (Catholic) church 117
St. Augustine's (Catholic) church
    115, 116
St. Augustine's Episcopal church
    117
St. Francis (Lithuanian Catholic)
    church 117
St. Francis school 110
St. George Syrian Greek Orthodox
    Church 118
St. James' Hall 109
St. John Baptist Russian Greek
    Catholic Church 118
St. John's Episcopal church
    115, 117
St. Joseph's school for girls 110
St. Joseph's Syrian (Greek Catholic
    Rite) church 117
St. Laurence's (Catholic) church 116
St. Laurence's school for boys and
    girls 110
St. Mark's Methodist Episcopal
    church 116
St. Mary's Catholic Church
    109, 114, 115, 117
St. Mary's High School 108
St. Mary's Parish 109, 115

St. Mary's Schools 110
St. Patrick's (Catholic) church
    63, 65, 115
St. Patrick's for boys and girls 110
St. Paul's Methodist Episcopal
    church 116
St. Rita's school for boys and girls
    109
Stafford, George W. 239
Stafford, John H. 239, 254, 255
Stafford, John S. 236
Stafford, Joseph H. 239
stagecoaches 143
Stanley, Frank J. 255
Stanley, George A. 222
Stanley Grain Company 221, 222
Stanley, James J. 233
Stanley machine shop 48
Stannard, James H. 237
Stansfield, George T. 234, 243
the Star 180
State Armory 139, 218, 259
State Board of Arbitration 72
State Board of Charity 142
State Board of Health 194
State Committee on Public Safety
    123
State Constitutional Convention 209
State Militia 70, 121, 139, 218
Statfford, John S. 232
steamer "City of Lawrence"
    39, 176, 193
steamer landing 15
Stearns, Artemus W.
    31, 144, 161, 168, 220, 232
Stedman, Samuel M. 232
Stetson, William I. 82
Steunenberg, Gov. Frank, of Idaho
    72
Stevens, Abiel 18, 19
Stevens, B. D. 86
Stevens' box shop 45
Stevens, Celia A., Pemberton victim
    62
Stevens, Charles W. 238
Stevens family 18
Stevens, Ivan 103, 231
Stevens, James 18, 229, 235
Stevens, Joseph 22
Stevens, Luther E. 236
Stevens piano case shop 17
Stevens Village 183
Stevens, Warren 237, 238
Stevens, William 38, 103, 250
Stevenson, Maynard W. 77
Stiegler, August 227, 234
Stiegler, Emil C. 77, 240, 241
Stillwater pond 20
Stockton, Howard 27
Stockton Park 27, 133
Stoddard, Granville M. 238
Stoddard, Leonard 250
Stone, Andrew C.
    95, 237, 238, 250, 253
Stone, I. H. 169
Stone, John 237
Stone Machine Shop building 58
stone quarry 63
Stone, S. E. 231
Storer, James A. 237
Storrow, Charles S.
    26, 27, 40, 43, 60, 103,
    106, 136, 165, 231, 246
Storrow Park 27, 133, 194
Stott, David 222
Stow, John 237
Stowell, Joseph 236
Stowell's shop burned 257
Stratton, Lewis 237
Stratton, Thomas S. 232, 235, 257
Street, Jackson 196
Street lights 96
street railway 143
Strike of 1912 68, 69, 72, 75
strikers 72
Sts. Peter and Paul (Portuguese

Catholic) church 117
Sturgis, R. Clipston 131
Sturgis, William 26
Sugatt, C. H. 172
Sugatt, Henry E. 240, 241
Sugatt, R. H. 77
Sullivan, A. M. 220
Sullivan, John F. 242
Sullivan, Ann, Pemberton victim 62
Sullivan, Cornelius F.
    107, 239, 241, 255
Sullivan, Dennis A. 254
Sullivan, Frank A. 243
Sullivan, John J. 73, 250
Sullivan, M. A. 172
Sullivan, Margaret, Pemberton victim
    62
Sullivan, Michael F. 240, 242, 255
Sullivan, Michael J.
    77, 172, 220, 241, 247
Sullivan, Michael T. 220
Sullivan, T. J. 172
the Sun 180
the Sun-American 180
the Sunday Register 180
the Sunday Sun 180
the Sunday Telegram 180
Superior Court 38, 83
Supreme Court 120
Sutherland, Mrs. A. B. 220
Sutherland, Andrew B.
    77, 169, 170, 176, 220
Sutherland Company 31
Sutton, Eben 61
the Swamp 191
Swan, David S. 237
Swan family 18
Swan house 16, 20
Swan, William 229
Swedish Lutheran Church 118
Sweeney, Catharine, Pemberton
    victim 62
Sweeney, Cox & Sargent 203

Sweeney, John J. 124
Sweeney, John P. 249, 253
Sweeney, Patrick
    180, 220, 239, 254
Sweeney, Peter M. 241
Sweeney, Y. P. 170
Sweetser, Col. E. Leroy 72
Sylvester, Fred A. 241
Sylvester, Sewell 235, 236
Syrian Protestant Church 118

T

Taaffe, Rev. James H. D. 112
Taft, President 197
Tarbox family 18
Tarbox Grammar School
    104, 133, 200
Tarbox house 20
Tarbox, John K.
    18, 20, 120, 179, 203, 231,
        246, 253, 254
Tariff of 1867 155
Tatham, John W. 242
Taylor, Zachary 81
Taylor, Fred W. 233
Taylor, L. Morton 244
Tenney, John 88
Tetler, James R. 202, 243, 253, 256
Tetler, Senator 202
Tewksbury, Mrs. Robert H. 11
Tewksbury, Robert H.
    11, 29, 57, 130, 168, 193,
        231, 246, 248
Theberge, George 242
Thomas, Jane, Pemberton victim 62
Thomas, William 232, 236
Thompson, Henry B. 233
Thompson, Robert 241
Thompson, Samuel I. 251
Thompson, William L. 237
Thornton, William 66
Thwing, Joshua 17
Tiger Fire Association 91

Tighe, Cornelius J. 238
Tobin, John 234, 235
Todd, John S. 244, 245
Todd, Robert T. 171
tollhouse 23
tolls, Andover bridge 22, 24
Toomey & Demara Amusement
    Company 223
Toomey, Thomas 223
tornado of 1890 63
tornado of 1910 65
Tosney, Joseph A. 243
Tower Hill 15, 19, 21, 37, 42, 43,
    90, 102, 104, 183
Tower Hill Congregational church
    115
Town Hall 95
Town House 82
Towne, Asa 18
Towne, Lizzie, Pemberton victim 62
Towne, Stillman 235
Townsend, Benjamin 124
Townsend, Milton B. 240, 254
Trades and Labor Congress of
    Canada, 200
Training School 20
Treat, James A. 168, 232, 233
Tremont street 32, 102, 257
Tresca, Carlo 72, 76
Trinity Congregational Church 114
trolley lines 143
Truell, Byron
    130, 170, 237, 246, 253, 254
Trumbull, Charles A. 239
Trumbull, Charles E. 227
Tuberculosis Hospital 52, 140
Tucker, Thomas F. 246
Tufts College Medical School 217
Turner, Frank S. 241
Turner, Margaret, Pemberton victim
    62
Turnpike street
    31, 32, 91, 113, 184, 257

Turnpike Street, No. 5 112
Twiss, Fred E. 126
Twiss, W. D. 169
Tyler, William M. 235

U

U. S. Bobbin Co. 259
U.S. uniform cloth 150
Ulrich, Albin 244
Union Evangelical church 116
Union Park 27, 133
Union street 17, 20, 24, 71, 90
Union street bridge 258
Unitarian church
    32, 42, 104, 112, 113, 257
United Congregational church 115
United Presbyterian church
    115, 118
United Shoe Machinery Company
    212, 213
United States Hotel 32, 42, 257
United States Worsted Co. 48, 164
Universalists 112
University, Harvard 136
Upper Pacific Mill 27
Uswoco Mill 48

V

Vacation club 173
Valpey, Samuel S. 232
the Vanguard 179, 180
Varnam, Adelbert C. 234
Varney, Samuel J. 35
Vaudreuil, Arthur 124
Verein, Ruth 141
Viger, Simeon 77, 234
Villanova College 214
Vine street 116
Vose, Clinton P. 250

W

W. F. Rutter & Company 211

W. H. Godfrey's storehouse 258
Wade, Asa M. 237
Wade bobbin holder 47
Wade, Edward J. 77, 214, 229
Wadleigh, John C. 235
Wadsworth, Horace A. 11, 180
Waldo, George A. 35, 253
Walker, Dr. James 136
Walker, James R. 235
Walsh, William A. 11
Walton, George A. 232
Walton Shoe Company 48, 212
Walworth Bros. Inc. 164
Walworth, C. W. 170
Walworth, Joseph E. 259
Wamesit tribe 13
Ward, Edward J. 243
Ward, John R. H. 241
Ward, Patrick C. 240
Ward, Richard 161, 212
Wards
    Five 19, 51, 183, 191
    Four 17
    One 53, 133
    Six 63, 133
    Three 17, 183
    Two 17
Warren, Albert 40, 231, 232, 246
Warren, Fred R. 241
Washburn, William B. 89
Washington Corporation 258
Washington, George 22
Washington Mills
    48, 70, 71, 84, 149, 150, 200, 257, 258
Water Power Association 135
Water street
    27, 116, 117, 185, 192, 259
water supply 43, 51
water tower 90
waterpower 20, 25, 30, 45, 54
Watson, Benjamin F.
    179, 193, 246, 253
Watson, Fred J. 243

Watts, James 238
Watts, Joseph E. 240
Weatherbee school 51
Webber, Henry G. 98
Webster, Abel 236, 237, 238, 254
Webster, Daniel B. 196, 233
Webster, Henry K.
    131, 170, 231, 239, 246, 259
Webster, John L. 238
Weed, Dan 102
The Weekly Messenger 179
Weeks, Benjamin L. 234, 243
Weidner, Anton L. 243
Welch, John 124
Welch, Michael Jr. 243
Welch, Thomas A. 244
Weldon, James H. 240
Well, Nathan 19
wells 194
Wells, Nathan 18, 229
Wentworth, David 232, 235
Wentworth, Eli 236
West Parish road 63, 183
Western Electric Company 212
Weston, Eldridge 60, 235
Wetherbee school 63, 104
Wheeler, Frank E. 238
Wheeler, Joseph H. 240
Wheeler, Leonard 236
Wheeler, Orange 236
Wheelwright, Richard 238
Whelan, Frank J. 241
Whig party 39, 40
Whitcomb, Baruch C. 236, 237
White, Arthur A. 242, 243
White, Capt. 18
White, Daniel Appleton
    18, 135, 136, 185
White, E. P. 172
White, Fairfield 18, 42
White Fund 18, 136, 137
White, Harvey 235
White, J. Clinton 233, 239

White, Joseph 77
White, Miss Elizabeth W. 135
White, Mrs. Nathaniel G. 135
White, Nathaniel G.
    40, 136, 165, 166, 232, 235, 246, 248
White Pups Bridge 184
White, Samuel 238
White street
    73, 91, 95, 109, 112, 113
White, William P.
    210, 231, 234, 247
Whitehead, Cornelius 239
Whitehouse, Josiah S. 234
Whitman Corporation 160
Whitman, William
    49, 155, 158, 159, 160
Whitmarsh, William H. 236
Whitney, Charles C. 238
Whittaker, Abner N. 235
Whittemore, Harry 240
Wholley, Dennis 251
Wickersham, General 73
Wiesner, William F. 238
Wiggin, George K. 237, 251
Wiggin, James B. 239
Wiggin, P. C. 170
Wilde, Emil H. 242
Wildes, Henry H. 243
Wilkins, E. R. 180
Wilkins, George Jr. 236
Wilkinson, Albert 243
William Oswald Company 221
William Whitman Co.
    156, 158, 159
Williams, Cyrus 232, 235, 238, 254
Williams, George S. 239
Wilson & Allyn steam mill 42, 257
Wilson, Allen 236
Wilson, Isaac N. 241
Wilson, Nathaniel 31, 248, 253
WIlson, Woodrow 196, 208
Winch, Elisha 235
Wingate, Charles E. 241

Winkley, Alonzo 232, 236, 237
Winn, Alonzo S. 237
Winn, Thomas S. 236
Winnepucket, a sachem of Saugus
    13
Winnipesaukee tribe 13
Winter street 184
Winthrop Avenue 133, 184
Withington, Henry 60, 235
Woburn, Mass. 193
Woekel, Carl A. Jr. 235, 243
Woitena, Michael 66
Wonolancet 14
Wood, Duncan 238
Wood Home 142
Wood Memorial Free Baptist
    church 117
Wood, William M. 47, 49, 149
Wood Worsted Mills
    48, 52, 71, 149, 150
Woodbury, Moses E. 240
Woodhall, Joseph A. 234, 242
Woodman, Franklin of Haverhill
    145
Woolen mill 39
Worcester, Mass. 54
Workingmen's Compensation Act
    201
World War I 54, 123
World's End Pond 17, 20
Wright, Algernon S. 161, 236
Wright, G. L. 170
Wright, L. A. 57
Wright, L. W. 103
Wright Manufacturing Co.
    161, 212, 258
Wright, Thomas 246, 253
Wright, William H. P.
    95, 192, 231, 246, 250, 251, 254
Wylde, Harry 169
Wyman Street 116

X

Xaverian Brothers 109

Y

Y. M. C. A. 99, 114, 118, 125
Y. M. C. A. Red Triangle War Fund
 125
Y. W. C. A. 118
Yeaton, Philip 236
Yeaw, Albin 238, 239
Young, Bartholomew A. 242
Young, Charles T. 237
Young, John F. 234, 243
Yunggebauer, Herman 227